Advance Praise

A Congressman's Lifelong Fight Against
Bigotry, Famine, and War

SPEAKING OUT

PAUL FINDLEY

Foreword by Helen Thomas

Lawrence Hill Books

B
Findley
7

Library of Congress Cataloging-in-Publication Data

Findley, Paul, 1921–
  Speaking out : a Congressman's lifelong fight against bigotry, famine, and war /
Paul Findley ; foreword by Helen Thomas.
      p. cm.
  Includes bibliographical references and index.
  ISBN 978-1-56976-625-5 (hardcover)
 1. Findley, Paul, 1921– 2. Findley, Paul, 1921—Political and social views.
3. United States—Politics and government—1945–1989.   4. United States—
Politics and government—1989–   5. Legislators—United States—Biography.
6. United States. Congress. House—Biography. I. Title.
  E840.8.F56A3 2011
  328.73'092—dc22
  [B]
                                    2010053899

Interior design: Sarah Olson

© 2011 by Paul Findley
Foreword © 2011 by Helen Thomas
All rights reserved
Published by Lawrence Hill Books, an imprint of
Chicago Review Press, Incorporated
814 North Franklin Street
Chicago, Illinois 60610
ISBN 978-1-56976-625-5
Printed in the United States of America
5 4 3 2 1

Contents

✕✕✕✕✕✕✕✕✕✕✕✕✕✕✕✕✕✕✕✕✕✕

Foreword

HELEN THOMAS

Former Dean of White House Correspondents

This book by former Representative Paul Findley, an Illinois Republican, is a revealing and fascinating autobiography of a twenty-two-year veteran on Capitol Hill who called them as he saw them—a true profile in courage.

Findley was one of the few members of Congress who had the audacity to meet with the late Palestinian leader Yasser Arafat and express his sympathy for the plight of the Palestinians and dismay at the help given by the United States to "scofflaw Israel [to] destroy an entire nationality."

In *Speaking Out*, the author takes issue with the U.S. government trying to police the world and urges a multinational federation "strong enough to enforce world law." He reminds President Obama of President Eisenhower's warning against "the danger of the military industrial complex" and recommends a sharp cut in the defense budget. He writes that since Obama took office "there are disturbing signs that he is surrounded by generals [and] has been misled into the illusion that violent insurgents can be defeated by bombs and missiles. Instead of halting U.S. combat operations, he brandishes new swords and calls for victory in Afghanistan."

Findley predicts: "Insurgent violence would quickly diminish if our leaders halted all U.S. combat operations . . . and terminated our complicity in Israel's abuse of Arabs." He notes, "History demonstrates that suicide bombings occur almost entirely in countries like Iraq and Afghanistan where foreign troops hold the upper hand."

It is Findley's second book that takes a big whack at the Israeli lobby's power in America's foreign policy centers—in the White House and Congress. It follows his remarkable breakthrough treatise, *They Dare to Speak Out: People and Institutions Confront Israel's Lobby.* He discloses how untouchable Israel became, even after it attempted to destroy the USS *Liberty,* a U.S. intelligence ship, and its crew during the Six-Day War between the Israelis and Arabs in 1967. He adds that President Lyndon B. Johnson, by issuing orders calling off a navy rescue mission and imposing a tight cover-up of Israel's guilt, "ignored murder and sanctioned perfidy, malfeasance, and deceit." He asserts that Israel repeatedly violates the Arms Export Control Act that prohibits use of U.S.-supplied weapons beyond legitimate self-defense.

A series of episodes convinced him that "goodwill for Palestinian human rights never existed among Israeli administration officials at any time during the Jewish state's half-century history. . . . They did not want good faith negotiations." Instead, he writes, Israelis wanted to prolong talks indefinitely while they expanded their settlements to overrun and obliterate occupied Palestine. When Findley urged support for a homeland for Palestinians in a White House exchange with Ronald Reagan, the president responded astoundingly: "But where would they go?" You could not find anyone more pro-Israel than Reagan.

In light of America's "subservience" to Israel, Findley sees little hope that Washington will soon force Israel to agree to a viable independent Palestine. While not holding his breath, he believes the only hope for early peace in the Holy Land lies in resolute leadership by wise citizens within Israel and Palestine inspired by South Africa's recent termination of apartheid. "If white Afrikaners and black Zulus can be brought together in equal political standing, Israeli Semites and Palestinian Semites can find a similar, useful, and durable accord. To do this, both sides should take control of public policy and organize a mutual program of confession, forgiveness, and reconciliation."

Findley began his political career as a congressman in 1961, focusing on the agricultural problems of his constituency in rural Illinois. But his position as ranking Republican member of the Middle East Subcommittee of the House Foreign Affairs Committee was an eye-opener to the global picture and U.S. involvement. He soon learned that it would cost him to have an independent view and take the path least taken to find out for himself, despite the propaganda onslaught against a free thinker on Capitol Hill who shunned the party line. Findley became a major target for the American Zionists, who succeeded in defeating him in 1982.

He writes, "The time has come for plain talk and clear-headed action. Our society pays a terrible price for policies that magnify and multiply religious bias and acts of war. We must liberate ourselves from fear of Israel and its partisans, and retrace our steps to moral high ground where America belongs."

Findley's brave and unfortunately almost unique political stand for an American politician—despite "the slings and arrows" he sustains, even death threats—were worth it as he reflects on his efforts to weigh in on worthy causes on Capitol Hill.

He was chosen a Lincoln Laureate and lived up to the great honor by being a strong defender of civil rights legislation. He also was on the right side in opposing the Vietnam War and spoke out in opposition when President Johnson waved the Tonkin Gulf Resolution to justify the sending of U.S. ground forces without limits to Vietnam. President Obama should read this book to gain more insight into the pressures he is succumbing to at the cost of U.S. interests, lives, and treasure. It's not too late to learn from Representative Findley, a man of good conscience who is daring to tell the truth.

Prologue

Excitement in the Village

In a small Midwest county seat, excitement was rising election night, November 7, 1960. It centered in my Findley-for-Congress headquarters in a storefront on the south side of the public square in Pittsfield, population four thousand, where veteran volunteers of the campaign struggle on my behalf were gathering. A place on the sidewalk just west of the headquarters gave the neighborhood a historic touch. There, a decade after serving a term in Congress, Abraham Lincoln addressed a crowd, and then posed for a portrait that became known as The Pittsfield Lincoln. Several of the counties he represented in Congress were in the district I hoped to serve.

In late fall, local attention usually focused on high school basketball and football, not on politics. This was different. Instead of an hour or so of struggle between teams of five or eleven players, this one lasted for a year, involving hundreds of volunteers and thousands of voters in fourteen counties.

When I announced my candidacy for the Republican nomination a year earlier, I may have been the only one in Illinois who thought I had a chance to be nominated, much less elected. From the beginning, odds were against me. Montgomery Carrott, my Democratic opponent, was a popular businessman who lived in Quincy, population over forty thousand. It was ten times the size of Pittsfield, the town my family had called home for thirteen years. I had no experience in elective or appointive office, nor was I a leader for activities of the Republican Party. No Republican county chairman announced support for me before the primary election. Our family financial resources were modest—a mortgaged small residence and a weekly newspaper, the *Pike County Republican* that, despite its name, I pronounced independent. Although born and reared in nearby Jacksonville, a town of eighteen thousand, I had not lived there for seventeen years.

At campaign headquarters election night, I spent the early hours thanking individual supporters for campaign help. Like scores of people in other counties, they had become my friends and would remain so, I believed, no matter how voting balanced out. All were volunteers. None received expense money, much less a salary, for their endeavors. The only paid employee during the entire year was a typist who had worked long nights for one month. She had prepared personalized campaign letters mailed just days ahead of my surprising victory in the four-way March primary election contest.

The room buzzed with conversation and laughter. Among those taking part were my wife, Lucille, our two children, Craig, twelve, and Diane, six, and my mother, Florence Nichols Findley, seventy-eight. The evening ended a long, challenging race to decide a two-year membership in the United States House of Representatives. As the clock passed ten, the room was crowded with people, mostly volunteers.

Everyone kept glancing at a large television set where election updates were announced periodically from a station in Quincy. There was avid interest in other races as well, especially the presidential contest, in which Republican Vice President Richard M. Nixon was challenged by Senator John F. Kennedy. Democrat Otto Kerner seemed safely ahead in his bid to be governor of Illinois. Republican committeemen arrived one at a time, each bearing returns from his precinct. Sandwiches and donuts, compliments of M and D Grocery, disappeared quickly. Polls had closed four hours earlier; time enough, I mused, for officials to count and report all ballots.

Suddenly, the words from a televised update brought silence: "We now have complete returns for the Illinois twentieth congressional district, totals from all fourteen counties. Paul Findley is the winner. Findley is the congressman-elect." A shout went up, then sustained applause. It was news I had longed to hear, but I had trouble believing that I had won. Did this really mean our family would soon pack up and head for Washington, D.C.? Was I dreaming?

The crowd, jubilant that the contest ended in victory, drifted away to bed. So did the Findleys. Before retiring, I expressed wonderment to Lucille. I did not grasp reality until the next morning when the banner headline across the top of my newspaper's front page announced "Kennedy, Kerner elected, Findley Wins." A few weeks later, my artist neighbor Ollie Noll delivered a handsome oil painting of that front page with its confirming headline.

As we prepared for the move to Washington, there was no hint that election night had set me on a half-century career, in and out of office, sweeping me within powerful political storms of national and often worldwide impact. I had no thought of becoming a close observer, occasionally at the center of fateful forces and events, even crime at highest levels and premeditated murder of U.S. citizens by a close ally. I had no inkling that religion-based bias in foreign policy would become so severe it would lead to a bloody suicide assault on America and lure the United States government into initiating two costly wars and restricting civil liberties of U.S. citizens.

Major planks in my campaign platform were protecting farmers from government mandates and establishing an international institution strong enough to prevent wars. Washington, D.C., was the action center of the world, and I dreamed of being part of that action. My agenda was not detailed. I wanted to advance what I called good government. My strongest single motivation for seeking election was a book I read during college days. Written by *New York Times* foreign correspondent Clarence K. Streit and titled *Union Now*, it proposed a federal union of democracies strong enough to enforce world law and prevent war. In Congress, I hoped to advance consideration of the proposal. I considered war a grisly folly that must be ended.

I knew nothing about Israel-centric U.S. foreign policy, Islam, the Middle East, or presidential deceit and cover-up—issues that would come to dominate my life. I had no hint that years in Congress would find me heavily involved in swift changes at the presidential level, antiwar protest, freeing a constituent from prison in remote South Yemen, and sustained personal dealings with a Palestinian leader widely denounced as a terrorist. Nor that I would find my name prominent in legislation to advance normalization of relations with Communist China and the employment rights of seniors, and other laws to prevent famine and curb preemptive war measures presidents might order. I had no inkling that in my post-Congress years I would find myself confronting religious bigotry on a vast scale and fighting the impact of unwarranted religious fear in the formulation of U.S. foreign policies.

In Congress, I wanted to halt the trend toward government management of farming and encourage projects that would advance the rule of law, not force, in settling international disputes. I would have a lot to learn, but I was determined to be a fast learner.

Part I

GROWING UP

1

✧✧✧✧✧✧✧✧✧✧✧✧✧✧✧✧✧

Fun on Edgehill Road

On good authority—my mother—I arrived into the world uneventfully on June 23, 1921, and caused her little discomfort despite weighing nine and one-half pounds. The cottage where I was born still stands at 927 Edgehill Road, Jacksonville, Illinois, just two blocks from where Lucille and I now reside.

My eldest sister Miriam was distressed that my legs were bowed badly at birth. She and Mom tried unsuccessfully to straighten them by wrapping them in wooden splints. They remained bowed until I reached the age of eighty, when the left one became straight thanks to the skill of the surgeon who was installing a replacement knee. Now I am half-straight—in my legs, that is.

My birth occurred soon after my father's career with the YMCA came to an end. He worked for the organization in Logansport, Indiana, when he and Mom were married June 8, 1911. He had attended nearby Purdue University for one year. In my curio cabinet is an exquisitely turned wood goblet, a souvenir of his skill at the lathe during that student year. Leaving Logansport, he managed the Y in Mankato, Minnesota, where my parents' first two children, William and Miriam, were born. Shortly after World War I, they all moved to Jacksonville, where management of the local YMCA beckoned Pop as a step up the career ladder. My sister Ruth was born on Edgehill Road just two years before my arrival. Of five children, only the youngest, Barbara, made a grand entry on a hospital bed.

3

The first four Findleys arrived in Jacksonville as Methodists but soon became Presbyterians. A committee from State Street Presbyterian Church persuaded my father to serve as interim minister. When a permanent pastor was hired months later, the Findleys were so accustomed to the State Street Church community they stayed on as Presbyterians.

By the time of my birth in 1921, Pop's YMCA career was over. The local board of directors had sold its aging property to the Elks Club, intending to use proceeds to finance a new building. The board was suddenly confronted with hard times in the depression that followed World War I. Acting against my father's recommendation, the board began spending the building fund on current expenses. This troubled my father so greatly he ended his YMCA career by resigning.

Another career setback followed immediately. He had a short, bad experience operating a farm owned by my mother's parents, Augustus and Elsie Nichols, near Princeton, Illinois. The move to farming was big step for our family. At the age of two, my world was limited by an unpaved road that divided the farm and became impassable after rains. I have few memories of farm life, but one is vivid. I was riding with my father in a car with no side windows or curtains. It was a gloomy, rainy night appropriate to his mission. His two-year experiment in farming was a financial failure that caused intrafamily strains. In the end, he quit and had to sell his farm equipment and animals. That night he was nailing up notices inviting passersby to a public auction.

Pop brought his family back to Jacksonville, where he became a salesman for Metropolitan Life Insurance Company. Six days a week and most evenings he made house-to-house rounds, carrying a large bound volume known as a debit book. He never bought a new car. His used ones were frequently in a garage for repair. When we made the annual eighty-mile trip to visit Mom's parents and other relatives in Princeton, we could be certain the journey would include at least one stop to fix a flat tire or correct a mechanical problem.

At home, we saw little of my father until late evenings and Sundays. A large oak rocker with upholstered seat, now in my office, was reserved as Pop's chair. Each Saturday evening he and Mom were engrossed at a roll-top desk in the hall, where they counted and recorded the week's money collections. Family income was hard earned.

Our family lived at financial margins, but we did not consider ourselves poor. We viewed tramps that occasionally begged for food at the back door—and always received at least a sandwich—as the truly poor. The Great Depression was underway, and most people in our little city lived on tight budgets. Despite the shortage of cash, the Findley kids had a sense of vibrant community and wonderful childhood. For several years, the 900 block of Edgehill Road bounded most of my world.

Sunday school and worship services were major family events. The Findleys were at State Street Presbyterian Church every Sunday morning from nine to noon. Opening exercises in Sunday school often included recitations. Children were expected to memorize the Apostles' Creed and the names of the books of the Bible. At any moment, one might be called upon for recitation. Sunday school ended just a few minutes before the beginning of worship services in the sanctuary, a large, beautiful auditorium that had entered the threadbare era years earlier. Presbyterian membership was routine, like starting to shave or graduating from junior high school. There was no discussion of other denominations and faiths. My parents were Presbyterians, so I became one. I later learned that adopting the faith of one's parents is a deep-seated custom worldwide, a fact that should disincline everyone from self-righteous posturing.

After the Sunday noon meal, sometimes with close friends, our family piled into the family car. The ride—always a happy time— included a stop at Merrigan's, a local candy store, where we waited in the car while Pop bought an ice cream cone for each of us.

The large screened back porch served as sleeping quarters for my sisters and me. William occupied one of the residence's two bedrooms, our parents the other. When Barbara arrived in 1927, she joined us on the porch, where roll-down canvas curtains provided privacy and some relief from bad weather. On cold nights, Mom eased the shock of climbing into frigid beds by placing between the sheets stones she had warmed in the kitchen oven.

The backyard included fruit trees and a shed for chickens that later became the main course for many dinners. One day I had the chore of using a hatchet and tree stump to decapitate a chicken. I skipped eating the fried chicken served at the next meal. My aversion to capital punishment began when my hatchet severed the chicken's head.

The highlight of one summer was the Edgehill Circus, organized and directed by my sister Ruth, a natural leader. Children of the neighborhood joined in a fun afternoon featuring homemade costumes—mainly pirates and Indians. I was attired as a clown, my sister Miriam an Indian. The future dean of Jacksonville lawyers, three-year-old Bob Bradney, was a spectator. My mother remembered him wearing, in summer, only a diaper that "tended to drop south."

One evening, I visited the Lipsmeier family across the street where I had the thrill of listening to a crystal set, the primitive forerunner of the radio. A cooking bowl served as amplifier. Amid constant static I heard a few words from a faraway Chicago station, clearer ones from one in St. Louis. To me, the set was a marvel of scientific advance.

The greatest evening fun came when our mother read aloud with her children gathered at her feet. Any novel would do. When she fell asleep while reading, as she often did, she was quickly aroused with the chorus, "Read, Mom, read." One of my favorites was a small volume titled *Log Cabin to White House*, about the life of Abraham Lincoln.

Just west of our house was a large vacant lot that my mother rented and transformed into an immense vegetable garden. It yielded large supplies of potatoes, sweet corn, peas, green beans, and lettuce. Some of it was sold door-to-door by Miriam and Ruth, some consumed fresh by our family, and the rest canned for winter months. I liked to eat raw peas out of the pod but found no joy in digging potatoes or picking vegetables. Garden duties were apportioned each spring. I vowed that when I left home I would never again work in a garden.

A thrill even exceeding the crystal set experience came when Charles A. Lindbergh made his solo flight from New York to Paris. I was in first grade at the time. Our class celebrated joyously. He was the preeminent hero of my youth. The license number displayed on the wing of his plane, the *Spirit of St. Louis*, remains fixed in my mind. It was N-X-211. In a homemade scrapbook I placed keepsakes, among them sticker souvenirs of the flight. I relished every word of *We*, his account of his flight.

When I was nine, we moved to 236 Park Street, where I acquired my first trombone, a dented used one. It was borrowed, but I considered it mine. The first night, I took it to bed with me. After school I often played unsupervised football—tackle, not touch. One evening a game brought something rare—a stern scolding. My mother had told me to come straight home from school that day to prepare for playing the trombone in a school band concert that evening. After school I forgot her instruction and enjoyed a football game. When I arrived home she said, "I should keep you home from the concert as punishment, but I know this would disappoint Mr. Von Bodegraven [the band director]. In the future pay careful attention to what I say." It was the only time I recall receiving a scolding from her. Usually, she didn't have to state a word of direction to any of us. She led by example. We all knew how we were expected to behave.

Our parents seemed busy each waking hour, but both had calm personalities, no matter what happened. Pop's strongest expletive, at least the strongest I heard, was "oh, shaw." I heard Mom say "damn" just once. Profanity was considered in poor taste, evidence of an inadequate vocabulary. Grammatical errors were quickly corrected. My father surprised me one day when he brought home a two-piece suit that fit perfectly and made me feel grand.

Another day he took me to Myers Brothers department store where he bought me something new in my life—an athletic supporter. The move to Park Street had opened the world of tennis. Beyond bushes across the street, I discovered a clay court that required periodic doses of lime to keep the lines visible. My pals and I didn't let a little rain or slick clay interrupt a game. We wore tennis balls down to the core and bought inexpensive rackets with steel strings. We called them rainy day rackets. The sport became a passion. I dreamed of having a tennis court in my own backyard. At the age of sixty-seven I achieved the dream, and tennis became nearly a daily routine that lasted until my eightieth birthday. That day, my left knee gave way during a game with physician friend Dr. Chandupatla Prabhakar. I have often wondered if my knee would have remained sound if I had somehow been able to skip my eightieth birthday.

Life on Park Street was enlivened one day when Washington School, where I was attending fourth grade, burned to the ground. For me, it was a thrilling adventure. The alarm sounded during afternoon classes when a blaze was discovered in the attic. Our class calmly left the building by walking down two flights of stairs to ground level. I watched from a safe distance until my dad arrived a few minutes later. To my surprise, he took my hand and, in a clear violation of common sense, escorted me back into the burning building. As we entered, I asked, "Pop, are you sure we should go in?" He smiled, patted me on the shoulder, and said, "We will be all right." We walked upstairs to my classroom, where he helped me gather books and other supplies from my desk before rejoining the crowd outside. We stood together on the lawn and watched from a distance as flames licked at the lower floors. It was a rare moment with my father that I cherished greatly, especially the excitement of entering the burning building.

Barbara Hart taught both fifth and sixth grades at Lafayette School, where many students were transferred after Washington School burned. Miss Hart won student affection by starting each afternoon session by reading aloud a chapter from the book series in which Tarzan, adopted by apes, had many thrilling jungle adventures.

One evening, my father thrilled the family by bringing home a table model Emerson radio. It provided exciting entertainment for all of us. We became acquainted with fascinating characters through weekly radio dramas. Most popular ones for me were the Lone Ranger and his horse Silver, the comedy couple Fibber McGee and Molly, and a hilarious African American pair named Amos and Andy. In just seven years, scientific advance made a giant step from the primitive crystal set that stirred excitement on Edgehill Road.

Gloom descended one afternoon in the spring of 1934 when Pop showed symptoms of Parkinson's disease. After driving around town all day with his debit book, he showed me his fingers. They were stiffly curled to conform to the rim of the car's steering wheel. He was forty-eight and became severely handicapped before the year was out. Walking became difficult. He needed help getting dressed. Unable to manage foot pedals, he had to sell the family car and quit work. Sometimes his hands shook uncontrollably. I occasionally heard bits of quiet conversation between him and Mom on what lay ahead for the family.

2

◇◇◇◇◇◇◇◇◇◇◇◇◇◇◇◇◇◇◇◇◇◇◇◇

Leaving Hard Times

No medications were available that could control or even slow the progress of Parkinson's disease. My father's disability qualified the family for an insurance pension of fifty dollars a month, a major help, but rigorous challenges lay ahead, especially for my mother. For a short time, he could wash dishes and take short walks on his own. Soon he could do nothing for himself or by himself. Each word came with difficulty. His emotions were always close to the surface.

I rarely stopped to converse with him. I don't recall ever having a long, satisfying chat with him. I was always busy, but I could have made time to be with him even if just to tell him my experiences of the previous day. I did not. The memory of that neglect is still painful.

Each passing year intensified his handicaps, but Mom kept him from being bedridden until a few months before his death years later. I remember her walking backward as she led him, shuffling, slowly from room to room. She was still getting him up and dressed each day. By then my parents had moved to the former home of Mom's parents in Princeton, Illinois. Before I began my job managing a weekly newspaper in Pittsfield, he managed to say, "You can be another William Allen White." He smiled, then became choked with emotion. White was one of my heroes, the editor of the *Emporia* (Kansas) *Gazette* and nationally popular as a writer and commentator. I should have stayed and told Pop the dreams I had for my own future.

After Lucille and I moved to Pittsfield, my parents visited us briefly but only part of one day. They had glimpses of the newspaper office and the house where we occupied an upstairs apartment.

During Pop's long illness, I recall only one occasion when he and I were together privately. By then he was hospitalized with pneumonia and unable to utter a word. I spent a long evening at his bedside, holding his right hand. I asked him occasionally if he wanted a sip of water. He usually managed a nod, and I provided it through a straw. We exchanged no words. He died an hour after I left for the night.

Mom was an angel for all of us, serving as homemaker for a family of seven, driving spirit and inspiration for five children, sole caretaker of a disabled husband, and chief breadwinner for the family. I did not hear her complain even once—never a discouraging word, always beaming a smile. She chuckled; for some reason, she had trouble laughing, but she had an abundance of smiles. For several years she managed the high school cafeteria, starting at fifteen dollars a week, later increased to twenty-five. While a student, I earned lunch by serving as cafeteria cashier. Ruth helped in the kitchen. By then, my sister Miriam was studying at a teacher university. Dozens of other students earned lunch by performing tasks under Mom's supervision. She took a personal interest in each and maintained lifelong correspondence with several former helpers. Although afflicted with sore feet, she walked ten blocks from home to school and back each school day.

My mother did housework and laundry for a physician living nearby. During summers she managed a Prairie Farms ice cream store located south of the public library. Two years before the move to her mother's former home, she purchased a house from the Jacksonville Savings and Loan Association. Real estate prices hit rock bottom. The Great Depression was in full force. I do not know how she managed the purchase.

To help ease the family budget, all Findley children found ways to earn money for their own personal expenses. Starting in the sixth grade, I mowed lawns and did odd jobs. Mowing a large lawn brought me seventy-five cents, smaller ones thirty-five to fifty cents. Power mowers were still in the future, and keeping the reel blades sharp on my push mower was a never-ending challenge. One summer I helped Glen Hickle, a high school teacher, dismantle a house. My pay was fifteen cents an hour. One morning, a single lady we knew as Miss Prince called me to her house on Grove Street. Considered an aristocrat by some, an eccentric by others, she did not trust the postal service. She asked me to deliver a letter across town. I made the delivery and received a dime for doing so.

As an eighth-grader, I bought a typewriter and mimeograph from Earl A. Davis, owner of an office supply firm. Both were used, of course, and cost, as I recall, about five dollars each. Owning them put me in the printing business. I was self-employed, my own boss. I liked that way of earning needed funds. For modest fees I produced church bulletins, recital programs, and on one occasion duplicated a master's degree treatise for a local educator. I occasionally had my sister Barbara's help.

In high school, I had several other sources of income. With the principal's permission I mimeographed programs and sold them to fans at football and basketball games. They included merchant advertising I solicited. A scrapbook records a profit of twenty-five dollars for the season. I also received permission to sell chewing gum to students between classes. That project netted forty dollars. Evenings, I sold ham-salad and egg-salad sandwiches, as well as candy bars, at a girls' dormitory at Illinois College. Sandwiches were fifteen cents each, and candy bars just a nickel. Mom made the sandwiches. After paying Mom for ingredients, I cleared about a dollar each evening.

In 1936, national politics got my attention. I was a high school freshman when Republican Governor Alf Landon of Kansas, nominated to oppose the reelection of Roosevelt, became my hero. To boost his candidacy, I joined several neighborhood students in literally tooting the horn. Carrying Landon signs, we played march music for several blocks each evening. During the campaign I met Harry Montgomery, a young Winchester businessman who was Republican candidate for Congress. He unsuccessfully challenged U.S. Representative Henry T. Rainey of Carrollton. My collection of campaign literature includes a Montgomery for Congress sign. At the time I had no inkling that twenty-four years later, when I became Congressman-elect, Montgomery, by then a Winchester realtor, would give me useful advice on how to handle my new responsibility. He urged me to hire several secretaries immediately so I could acknowledge, even if only with a single sentence, every letter the day it arrived. When I reached Capitol Hill, I put his recommendation into operation.

Despite our efforts, Roosevelt carried Jacksonville and won reelection in a national landslide. Landon carried only Maine and Vermont. Although his candidacy was unsuccessful, the Landon campaign whetted my appetite for politics. Suddenly, I became a political pundit. Armed with typewriter and mimeograph, inspired by the career of crusading pamphleteer Tom Paine of American Revolutionary War fame, and at fifteen a self-proclaimed Republican, I issued my own comments and advice on public policy. They were presented on half sheets of letter-size paper, printed both sides. I routinely mimeographed about twenty copies of each commentary and distributed them to any outstretched hand on the sidewalk or at school.

The next year, 1937, was a very busy time. I tried my hand at personal candidacy and won the class presidency in a race against two friends. I received a plurality of votes cast—not a majority—but they were enough. Both opponents were very popular, and, reflecting on the outcome, I was glad that both of them had, at my urging, entered the contest. If I had run against just one of them, I believed I would have lost.

Early that year, I got inside the *Jacksonville Journal-Courier* newsroom. On a hunch I stopped to see publisher W. A. Fay and told him I wanted to write news about events at the high school.

Although taken aback at my rather aggressive step, he agreed and, to my surprise and delight, said he would pay me five cents for each column inch published. Soon I was contributing a weekly column, High School Notes. As I gained confidence of the editors, I received occasional reporting assignments in sports.

By my senior year I was a part-time cub reporter, covering mainly school events and sports. Political meetings were my favorite assignments. The pay stayed at five cents an inch, but I gloried in seeing my written words published. It was a satisfying experience. A scrapbook contains dozens of clippings of my reports, including those covering a lecture by a visiting Indiana professor, Dr. J. Raymond Schulz, who said the United States was the world's only surviving democracy; a talk by Ella Enslow, author of the bestselling *Schoolhouse in the Foothills*; and a lecture by architect-artist Karl Bolander. On the margin of each page of the scrapbook I entered the total column inches displayed. It was useful proof-of-publication when I collected my five-cents-an-inch fee.

During the summer, I had a delightful break from journalism. My brother William, who was twenty-one, drove my sisters Miriam and Ruth and me to the Colorado Rocky Mountains where we enjoyed a week of pure fun. He rented a rustic cabin and paid all our expenses himself. On a side trip to Colorado Springs, where Pop's two unmarried teacher sisters, Grace and Bess, lived, I damaged Grace's new sedan by driving it into a high curb. To my surprise and relief, she didn't scold me. The next summer, William paid my tuition at a summer music camp sponsored by the University of Michigan at Ann Arbor, providing another chapter in my preparation for the public stage.

That fall, I entered the publishing business on a small scale. I used my typewriter and mimeograph to issue a small monthly newsletter, *Hi-Y Record*. It consisted of a single legal-size folded sheet that featured past and coming activities of the people active in Hi-Y events. One issue reported a meeting with State Representative Hugh Green, who explained the new federal program for senior citizens called Social Security. It foreshadowed my varied career in maga-zine and newspaper publishing. Fingers stained by mimeograph ink would soon be stained by printer's ink from the composing rooms of the *Jacksonville Journal-Courier* and still later the composing room of my own newspaper, the *Pike County Republican.*

Late that fall, without even lifting a finger, I attained another presidency. YMCA headquarters in Chicago sponsored annual statewide Older Boys Conferences, usually attended by about a thousand high school boys. While attending the one in Elgin in December 1937, I was asked, to my surprise, to conduct a respon-sive reading during a plenary session. Before adjourning, delegates elected me to serve as president at the next conference, to be held in Peoria. I was astounded. It was the easiest election of my life. I did not know I was a candidate until voting began. The next year, when I left home for Peoria, my mother was beaming broadly. She had deep allegiance to the YMCA, dating from the early years of Pop's career. My election as president of the Older Boys Conference may have given her greater joy than my later election to Congress. The conference was a flawless, uplifting experience for me. It gave me experience in addressing large crowds and helped convince me that public service could be satisfying.

One evening in the family living room, I was typing a critique of President Roosevelt's controversial proposal to increase the size of the Supreme Court. The court had blocked several of Roosevelt's New Deal proposals. By appointing three additional justices favor-able to Roosevelt's political views, the president could expect future court decisions to turn more in his favor. While I pecked noisily away, my father was trying to listen to the president explain his court proposal in a "fireside" radio address. By that time my father was having difficulty expressing words, but, in halting speech, he was able to ask, "Why don't you let Roosevelt finish before you criticize him?" I stopped typing until the president concluded. I did not ask Pop what he thought of the president's proposal, though. I already had my own firm opinion.

The next day I distributed a statement called "Democracy to Dictatorship." In the text I deplored Roosevelt's move and accused him of subverting the Constitution. I warned, "He has already made Congress his tool" and added that his "court-packing scheme" was a "mad rush for supremacy." The public agreed with my disapproval, and stirred wide public protest—it was one of the few Roosevelt initiatives that failed.

In a later, milder broadside titled "A Stable Currency," I warned against "deficit spending" and declared that "one of the necessities and obligations of a central government is providing a sound and nonfluctuating currency." I wrote that seventy-three years ago, but it sounds like wise counsel for today. Tom Paine may be smiling.

One day I lost my bearings. I circulated a commentary captioned, "Evidence of Communism in Jacksonville." I decried the decision of city fathers to construct a city-owned power plant, a move I deplored as a "firm foundation for the Communists as government-ownership is one of the things [they] emphasized." It probably prompted a few laughs around town. The manager of the privately owned Illinois Power and Light Company, the firm that long served Jacksonville power needs, wanted extra copies.

The summer of 1938 was exciting. In June, I hitchhiked to Washington, D.C., my first visit there, staying with the Vannier family who formerly lived across Edgehill Road from my family. My tour included Capitol Hill, where I received a pass to the visitors' galleries from the office of my congressman, Representative Scott Lucas of Havana, later Senate majority leader. I was thrilled to tour the Capitol building and visit both chambers of Congress. In the Senate gallery, I sat transfixed, studying the chamber below. The dapper Senator Robert LaFollette Jr. of Wisconsin was seated at his desk sporting a prominent bowtie. Also on the floor was Senator William E. Borah, the "lion of Idaho." Both were Republicans, with LaFollette in the progressive wing and Borah in the conservative. I thought of how grand it must be to serve in Congress.

Back home, not all my public statements were calmly received. One aroused ire of students and faculty at Jacksonville High School. In "Collapse of Conscience," an article in the December 8, 1938, issue of the mimeographed student newspaper, the *Herald,* I applauded the acting skill of participants in the annual faculty-student minstrel show but lamented its "gutter filth" obscenities. A handwritten "open" letter arrived in the mail several days later. Although unsigned, it was identified as being from "students of the minstrel and teachers who took part in the production." The text warned, "The time will come when you will need the friends you have lost by writing that editorial." Convinced I was right to complain, I felt no concern over the warning. On the scrapbook page displaying evidence of the episode, this marginal note announced: "Future minstrels contained no obscenities."

These experiments in speaking out elicited no apparent reaction from my parents or my siblings, possibly because they learned not to read them. My parents were Republicans. I know they took an interest in public affairs, but I cannot recall when either of them expressed a personal opinion, except on behalf of a bond issue to finance four new elementary schools. For news, inspiration, and opinion, I leaned mainly on the local daily newspaper, the magazine rack at the public library, and articles in the *Literary Digest.*

Early in the summer of 1939, I had a sobering business experience. Jimmy Johnston, years later the editor of the Bloomington, Illinois, *Pantagraph,* joined me in an ill-fated attempt to make a few dollars at two county fairs in southern Illinois. We sold advertising for programs we prepared and mimeographed. We then sold them for ten cents a copy in stands at horse shows. The project ended during the second fair when Johnston, lured by a professional gambler into a shell game, lost every dime of our profits. He came to our rented room that evening in tears. Fortunately, our room fee was paid in advance. We returned to Jacksonville determined to keep a safe distance from shell games.

Seeking a college scholarship, I started at the top, writing to Oxford University in England and Harvard, as each impressed me as a neat place to study. I received friendly turn-downs from both schools, as well as from several others in the Ivy League. My appeal to DePauw University in Greencastle, Indiana, and Illinois College in Jacksonville brought good responses. DePauw offered a four-year tuition-only scholarship. This prompted me to hitchhike to Greencastle and arrange to do household work to pay for a room beginning in September. On returning to Jacksonville, I reconsidered in favor of Illinois College. It was easier and less costly to live at home—for awhile, that is. My parents moved to my mother's childhood home in Princeton during my sophomore year.

In September 1939, wearing a green skullcap that marked me a freshman, I had the good fortune to meet sophomore Charles Menees of Virginia, Illinois. Handicapped by injuries from a car accident several years earlier, he limped and always used a cane. He took me under his wing, persuaded me to join Phi Alpha Literary Society, and, on becoming the editor of the *Rambler*, the student weekly newspaper, he welcomed my op-ed pieces.

By then, I was well established as a reporter at the *Journal-Courier*, devoting many hours each week to covering lectures, writing sports, and proofreading. I loved the pressure of deadlines and the constant clatter of the teletype that brought Associated Press dispatches into a booth in the room. Erland Ericson, a friend and recent Illinois College graduate, was night wire editor. Inside the booth, the AP news was printed on continuous paper fed from a box on the floor. When Ericson was in the booth removing the latest output of wire news, he usually sang at the top of his fine baritone voice. I enjoyed it as background music.

The newsroom became my home. I loved being there. I relaxed sitting at a steel newsroom desk with my fingers on a typewriter keyboard. I enjoyed typing news on a continuous steam of paper like the one in the teletype booth.

After approving one of my reports, the copyeditor would hook it to a line accessible to the composing room above. Once set in type, a proof was sent back on the same clip line for checking. It was the era of hot type from linotypes. The lines of type were placed in heavy page forms, and then converted into metal cylinders before being locked on a large press for newspaper printing. News and composing rooms today, by contrast, are neat and almost silent. Gone but not forgotten, by me at least, is newsroom magic, a place of clatter, hustle, clutter, and smears of printer's ink.

Each issue of the *Rambler* was prepared in the upstairs *Journal-Courier* composing room, so I soon found the newsroom situated below a handy site for composing opinion columns for the campus newspaper. My opinion contributions, initially called Highlights and Shadows, later Findley's Uncensored Prejudices, produced no financial income—not even five cents a column inch—but valuable experience in speaking out. In the September 30, 1942, issue of the *Rambler*, while deploring the plight of people suffering brutality under Japanese conquest, I quoted a victim of Britain's imperialism in India. At that time, India was still a colony, with its inhabitants denied many of the freedoms British citizens enjoyed. Much of the fruit of Indian labor went to London, not into producer pockets. In a column a week later, I lamented the fate of U.S. citizens of Japanese ancestry living on the West Coast who were forced into internment camps simply because of their national origin. I wrote, "Thousands of the interned Japanese were born in the United States, some of them of parents who were born in this country."

Campus life included fun. Despite the Depression, dress-up proms were so common that I bought a fourteen-dollar tuxedo. Phi Alpha members enjoyed serenading dormitories at MacMurray College, then a girls' school. Wilbur Moore, who rented the room near mine in a private home, occasionally joined me in entertaining a MacMurray girl or two with a duet over the telephone—Wilbur playing the saxophone and I the trombone.

In history classes I attended, professor Joe Patterson Smith needed no proctor. Although blind, he maintained absolute control. As he lectured, he seemed to know where each of us sat and what each was thinking. Menees was one of his special wards; I was not. Perhaps he thought my commentaries in the *Rambler*—he was its faculty adviser—were juvenile or worse. One day, while seated in his paper-strewn office, Smith said, "Findley, your harness squeaks. It needs oiling. You need to loosen up your mind." I took no offense. I knew Smith had a valid point, although I didn't mention my agreement. As my comments continued, they showed, at least to me, some progress toward thoughtful reflection. One day in class, Smith said the United States should immediately declare war against Germany. I disagreed. In a column published in the *Rambler*, I complained that America was once again "pulling British chestnuts out of the fire."

Shortly after that isolationist comment, I took a different tack, recommending immediate, common citizenship with Britain and a few other democracies. This abrupt, major change in opinion reflected a startling, profound event—the Japanese assault on Pearl Harbor. A foreign power had delivered a powerful blow on American territory. The situation had nothing to do with chestnuts. U.S. territory suffered heavy losses of lives and materiel. Any government whose territory is assaulted has the right and duty to respond. War was thrust upon us.

That day, December 7, 1941, was a personal awakening. I was walking downstairs that Sunday morning from my rented room near the college campus, expecting to walk to church. Instead, on reaching the first floor I stood spellbound, listening to President Roosevelt's voice as he announced that the United States was at war. I knew military service lay ahead. The Japanese assault and the state of war against Hitler's Germany put isolationist thoughts out of my mind.

Early in 1942, I joined two other Phi Alpha members in signing up for navy flight training. I also signed up for summer school at the University of Chicago Law School, helped by a warm note to the dean from Professor Smith. I was surprised and grateful for the letter. Perhaps he found my harness better oiled than before. I wanted to receive my college degree before putting on a uniform. Transferring credits from a summer term at University of Chicago Law School would qualify me for a bachelor's degree at Illinois College in January 1943.

Enlisting in the cadet program would enable me to remain a civilian until February. I also hoped the summer study at Chicago would help me decide whether I wanted to study law. That year, Illinois College had a January graduation for students like me who had enough credits to graduate early. All my grades at Illinois College were As. Luckily, my law school grades—two Bs and a C—arrived at Illinois College after I was invited to membership in Phi Beta Kappa.

I graduated debt free, thanks to my employment two previous summers, plus scholarships and earnings from the *Journal-Courier*. One year, thanks to a federal youth program, I received $120 for directing the Illinois College band. This suggested desperation in the college music department, as my only claim to musicianship came from my mediocre performance on a trombone and serving one year as student band director in high school. My siblings Miriam, Ruth, and Barbara were far more skilled, talented in both voice and piano. Under my direction the college band provided a chapel program and later an outdoor concert—both notable only for length.

I gained lasting friendships and valuable public speaking experience at Illinois College, especially through membership in Phi Alpha. Supporting the college became a lifelong passion that seems to grip me tighter with each passing year. For thirty years I served on its board of trustees, and at eighty-nine still serve as "den father" for student members of Phi Alpha.

On February 1, 1943, I headed for Monmouth, Illinois, as a naval aviation cadet. I could not swim, had never been in an aircraft or viewed an ocean. This did not make me an oddity, however, as the navy was already well stocked with "ninety-day wonders," young-sters who had seen little but cornfields prior to becoming sailors. When I enlisted, the navy wanted two thousand more air cadets. Illinois College recruits were part of the navy's initial sign up of six hundred. I wanted to serve overseas in military uniform.

3

∞∞∞∞∞∞∞∞∞∞∞∞∞∞∞∞∞∞

War and Romance

My service in World War II lasted nearly three years. The first ten months were spent on training bases in the United States, and the balance in the far Pacific where I served as a Seabee supply officer in the liberation of Guam and briefly during occupation of Japan. While on Guam, a Navy Department wire automatically advanced me and hundreds of other ensigns to lieutenant junior grade. Ensign Lucille Gemme, a beautiful flight nurse from the Boston area who later voluntarily changed her name to Findley, achieved the extra half-stripe two months before I did. By war's end, she wore two battle stars, one each for Iwo Jima and Okinawa. I lagged behind with just one for Guam.

During wartime service, hostile fire was never directed at me. One night friendly fire penetrated my tent and a bullet came to rest in a floor plank just inches from the bunk where I was sleeping. It was fired by a Seabee helping pals in reckless celebration of New Year's Day 1945. They fired carbines and revolvers aimlessly in the air. Perhaps I should have dug the bullet from the plank as later proof to grandchildren that one night I nearly got shot.

Wartime was one of the most profound experiences of my life. While on Guam, pure happenstance led me to Lucille, who became my loving wife and companion in January 1946 and soon after the mother of our children, Craig and Diane. At a party one night when her army pilot escort became too drunk to drive, Lucille let me provide a jeep ride to her quarters. Winning Lucille was, for me, more significant than the liberation of Guam, but the two campaigns intertwined.

Navy duty was my first disciplined lifestyle. It also entailed an occasional touch of leadership. From my first day as a cadet, I enjoyed discipline—a regular personal schedule day and night, close order marching drill, and even the requirement to turn square corners while walking to class at preparatory schools.

When I became an ensign I had responsibility for conduct of others but rarely needed to exercise it. On Guam I was responsible for about $200,000 in cash. I kept funds in a safe in my tent office. As I received deposits from Ship's Store and conducted paydays, I watched pieces of torn and patched currency circulate time after time through the battalion's tiny economy. Since mustering out of the navy and transferring cash to another officer in December 1945, I have wondered if anyone in the long navy chain of command ever balanced my accounts.

I had personal satisfaction in having a part—small though it was—in defeating the Axis Powers. Had I been unable to be in uniform and serve in a combat area, I would have felt disadvantaged. The war had become one of the most important and violent events in human history. It was also perhaps the most gigantic failure of human beings. Although I deplored the failure, the consequences were inescapable. I did not want to be a spectator. The nation was mobilized and united for the war. Public spirit was higher, I believed, than any previous times in American history. The war had to be won, and I wanted to be a participant.

My first duty station was Monmouth, a small town of about eight thousand just a few hours drive from my parents' home in Princeton and my college home in Jacksonville. On the Monmouth College campus the navy established a three-month flight preparatory program designed to keep cadets busy until major flight schools at Corpus Christi, Texas, and Pensacola, Florida, had room for them.

The course was not arduous. I still had printer's ink in my blood and enough spare time to help launch a cadet newspaper called *Wing Tips*. I served as editor and columnist. My scrapbook shows I could do twenty-three pushups without a break, a feat that I report with a mixture of incredulity and nostalgia. Before the course was over, the commanding officer announced a new, additional step for cadets before final flight training would begin. It was a three-month course with some flight training at St. Ambrose College in nearby Davenport, Iowa. There we had daily training in sturdy single-engine high-wing crafts called Aeroncas. We were soon doing wingovers, chandelles, dives, loops, and tail spins, most of which I enjoyed even during hours flying solo.

Shortly after arrival at Davenport, I learned another intermediate step would soon lengthen preparatory work after Davenport. You may have difficulty believing this, but I worried I would not be stationed in a combat zone before the war ended. I didn't want to push pencils at a stateside desk. That would be embarrassing. I wanted to be where great adventures were being undertaken. After the war was won—which I accepted as a certainty—I wanted to take pride in explaining to my family what I did.

In July, I requested and received a transfer to Great Lakes Naval Training Station north of Chicago, where I received physical exams and management duties while awaiting orders. During weekends in the Chicago Loop, I enjoyed dancing at the Trianon Ballroom where big bands provided music and the fee was only ten cents a set. Most of the men, me included, wore military uniforms and arrived without dates. Attractive girls gathered near the walls were always available for a spin around the floor.

Two weeks later a direct commission as ensign arrived, together with orders to report to Harvard Business School, where I spent two months training as a navy supply officer. While there, I had the pleasure of carrying home from the hospital my infant nephew Ronald, the first child of my eldest sister Miriam and her husband, Herbert Schaller, an army sergeant stationed in Boston.

After Harvard, I endured an exhausting train trip from Boston to Seattle. Movie star Gene Kelly brightened one afternoon by dropping by the club car where I was enjoying a friendly poker game with other sailors. A chair at our table was empty, and Kelly accepted an invitation to play a hand. It was seven-card stud, and for some reason I could do no wrong. I won handily. Kelly cheerfully congratulated me, paid up, shook hands around, and left. Meeting Kelly was a high point, as he was my all-time favorite actor-dancer. Except for the Kelly appearance, the trip was miserable. The weather was bitter cold, food terrible, and during frequent delays, some lasting several hours, train cars were unheated.

Worse was yet to come. At Seattle, I boarded a transport ship, joining several hundred other military personnel headed for Pearl Harbor. Seas were rough, and the ship bounced around like a ping-pong ball. I spent a lot of time heaving over the side. Even when my stomach was empty, I kept heaving. I tried to take my mind off innards by reading Tolstoy's *War and Peace,* but my alimentary canal did not return to normal until the ship docked at Pearl Harbor. I kept the book as a souvenir of misery.

During the next two weeks, I settled into new duties as disbursing and commissary officer for the 72nd Seabee Battalion. It was organized in Georgia and was being fitted out for assault on an unspecified island in the Far Pacific.

One afternoon, holding a piece of paper aloft, Lieutenant Commander Lester Clauburger shouted, "This is it." It was his dramatic prelude to telling the officers and crew that the battalion would soon take part in the liberation of Guam. A Dutch transport ship named the *Veltevreden,* captained by a brother of Nazi Germany's Marshal Rommel, would be our conveyance. It was soon fully loaded with varied equipment and supplies needed to build a navy air base on Guam.

The journey to Guam was expected to take five days. Instead, it took thirty-five. Along with scores of other vessels, our ship "swung around the hook" for thirty days at the tiny atoll of Eniwetok while awaiting orders to go ashore at Guam. I spent most of the days at a poker table. The chips were cheap enough so no one lost more than five dollars even during a long day. I was lucky during the early days and piled up winnings of over two hundred dollars. But the tide turned and by the time we reached Guam, I was down to a few dollars.

Landing was an around-the-clock process. U.S. Marines had secured most of the island, but bullets still whizzed around Agana, the main harbor at Guam, when the battalion crew began unloading equipment and supplies. Executive Officer Clauburger panicked and refused to go ashore. When a medical officer declared him fit for service, Captain Walter Blue, furious at his chief deputy's behavior, ordered him hauled ashore on a stretcher. A week later, he was ordered stateside.

The U.S. death toll, mostly marines, was about fourteen hundred. The Japanese lost over five thousand. The first thing I noticed, along with sporadic gunfire, was the stench of dead bodies rotting in tropical heat. I have never forgotten it. It came vividly to mind years later when Lucille and I toured the Highway of Death between Basra and Kuwait City in 1991 at the end of the Gulf War and saw—and smelled—decaying Iraqi bodies in tanks and trucks left at roadside.

On Guam, I knew personal danger could lie ahead. The island was within air reach of Japan. One of the bullets flying around might have my name on it, but despite the stench of death all around us, I do not recall giving even passing thought to the prospect of being killed or even wounded.

Our job was to enlarge a small hilltop airstrip into a major navy air base big enough to handle heavy traffic. As disbursing and commissary officer, I had little to do during immediate landing operations. A mess hall would not be erected until hilly ground was leveled for base quarters. A payday would not be needed until the Ship's Store began to function.

In the early days, I helped organize a hilltop storage area near Agana. Most of the battalion crew were men experienced in construction in civilian life. Almost all were in their late thirties or older. Most were married. At twenty-three, I was one of the youngest and was frequently told I looked like a high school kid.

During landing operations, I became hooked on coffee. The coffeemaker was primitive: a fifty-gallon steel drum that contained water and a large bag of ground coffee beans simmering over a wood fire. The result tasted great, especially after midnight. Food consisted of cold C and K rations, nourishing but impossible to relish. K rations were bars of dark stuff advertised as nutritious. C rations were varied food items in small cans. One of the first pieces of equipment put into operation was a bread oven. Eating fresh bread for the first time in days was pure joy.

Working in shifts around the clock, Seabees soon had quarters, offices, a mess hall—all in tents—and a large airstrip busy around the clock. Storage buildings and expanded parking space for planes were completed in days. Lieutenant Homer Barger, my tent mate at the time, supervised the erection of immense tanks for storing aviation fuel. He persuaded the battalion sign painter to post a sign at our tent entrance inspired by a popular comic strip. It read: "Lonesome Polecat and Hairless Joe." Homer was the polecat and I hairless Joe. Homer longed for former carefree days when he toured the Western Hemisphere erecting steel mills and tank farms. In the comic strip, Hairless Joe and Lonesome Polecat were an odd couple who engaged in whimsical, homespun antics.

During the long months on Guam, handling pay records and funds kept me busy most of the time at the disbursing tent, where my staff consisted of a chief petty officer and three yeomen. I kept personal custody and care of about $200,000, conducted paydays, and signed all pay cards. Occasionally I conducted payday aboard a nearby navy ship that was too small to have a paymaster. This usually involved climbing aboard ship via a rope ladder, sometimes in a rough sea.

But it wasn't all work and no play: under Chaplain Hambrick's leadership, a softball diamond and a tennis court were soon in operation. I was the regular catcher in softball even though my batting average was low. A right-hander, my swing was always lethargic. On those rare occasions when I hit the ball, it fell in right field, just inside the first base line. Most of my exercise occurred on the tennis court.

Days were hot and humid. Nights were just humid, and mosquitoes were abundant and well armed. Overweight frogs were everywhere, and each morning we shook fast-moving lizards from shoes and other clothing as we dressed. News was scarce. So were books and magazines. Even reports on the Pacific military campaign were rare and skimpy. The small island—twenty miles in its longest dimension—was my world.

It quickly became a beehive of construction. Several large army air bases were underway and roads improved. Although I did not realize it at the time, Guam was becoming a major center of gigantic military preparations. Building and maintaining the navy air base at Agana was a comparatively small operation, but it was a vital link in a vast chain that spread from the U.S. mainland to battle lines close to Japan. Guam became essential to a vast armada of big bombers that dropped bombs on Tokyo and other Japanese cities, a violent prelude to the expected U.S. invasion.

Some bombers did not make it back to Guam. Others with personnel aboard were destroyed in crash landings. We could tell from engine whines and coughing which landing planes were damaged. A deep pit created by construction projects on Guam became the burial ground of wrecked planes.

Among early patrons of the new air base at Agana were Lucille and eleven other navy flight nurses, a unique group that pioneered air evacuation of wounded from battlefields. They took turns in trips on DC-3 hospital planes from Guam to Iwo Jima, where one of the bloodiest battles of World War II was underway. They drew straws to determine the order in which they would begin trips. Lucille was third in line.

On each flight a nurse and a corpsman accompanied twenty-eight fresh marine recruits who deplaned at a tiny airstrip often under hostile fire. They augmented forces already in combat. After fresh troops left the plane, the nurse and corpsman helped airstrip personnel load twenty-five badly wounded marines onto litters fastened four-deep inside cabin walls. They were a tight fit. About three inches separated one patient from the litter above. Deplaning and loading usually took thirty minutes.

Deplaning troops sometimes included one or two who resisted, some tearfully. As officer in charge, the nurse had the chore of demanding that all get off, tears or not. Marine losses in combat were so heavy that, for the first time in the corps' history, fresh marines were mostly draftees. Many of the recruits Lucille unloaded at Iwo were teenagers.

The flight took about six hours each way. Some days, several flights occurred in quick sequence. Each departed Guam just before midnight, scheduled for landing at dawn, a time that minimized risk of Japanese air assault during deplaning and loading. On one arrival Lucille had to join marines in a pillbox for about thirty minutes while the airstrip was under attack. When Japanese planes disappeared and airstrip potholes were filled, the plane with patients and crew headed back to Guam.

Nurse Gwen Jensen had a narrow escape when Japanese gunfire tore a hole in a wing. The pilot, fearing that wind might enlarge the hole, returned to Iwo. After landing, a leak in a fuel tank was discovered and repaired. Jensen said, "It's a good thing we returned to Iwo for repairs. Otherwise, we would have ditched a planeload of patients in the ocean."

Each wounded marine received a Purple Heart medal before leaving Iwo. One tried to give his medal to Lucille, but she persuaded him to take it home to his mother. Nurses offered sandwiches to the wounded. One nurse remembered slicing bread with a Japanese sword borrowed from a patient taking it home as a souvenir. To provide a touch of home, flight nurses usually wore perfume and lipstick. Patients loved the scent and sometimes said, "Walk past me again." While checking her lipstick, one nurse heard a patient say softly, "You look just like my mother when she puts on lipstick." Even though badly wounded, the marines would joke. Like all marines, they were instructed to address all officers as sir, and especially enjoyed addressing the nurses that way. One, with a grin, asked Ensign Mary Leahy: "Sir, may I address you as 'tootsie'?"

On return flights the nurse and corpsman had the challenging assignment of keeping twenty-five seriously wounded patients alive. The task was complicated because aircraft cabins were not pressurized, and pilots flew low to minimize patient bleeding. This made the trip bouncy. At Guam, the wounded were transferred to a local hospital for emergency care before being flown to a general hospital in Hawaii.

Years later, I asked Lucille and her flight nurse buddy, Ensign Leahy (now Hudnall), to estimate the total number of flights nurses made to Iwo Jima. They concluded that each of the twelve nurses made at least six round trips to Iwo. This meant each cared for at least 150 wounded marines on return trips. In aggregate, the twelve cared for about eighteen hundred marines on long flights to hospitals on Guam. Only one patient died en route, a record of care so remarkable the unit received a commendation ribbon from the chief of naval operations. After the battle for Iwo Jima, each nurse made at least three trips to rescue wounded marines from the bloody battle on Okinawa. That air trip from Guam required nine hours. Lucille also made a rescue trip to Samar in the Philippines.

Private Ed Busch, one of the wounded Marines tended by Lucille on an evacuation flight from Okinawa, remembered her only as "the redhead nurse." Sixty-six years later, through a hometown friend who, in a remarkable coincidence, had served as a wartime flight nurse with Lucille, Busch learned the redhead's name and address. He surprised and pleased my wife in January 2011 with a greeting card, photos, and grateful message. He told her she was the first pretty girl he had seen in months, and he was so captivated that he reached out from his cot when she walked by, intending to give her a gentle pat on the derriere. He pulled back when a sergeant in the cot above warned, "Don't do it. She's an officer. You'll wind up in the brig."

Nurses were resourceful in improving quarters on Guam. Returning from Iwo one afternoon, Lucille found the nurses' tent and all contents, including perfume and lipstick, blown away by a hurricane. She and her close friend and colleague, Ensign Myrtle "Homey" Hanna, hitched a flight to Hawaii for replenishments, with perfume high on their shopping list. Bunking overnight in navy quarters on Oahu, they noted with envy a mirror on the wall and decided it would better serve the war effort if transferred to their quarters on Guam. It fit neatly in a sea-bag they used as a travel suitcase. In informal navy terminology, the transfer qualified as a "midnight requisition." When they returned to Guam, they found the tent quarters replaced by steel structures called Quonset huts. This was a special treat for the nurses. The mirror was a perfect fit. A similar requisition occurred when two nurses acquired a refrigerator for their quarters during a visit for dinner aboard a destroyer escort temporarily anchored in Agana harbor. I won nurse applause by persuading a Seabee carpenter to make plywood clothespins for their use.

Lucille and Norma were invited to dinner one evening with five-star Admiral Chester W. Nimitz, supreme commander of Pacific fleet operations, in his hilltop quarters on Guam. The admiral obviously enjoyed the occasional company of attractive young ladies. Nimitz autographed Lucille's place card, now her cherished keepsake.

A few unorganized Japanese soldiers still roamed the tropical hillsides long after the fighting stopped on Guam. For security, nurse quarters were surrounded by a wire fence. The outdoor head (navy word for latrine) was about twenty feet beyond it. The path between fence and head was guarded at night by two marines. One nurse said the marines made her more nervous than the prospect of Japanese intrusion. She was of course joking.

The appearance of lone Japanese soldiers became commonplace in the months after liberation. Those I learned about were not hostile, although they sometimes encountered hostile fire. I viewed them as hapless human beings, no longer enemies. Years later at a reunion, a former Seabee recalled sitting astride a log having a bowel movement when he was approached by a Japanese soldier who said in halting English that he wanted to surrender. As constipation was not unknown on Guam, the Seabee told the would-be prisoner that he was too busy to take him into custody and directed him up the path to Chaplain Hambrick's tent.

One night I was awakened by gunfire. Rumors reached the officers' quarters that a Japanese soldier was prowling menacingly at the bottom of a steep hill nearby. The air was soon filled with noise and smoke as several officers fired down the hill where the Japanese soldier was rumored to be cornered. The next morning I visited the focus of gunfire and found a bullet-ridden body. Beside it was a wallet containing a picture of a Japanese woman and three young children. It was a needless death. The soldier presented no danger to U.S. forces. Perhaps others felt as I did, but I did not hear it discussed. Those who fired aimlessly demonstrated a primitive, mob impulse. It was an exceptional display of abnormality that made me feel sorry for the victim and his family and ashamed of my colleagues.

I was surrounded by the horror and waste of war. Although I felt safe, I had some knowledge from Lucille's flights and from pilots of the price others paid. On Guam, cemeteries for U.S. dead were slowly taking shape. War seemed folly, a dreadful waste of human beings and physical resources. I had long thoughts, wondering how wars could be prevented in future years. Like millions of other Americans in uniform, I voted by absentee ballot in 1944. My vote was against Franklin D. Roosevelt's election to a fourth term. For one thing, photographs showed him to be a sick man. For another, twelve years was far too long for any person to bear the enormous burdens of the presidency. Another four years was unthinkable. In addition, I preferred the mainstream positions on public policy favored by the Republican Party.

But I recognized Roosevelt's record and ability. I was deeply shaken by this death. The man who had served as president since I was twelve years old was gone. When Vice President Harry S. Truman took the presidential oath, I wondered if this inexperienced man could handle the job.

Late in the summer of 1945, the 72nd U.S. Naval Construction Battalion began packing up, preparing to participate in the planned invasion of the Japanese mainland, an operation expected to be fanatically resisted by the island nation's entire population. Enormous U.S. casualties were anticipated.

Suddenly, the armed services radio reported a huge explosion at a city named Hiroshima, Japan, then another at nearby Nagasaki. The U.S. Air Force had dropped atomic bombs on each city. In their fiery wake, Emperor Hirohito ordered the end of Japanese resistance. Admiral Nimitz, Lucille's onetime host at dinner, and General Douglas MacArthur soon accepted Japanese surrender in ceremonies in Tokyo harbor aboard the USS *Missouri*. With Hitler dead and Germany hoisting the white flag in Europe, the mightiest and costliest military engagement in human history came to an end.

Two days after the surrender, a lone, hungry Japanese soldier who obviously did not know the war was over sneaked to the door of the nurses' Quonset plainly begging for something to eat. Lucille was one of the nurses who buttered a few slices of bread and handed them to the visitor. Bread in hand, the soldier scampered into thick undergrowth nearby.

The 72nd soon completed loading aboard ship for the trip in Japan. Without firing a shot or receiving hostile fire, we moved ashore as occupation forces at the Japanese Naval Base at Sasebo Harbor, Kyushu, Japan. By then I was one of the few remaining battalion officers who took part in the liberation of Guam. The others had been returned to the United States in normal rotation. My rotation wasn't up yet, as I did not join the 72nd until it had already arrived at a temporary transit point near Pearl Harbor.

As our ship moved into the Japanese harbor, we noted the hill-sides bristled with fortified pillboxes and caves. The harbor was festooned with cannon. All of us heaved a deep sigh of thanksgiving that Truman had gained unconditional surrender of Japanese military forces by ordering atomic bombing of two large cities.

In the cold calculus of war, Truman may have saved more lives than the two bombs destroyed. One life saved may have been my own. A conventional bombing and invasion of the mainland would likely have killed hundreds of thousand of Japanese civilians, and many thousands of military personnel on both sides. Landing at Sasebo, the battalion occupied quarters formerly used as a Japanese naval cadet training center and immediately enjoyed hot meals from steam tables the Seabees built before leaving Guam.

One morning, my friend Lieutenant David Wood and I rode a jeep to nearby Nagasaki, scene of the second atomic bombing, the blast that finally prompted Japanese surrender. The visit was risky so soon after the bomb was dropped, but we decided it was worth the risk. It was the chance of a lifetime to visit the site of history-making action.

The scene was pure devastation and desolation. No human beings were in sight. Nothing was left of a great industrial city except baseball-size rubble and steel beams twisted like wet spaghetti. We walked to the center of the blast and looked around. The space was empty for more than a mile in each direction. When the bomb exploded, an estimated 73,000 human beings died instantly and thousands more were disabled for life.

From my stay in Pearl Harbor and the heavy death toll during the liberation of Guam, I had a glimpse of war's cost in human misery. In conversations with Lucille, I received details of the awful human ordeals on Iwo Jima and Okinawa. At Nagasaki, Wood and I saw no dead bodies. Not one. Most had been consumed in the awful firestorm, the others hauled away. The enormity of war's costs began to hit me forcibly.

It was a profound moment. On both sides of World War II, millions of young men and many women died in uniform. Hundreds of thousands of civilians also perished. Millions of families were forever blighted. The cost in human misery is incalculable. I was one of the lucky people. I survived unscathed, a fact that made me feel humble and grateful. It also made me accept a deep obligation. Pondering evidence of innocent lives lost that I witnessed firsthand at Pearl Harbor, Guam, and now Nagasaki, I vowed to do what I could in civilian life to banish "this mighty scourge of war," as Lincoln called it. I wondered what, if anything, a young man from the cornfields of Illinois could do to influence great decisions like war and peace. I determined to keep the goal of war prevention foremost in mind as career opportunities unfolded.

Much of my time on Guam was almost serene, hardly grim duty and hardship on a bloody battlefront in a worldwide conflict. It was not the life I expected when I enlisted in the navy. Still, death and destruction were everywhere, experienced far more regularly and directly by Lucille than myself. Inspection of the body of a Japanese soldier killed the night before by pointless rifle and pistol fire by a gaggle of fellow officers, and inspection of a family picture I found on his body, stuck in my memory. At the time, the island was flooded with grim evidence that arrived daily on and off the air base, and in and out of the harbor. Seeing Nagasaki firsthand was a grim reminder of ugly events on thousands of far-flung battlefields worldwide.

Driving the jeep back to Sasebo Harbor, the realm of political action began to tug. I knew I would be able to leave the navy soon. I wanted to return to civilian life as soon as possible. Where would I start? Law practice? Journalism? How could I begin? First things first: engagement and marriage with Lucille, if she would have me. I had already told her that making money was not a high priority in my dreams for the future. I wanted most of all to make a difference in public policy—yes, to prevent wars.

4

Country Editor

When orders for my return to the States arrived, the battalion executive officer said he could arrange a leisurely trip through the main cities of China before I flew home. It was a tempting offer, but other tugs were stronger. Instead of going to China, I hitched a flight to Guam. As the plane landed, I had a full view of hillsides decorated with neat rows of crosses and shore depots filled with bulldozers, pans, and scrapers—big machines readied for the expected invasion of Japan. The view projected a note of finality, a sobering glimpse of lives lost as well as evidence the war was over.

After spending the night on Guam, I boarded a flight to Hawaii, where I bought Lucille a small diamond ring in the Ship's Store. I then hopped rides to the navy air base at Olathe, Kansas, where she and other flight nurses were expected to gather. On arrival I found other nurses but not Lucille, who was snowbound at an airbase in upstate New York. Her nurse friend Norma Harrison approved my ring selection. With it tucked in a belt pocket I headed for a rendezvous at Lucille's home in Stoughton, Massachusetts. Once again she was elsewhere due to bad weather. I introduced myself to her parents, sister, and brother-in-law.

We had a simple wedding at the local Catholic priest's home. We wore winter blues, the main items in our wardrobes. After a brief wedding trip to snowy New Hampshire, we parted once again; Lucille to San Diego for her discharge from the navy, while I, already discharged, took a train to Washington, D.C., to find housing and decide how to take the first step in my peacetime career. We chose Washington because it was the world's center of action; the site of several law schools; the home of Erland Ericson, my former newsroom colleague of *Journal-Courier* days in Jacksonville; and the office of Clarence K. Streit, already the hero of thousands of veterans. They admired him as the author of a plan I believed could prevent future wars. I had exchanged correspondence with him during the war, and I was interested to know his plans for the future.

I enrolled in the George Washington University School of Law, then called on Streit, who was organizing a new monthly magazine to be called *Freedom and Union.* He offered me the job of assistant editor at forty dollars a week. With Lucille's approval, I accepted the job and dropped my law school plans. I decided editing a country newspaper, instead of studying law, would be my best first step forward. The job with Streit would enlist me in a worthy cause while I cast around for the right newspaper opportunity. A few weeks later, my pay climbed to fifty dollars a week. The office was a modest second-floor suite reachable by a stairway. All of us were amateurs engaged in on-the-job training in magazine publishing. Streit, noted for his spartan lifestyle, leaned heavily on free advice from supporters of the federation already engaged in publishing magazines. Henry Luce, founder of *Time,* and his wife were among them.

My military mustering-out pay from the state of Illinois was two hundred dollars, and Lucille's from Massachusetts was five hundred. I persuaded her to pool our modest funds in a single bank account, which prompted her to observe with a smile that I married her for her money. Housing in the Washington area was scarce. Our first home was a rented basement heated by an erratic oil burner. One morning we awakened to find our nostrils covered with oil-burner soot. Thanks to a Streit supporter who owned property in northern Virginia, we soon moved to a modern apartment near Arlington Cemetery. Our initial furnishings consisted of a mattress, a card table, and two folding chairs.

One day, Streit asked us to accompany him to New Jersey by way of Manhattan to meet two men, an expert on magazine design, and Leonard Drew, the man who would be business manager of *Freedom and Union*. At a ferry landing, we parted ways with Lucille without arranging when and where we would meet later in the day. Lucille attended a performance of a popular musical at Radio City Music Hall, then boarded a Manhattan bus without knowing where to go. When the driver finished his route, Lucille was still on board. Informed of her plight, he drove her to the ferry landing where we had parted earlier in the day. I was already there, praying she would miraculously appear. We seemed to be tied closely to this thing called luck but vowed never again to be so careless in making plans, especially in New York City.

Back in Washington, I drafted an ambitious plan with Ericson. It proposed a newsmagazine to be called *The Record* that would compete alongside my old employer, the *Jacksonville Journal-Courier*. At the time, Ericson was night photo editor for the Associated Press in Washington, a step up from his job as wire editor of the Jacksonville newspaper. A college friend, Charles Menees, a staff member at the St. Louis *Post-Dispatch*, agreed to be an adviser. Ericson contributed much of the text. *The Record* might have succeeded, but it did not get beyond the prospectus.

A month later, two Jacksonville men I had known and admired in prewar days invited us to move to Pittsfield, thirty-five miles west of Jacksonville, where I would manage the *Pike County Republican*, a venerable weekly they wished to add to their small chain of newspapers. The men were Richard Yates Rowe Sr., then serving as treasurer of the state of Illinois, and Reaugh Jennings, business manager of Jacksonville State Hospital, an institution for psychiatric patients. I would be expected to buy one-third of the shares in a new corporation that would own the newspaper.

The Pittsfield newspaper was a going concern: old, venerable, respectable, established. *The Record* was only a possibility, a hope. The Pittsfield offer impressed me as a rare opportunity. The

Jacksonville men obviously saw in me the capacity for management. They wished to invest in property with me at the helm. They protected their interest by establishing me as a minority stockholder. If they found reason to fire me as manager, they could easily and quickly do so.

From early years I had shown a willingness to take chances and get things done. I also sought and established experience in sharing my views with others. I was thrilled. The Pittsfield offer seemed a perfect opportunity. Although inexperienced as an employer and businessman, I had self-confidence. I never doubted for an instant my ability to succeed. Lucille and I discussed the offer at length. She gave me the green light, so I quickly accepted. I was confident the newspaper would offer me the opportunity to acquire valuable experience, develop acquaintances, help rear a family, and share my views on public policy to a sizeable audience.

To buy my shares, I needed seven thousand dollars plus a fund as working capital. Lucille's parents loaned me two thousand dollars. My parents did the same. William Dodsworth, a Jacksonville area farmer I had never met, loaned me four thousand. He did so on the recommendation of Reaugh Jennings, one of my new partners and his longtime friend. All loans were unsecured with interest at 4 percent. I established a firm relationship with banker Earl Grigsby, providing to his temporary custody endorsed shares of my one-third interest in the new corporation called The Pike Press. The shares were security for future corporate and personal loans.

Before leaving Washington, we bought a 1936 Chevrolet sedan for three hundred dollars—this was August 1947, when even used cars were scarce—and headed for Pittsfield with our worldly possessions tied on the top and packed in the backseat. The trip was uneventful except for the moment when all of Lucille's clothes parted from the car top at an unknown spot on U.S. 36.

Thus began a thirteen-year adventure in corn and hog country.

5

◇◇◇◇◇◇◇◇◇◇◇◇◇◇◇◇◇◇◇◇◇◇◇◇◇◇

Pittsfield and Politics

Pittsfield, Illinois, a great place to raise a family, had a bustling economy when we arrived. U.S. 36, the nation's main east-west highway at the time, passed through the center of town. It was the residential hub of several transcontinental trucking firms, a major center of agricultural production and distribution, and county seat for over twenty thousand people. In Pittsfield our two children, Craig and Diane, were born and the four of us made many lasting friendships that still enrich our lives. A few years after our arrival, banker Grigsby helped us buy a residence, arranging a mortgage and even loaning us the required down payment.

My new job had special appeal because the *Pike County Republican*'s ancestry could be traced to the *Pike County Free Press*, the weekly newspaper once owned and edited by John G. Nicolay, who became a confidant of President Lincoln. Nicolay was the only paid employee in Lincoln's 1860 presidential campaign, and then served as the president's principal private secretary. After his White House service, he joined John Hay, also a Lincoln secretary, as Lincoln biographers. Pittsfield was replete with historic personalities and homes important in Lincoln saga.

I was thrilled at the prospect of managing a newspaper amid such rich associations. I joined the Rotary Club, American League, Chamber of Commerce, and the Congregational Church and expanded my acquaintance in the community, as did Lucille, who

41

joined St. Mary Catholic Church congregation and the Wednesday Bridge Club. We parted on religious affiliation, a division that arose from personal conviction. We made it work smoothly and occasionally joined each other at worship.

Craig was born a year later. At the age of four, he was fascinated with fire engines and seized every opportunity to ride with Chief Virgil Kriegshauser when he drove back to the firehouse after answering an alarm. As a first grader in 1954, Craig had to be restrained by teacher Bessie Penstone from leaving the classroom one day when the fire siren sounded. He was a regular patron at the public library, where he read every volume of the Oz books. While still in elementary school, he developed a love of music, guided by band director Paul Rosene. As a result, we sometimes found horn parts soaking in our bathtub. Craig later attained professional skill on both the baritone horn and trombone and now heads the trombone section of Jacksonville Symphony Orchestra.

Diane was born in 1954, but complications from her delivery by Cesarean caused Lucille a year of pain. Lucille's only sibling, Lillian Bete, traveled from Boston with her infant daughter to help for several weeks. During a second surgery a year later, physicians discovered the cause of Lucille's pain: a sponge overlooked at Diane's birth.

Diane's most worrisome childhood accident occurred at Pittsfield's public swimming pool. She was five and a good swimmer, but one day she slipped on the diving board and fell twelve feet to concrete pavement, landing face down. Examination showed no fractures—a major miracle—but Diane was a sick girl for several weeks.

Her memories of Pittsfield are entwined with Shelly, daughter of Ruby Dively, Lucille's best Pittsfield friend. Until Diane joined— tearfully—in our trek to Washington in January 1961, the two were inseparable, day and night.

During our Pittsfield years, I helped launch the Pittsfield Community Center, the annual Pittsfield Fall Festival, Old Orchard

Country Club, and the Pittsfield Industrial Development Association. I was active in the Illinois Press Association, where I became acquainted with several newspaper editors, including Paul Simon, later a colleague in Congress.

My duties at the newspaper office included varied chores—selling advertising, reporting news, writing editorials, managing the staff, and assuming assorted janitorial challenges. Keeping the newspaper financially afloat was a constant challenge. Income from advertising financed most operating expenses, and many Monday mornings I wondered where I could find sufficient advertising for Wednesday publication to cover the week's expenses.

My typical work day began at 7:30 A.M. before printing equipment started clattering. I pecked out a humor column titled Bull Pike. After veteran editor Jess Thompson died, I also began writing unsigned editorials. They dealt mainly with community betterment issues with an occasional comment on national or world events. I applauded President Truman when he fired General Douglas for insubordination.

By 8:00 A.M., the staff arrived and I began a tour of retail businesses, seeking news tips as well as paid advertising. I had to stay alert night and day, competing as I did with an excellent weekly called the *Democrat-Times*. I worked six days a week, and often seven. At press time on Wednesdays, I helped make final decisions on page makeup. My fingers were well-stained with printer's ink.

Our newspaper equipment included an oddity, a twelve-page Goss rotary printing press. It and related equipment were crowded into a small storefront just off the public square. Cylindrical page plates were formed in hot metal. Lucille's father, Ovella Gemme, a skilled machinist, spent most of a summer holiday making repairs on the Goss.

News and advertising desks were crowded close to the plate glass front wall. Immediately behind were the Goss press and two linotypes. Big rolls of newsprint were squeezed through a back door, past small printing presses, type cases, page-form tables, and casting and metal equipment for fashioning the press cylinders. Each day offered at least a sample of bedlam.

After three years in cramped quarters, I decided on a major change. I found a buyer for the big Goss press in Tennessee, and moved the *Republican* to a larger rented building two blocks away. The new location was large enough to accommodate separate office space. I bought sight-unseen a more efficient, used flatbed web press from a dealer in New York City. Producing a newspaper by the flatbed web system could be defined as one damned thing after another. Any moment, especially in zero weather, the broad web of paper would break with a loud bang that sent a shiver down my spine. Pressman Jim Halpin always reacted calmly, removing the torn web from the press and rethreading it.

Patience and loyalty of staff were crucial. Printer Myron Tedrow rarely said more than a few dozen words each day, but he was, like Halpin, ever calm and efficient in moving the printing process forward. Tedrow and several other printers learned the trade with financial help from the GI Bill program Congress enacted at the end of World War II.

Sometimes a payday or a load of newsprint brought the *Republican* bank account close to zero, but thanks to the sympathetic cooperation of friendly banker Earl Grigsby, we survived.

One day in October 1948, Democrat Paul Douglas campaigned in Pittsfield for election to the U.S. Senate. He spoke from courthouse steps, pleasing me and many others by quoting from memory the poem "Banty Tim" from John Hay's *Pike County Ballads*. After following his campaign closely, my vote—cast without public notice—helped him defeat the reelection bid of Republican Senator "Curly" Brooks, whom I considered a pedestrian politician.

In 1952, I offended local supporters of conservative Senator Robert Taft in the upcoming Republican primary with an early public endorsement of Dwight Eisenhower for president. We adorned a picture window in our home with a huge Ike photo. I considered Ike a progressive leader, uniquely equipped to keep us safe and out of war and strongly committed against government control of agriculture. Moreover, I was certain he could win if nominated. I doubted that Taft could, basing my opinion on a conversation I had with the Ohio senator during his presidential campaign visit to Pittsfield.

The same year, an itch for elective office surfaced. It was caused partly by optimism in Republican ranks. I expected, correctly, that Eisenhower would lead the party to a sweeping victory. Even though odds were heavily against success, I decided to seek the Republican nomination for state senator, an office being vacated by the incumbent. Of the district's four counties, the largest was Adams, with Quincy, population forty thousand, as its county seat. It was also the home of a well-known, respected Republican attorney named Lillian Schlagenhauf, who had already announced her candidacy for the nomination. She was widely known in mid-America for her skills in oratory and debate. By the deadline for filing petitions for candidacy, I was one of three candidates, the last filing being a lawyer in Calhoun County.

Early in the campaign, I sought the advice of a Democrat in Pittsfield, an elderly and wise circuit judge named A. Clay Williams. His advice: "Shake hands with everyone. Be a good listener. That way, you will gain friends and come out ahead whether you win the office or not." I limited campaign spending to six hundred dollars from our family bank account. I don't recall receiving any contributions. I placed small paid advertisements in newspapers, including the one I edited. I had no advertising on radio or television. I distributed news stories on speeches I made to political groups. These produced favorable publicity at no cost. I shook every hand I could reach, kept track of names, and tried to listen well. I did not mention my competitors, even in Quincy.

In the March voting, I carried three counties—Pike, Calhoun, and Scott—but Schlagenhauf had a big enough margin in Adams County to cancel my lead in the other three. By following the judge's counsel, I lost the nomination but won many friends, even emerging with the goodwill of my opponents. Nominee Schlagenhauf, with my enthusiastic endorsement, was elected state senator in November. Eight years later, she supported my campaign for Congress. In a post-election commentary printed in the *Quincy Herald-Whig,* I described campaigning as "hard work" and urged readers to "try it sometime."

Later that year, I had a press gallery seat at the Chicago convention that chose Dwight D. Eisenhower as Republican presidential nominee. During a massive reception the evening before the final voting, I slipped under a rope so I could shake Ike's hand before he was rushed away by aides. He smiled, looked me straight in the eye, and acted as if he were delighted to meet me. It was an unforgettable moment in a remarkable political drama played out later in the Chicago stockyards arena. Ike prevailed in a stormy struggle over candidates that included General Douglas MacArthur, Senator Robert Taft, and Governors Earl Warren of California and Tom Dewey of New York. The Chicago event was one of the last presidential nominating conventions that actually made the decision on nominee. In later years, due mainly to the influence of early primary voting, nominees for president were usually selected well before the conventions occurred. In November, Ike was elected in a landslide, even topping the Democratic candidate, Illinois governor Adlai Stevenson, in normally Democratic Pike County.

After 1952, all area legislative and congressional positions were filled by popular Republicans with long life expectancy, so I put further personal candidacy out of my mind. My life was full with the activities of our young family and the task of building the *Republican* into a profitable, constructive community force.

Two years later, I had second thoughts. After counseling together, Lucille and I made a big decision. We would try to sell our business interests in Pittsfield and seek a new life abroad. We always had a yen to see more of the world and decided to cast around for opportunities. Before our dreams gained traction, the death of two unrelated people within a short span of time proved crucial to our future. One was Helen Nicolay, only child of John Nicolay, President Abraham

Lincoln's first private secretary. The other was U.S. Representative Sid Simpson, whose district included Pittsfield.

Helen Nicolay had important Pike County connections, and her death was thoroughly reported in the *Republican*. A distant relative still lived in Pittsfield and helped me assemble information for the obituary. It reviewed the life of Nicolay's father, an immigrant from Bavaria who had learned the printing trade on a Pittsfield weekly and later became its editor and owner. He also became acquainted with Abraham Lincoln, whose law practice brought him frequently to Pittsfield. Helen Nicolay willed her personal property to her housekeeper, Fay Elizabeth Beij, who died a few weeks later and left her estate to her daughter, Barbara Benoit, a schoolteacher in Center Harbor, New Hampshire.

The estate included a unique photo-painting, showing Lincoln with his two private secretaries, Nicolay and John Hay, Nicolay's friend from Pittsfield days. The photograph was taken in the Washington studio of Alexander Gardner on November 9, 1863, a few days before Lincoln spoke at Gettysburg. Only six prints were made from the negative. Nicolay acquired one of them and had an artist in Washington convert the black and white photograph into a watercolor painting. The artist tinted the figures with a few cosmetic alterations and replaced the plain background with a representation of the White House room used for cabinet meetings.

Learning that this photo-painting was now at the Benoit residence, I called at her home in June 1956 on a side trip while we visited Lucille's parents near Boston. At my request, Benoit retrieved the photo-painting from the attic. She said she had not thought about selling it and had no idea of its market value. After a conversation about my Pittsfield connections, Benoit was willing to talk about selling. I mentioned Frederick Hill Meserve, the world's foremost collector of Lincoln photographs who resided in New York City. Benoit agreed with my suggestion that I try to telephone him for an estimate of the picture's worth. To my surprise, I quickly reached him by phone. He said the photograph would be worth at least one hundred dollars if it proved to be an original. After a short discussion, Benoit agreed to sell it for two hundred dollars. Pleased and feeling generous, I gave her a check for $220. A few days later the photo-painting was proudly displayed in my office in the *Republican's* new quarters.

I notified John Hay Whitney of my acquisition. A wealthy descendant of John Hay, he was serving as President Eisenhower's ambassador to Great Britain. I did so because I knew that his family had previously expressed an interest in buying it. Whitney responded with this message: "If the *Pike County Republican* ever wants to part with this photo-painting, I would certainly appreciate your letting me know." At the time, I had no intention of selling, but it was nice to know of a wealthy man's interest.

A year later, in early October 1958, Representative Simpson spoke at a dedication of a new wing of the Pittsfield hospital. It was a month before the general election in which Simpson was expected to win his ninth term in Congress. Knowing that I had an acquaintance with Simpson, the committee asked me to introduce him. After concluding his remarks, Simpson sat down and slumped over unconscious. He was taken to the hospital emergency room a few steps away and pronounced dead.

That evening I told Lucille I wanted to try to take Simpson's place as Republican candidate for Congress. I am sure she did not take me seriously. During the next two days, I visited all Republican county chairmen in the district, either in person or by phone. None welcomed my initiative. They wisely persuaded Simpson's widow, Edna, to be the candidate. She won handily but, on arrival in Washington, told the Associated Press she would not seek reelection. Her announcement gave me and other candidates nearly two years to campaign for the Republican nomination in the March 1960 primary.

I quickly visited each Republican county chairman. At each stop, I said that I viewed the opening as the opportunity of a lifetime and promised to do my best to secure the nomination and win the election in November. None of the chairmen jumped with glee, but several were cordial. I won the best smiles when I mentioned my early support for Eisenhower, who was then midway in his second term as president. Although I received no commitments, I found my tour of county chairmen satisfying. I detected no objection. Within days, three other men stated their interest in the nomination: State's Attorneys Albert Hall of Jacksonville, and Alvin Ufkes of Quincy, and Clyde Baulos, a former Scott County sports star and recently a White House liaison official.

The fourteen-county district stretched over a hundred miles from east to west and included counties like Calhoun and Greene to the south and northern ones like Hancock and McDonough. Although Republican Simpson held the congressional seat for sixteen years, the district was normally Democratic. No single newspaper or television station reached the entire area. Radio stations were numerous and community based. I knew the odds were against me. Pittsfield was a small town. Each of my three competitors was better known than I.

To overcome my handicaps, I needed two things above all else: first, freedom to spend most of two years campaigning; and second, a nonpartisan speech good enough to be remembered by listeners months later when I announced my candidacy.

As a minority shareholder in the newspaper corporation, I could not expect my partners to be happy if I neglected my duties as newspaper manager for the next two years. Nor could I afford to resign, as I had no other income and was in debt for home and business. To gain the needed freedom to campaign, I needed to buy out my partners. As sole owner, I would have the freedom to use my time as I wished. I would have to have good staff support, of course, but I was confident I would receive it. Everyone on my staff seemed supportive.

Best of all, I found Abraham Lincoln in my corner. He helped me meet both challenges: financing the buyout and providing me a speech outline that would quickly widen my support throughout the district.

Part II

RIDING LINCOLN'S
COATTAILS

6

◇◇◇◇◇◇◇◇◇◇◇◇◇◇◇◇◇◇

Abe Leads the Way

I learned that sixteen thousand dollars would buy out other share-holders in the *Pike County Republican*. I had to raise it fast. Ambassador Whitney's expressed interest in buying my prized photo-painting immediately came to mind. I decided to sell it, pro-vided I could get a good price.

After I carried it to his Manhattan office—insisting on keeping it on my lap during each leg of the air journey—Whitney bought it for $8,500, a nice gain from my $220 investment. The ambassador immediately donated it to the John Hay Library at Brown University, Providence, Rhode Island. On an autographed portrait he wrote: "I hope that the sad departure of the Hay-Nicolay original will bring happy days to the *Pike County Republican*—and to you."

The sale to Whitney plus borrowing from two sources—farmer William Dodsworth, who had loaned money without security eleven years earlier, and banker Grigsby in Pittsfield—enabled me to become sole owner of the newspaper and thus gain independence to seek election to Congress. The buyout came in November 1958, but I did not wish to be viewed as a candidate until I filed my petition of candidacy a year later. If I announced candidacy immediately, I assumed that service clubs, school groups, and other nonpartisan organizations I would like to address would be reluctant to invite as a speaker a political candidate like me.

I needed a strong speech acceptable to nonpartisan audiences. I wrote one on the Constitutional Convention and another on the high price of monetary inflation. Neither text had the emotional appeal I needed. Abe Lincoln helped again. A perfect theme emerged from a letter John Nicolay wrote May 13, 1900, reprinted in a biography of his life by his daughter Helen. Addressed to the Bloomington Historical Society, his letter included these phrases:

> I had the good fortune to be one of the delegates from Pike Co. to the Bloomington Convention of 1856, and to hear the inspiring address delivered by Abraham Lincoln at its close, which held the audience in such rapt attention that the reporters dropped their pencils and forgot their work. In the Representatives' Hall at Springfield I heard him deliver that famous address in which he quoted the scriptural maxim that a house divided against itself cannot stand. . . . In the Wigwam at Chicago I heard the roll call and the thunderous applause that decided and greeted his first nomination for President. . . . On the East Portico of the Capitol at Washington, I heard him read his First Inaugural in which he announced the Union to be perpetual. . . . On the battlefield of Gettysburg I heard him pronounce his immortal Gettysburg Address. . . . I saw him sign the Joint Resolution of Congress which authorized the thirteenth amendment to the Constitution. . . . And once more, on the East Portico, I heard from his lips the sublime words of the Second Inaugural.

Nicolay had the remarkable opportunity to be present during each of these great moments in Lincoln's life, no doubt the only person so privileged. Best of all, my newspaper had a close ancestral connection with the newspaper Nicolay once owned. The letter was Lincoln's priceless gift to me, because it gave me the outline of a strong nonpartisan speech. I would tell the story of young Nicolay, an immigrant from Bavaria who struggled from the lowly position of printer's devil to become owner-editor of a Pittsfield weekly newspaper and later private secretary to President Lincoln. It would be a Nicolay-was-there speech. Following a reference to each historic speech, I would recite from memory the words Nicolay heard from Lincoln's lips. I would include two major events that he witnessed personally but did not mention in his letter. Nicolay stood beside Lincoln on the rear platform of a train car when the president-elect delivered his immortal, extemporaneous farewell to the citizens of Springfield in February 1861. As the train moved from the station, New York newspaper reporter Henry Villard asked Lincoln for the text of his remarks. Lincoln had no text. To accommodate the reporter, he took a pen and legal pad and began to write his recollection of what he said. When the car began to shake as the train picked up speed, Lincoln handed the pad and pen to Nicolay, who recorded the rest of the statement as Lincoln dictated. The original document survives, and it shows clearly where Lincoln's handwriting stopped and his secretary's began. The other momentous occurrence Nicolay failed to list was his great privilege as he dipped a pen in an inkwell and handed it to Lincoln for signing the Emancipation Proclamation.

The Nicolay story could be a captivating theme, subtly linking me with the Lincoln saga in a way that could be the perfect foundation for my later candidacy. I had good reason to believe it would be effective. A few weeks earlier, a visitor at Pittsfield Rotary Club told me the remarkable response he experienced when he recently addressed his home Rotary Club in College Station, Pennsylvania. He said he did not utter one word of his own during his presentation. All he did was read extracts from Lincoln speeches. The audience listened silently and when he finished, they stood in a long ovation. It was a powerful, emotional response to the magic of Lincoln's words.

In preparing my speech, I cited the words Nicolay heard Lincoln utter and wove them into the exciting experiences of the young immigrant. Entitled "The Living Lincoln," my speech required about twenty-five minutes to deliver, the right length for any service club or church supper program. When I tested it on the Pittsfield

Rotary club, the members seemed spellbound. No one coughed or shuffled feet. When I finished, they, like the Rotarians in Pennsylvania, stood and applauded vigorously.

The Pittsfield club secretary, at my request, sent a note to other Rotary clubs in the district, suggesting they put me on their program schedule. After I spoke to the local Lions Club, its secretary recommended my talk to other nearby Lions Clubs. Harold Voshall, the Pittsfield superintendent of schools and a Democrat, passed the word to other area superintendents. The Pittsfield Parent-Teacher Association president did the same to other PTAs. A dentist friend wrote to other dentists. Democrat Walter Plattner, the local coroner, wrote to other coroners.

Invitations to speak kept coming. No group was too small for attention. Audiences were silent as I spoke. No glancing at watches. They seemed to hang onto each Lincoln phrase. When I finished, all stood and applauded. The experiences were heady, energizing. I had to remind myself that I was only the messenger. The applause was for Lincoln, not me, but I hoped listeners would remember me gratefully for bringing Lincoln to them. By keeping track of those who heard me speak, I rapidly expanded a card file I knew would be useful when my campaign began. Each speech received newspaper coverage that Lucille kept in a scrapbook.

Before filing nominating petitions, I called on Illinois Governor William G. Stratton and Secretary of State Charles Carpentier, both Republicans I knew from earlier meetings. I explained my ambition, how I was proceeding, and showed my scrapbook of publicity. At my request, both offered suggestions on campaign literature I was preparing.

Carpentier was especially important, because as the state official dealing with elections he would control the position of names when ballots were printed. I made no request about listing, but when the ballot text was announced, my name appeared first. My literature immodestly proclaimed me "Top man on the ballot and top man for the job."

To my surprise, even after I announced my candidacy in December 1959, speaking invitations from nonpartisan groups continued to arrive. Joe Bonansinga, manager of channel 10, a Quincy television station that reached most of the congressional district, was in the audience when I spoke about Nicolay to the Quincy Rotary Club. Weeks later, he arranged for me to give my entire speech, illustrated here and there with photographs, in prime time on his station. On a file folder containing the speech text, I entered the places where I spoke. By Election Day in November 1960, there were over one hundred entries, an average of two a week.

To supplement names of people who heard me speak, I kept track of others I met casually. I kept a supply of blank three-by-five cards in my right jacket pocket. Each time I met someone for the first time, I pulled out a blank card while we talked and entered the person's name, address, and phone number, then filed it in my left pocket. As soon as I announced my candidacy, these cards became an instant file of Findley-for-Congress Advisory Committee members. Frank Penstone Sr., mayor of Pittsfield, agreed to be chairman. An early news release listed founding committee members: eighteen in Pittsfield, ten in Griggsville, five each in Perry and Barry, one in Pleasant Hill, two each in Quincy, Hamburg, and Elsah. The list of volunteers grew daily. By primary campaign time, I could identify over three hundred volunteers and over two thousand advisers. By Election Day in November, the lists contained, in all, nearly six thousand names. To my surprise and delight, no one listed requested removal.

As a first step in my campaign, I knew I needed to focus on the relatively small percentage of voters who cast ballots in Republican primary elections. They were usually loyal to party leadership and devoted to party success. At political gatherings I took care to salute Republican county chairmen, local precinct committeemen, and Eisenhower, whose presidency was ending. I pledged to continue the standard of service provided by the late Congressman Simpson and his widow. Alone among the four competitors for nomination,

I could present myself as a small businessman who had already worked closely with farmers and small town interests.

On TV and radio and in newspapers, I presented myself as the apostle of limited government, individual liberty, private enterprise, market-responsive agriculture, balanced federal budgets, and a militarily strong America. These themes may seem simplistic jargon these days, but in 1960 they were popular in country Illinois and expressed my personal views. My weekly column, Campaigning with Paul Findley, was published without charge by several weekly newspapers. My paid advertising focused heavily on liberating farmers from government control. It was a simple platform but well-received throughout the district.

After I addressed party meetings, I tried to shake hands with all attending. Many complimented me on my remarks. As the campaign progressed, I was pleased at the warm reception I was receiving.

Funds were limited, and I insisted the committee avoid obligations beyond cash in the campaign bank account. I had no wealthy supporter who paid campaign bills, no "sugar daddy." Help came from unexpected sources. A few days after I announced my candidacy, farmer Kenneth Stark of Nebo, a board member of the Illinois Farm Bureau, brought me a check for two hundred dollars, asking that it be used for billboards, his favorite form of campaign advertising. Later, he organized volunteers in Pike and Calhoun counties, then served as secretary of the Findley-for-Congress Committee. Before long, he was campaign manager.

Republican State Representative Hugh Green of Jacksonville, a former speaker of the Illinois House of Representatives and widely respected as an elder statesman, helped me choose brief phrases that would create a positive impression. I had known and respected Green since my high school days. In helping me, he may have neglected his own campaign. Up for re-nomination as a Republican candidate for state representative in the same primary on which I focused, Green was defeated by a narrow margin by Harris Rowe, the young Republican chairman of Morgan County and son of Richard Yates

Rowe, my former newspaper partner and then an insurance company founder.

To my surprise, most county clerks helped assemble names and addresses of people who voted in the Republican primary two years earlier. This was before the era of computers and computerized mass mailings, and several county clerks invested hours assembling information. My staff of printers prepared form letters. Betty Orr, a young Pittsfield mother, spent long night hours in the newspaper office, using my carbon-ribbon typewriter to fill in the blank spaces. She typed perfect fill-ins of names, addresses, and salutations on the letters, then inserted them in addressed envelopes with first-class postage affixed. I do not recall how many letters were prepared, but the total exceeded six thousand. They were mailed on Friday before the Tuesday election.

The vigorously contested primary campaign cost about nine thousand dollars—a budget today's politicians would view with disbelief.

My primary election victory was surprisingly strong. District-wide totals were Findley 12,157; Albert Hall 8,062; Alvin Ufkes 6,177; and Clyde Baulos 5,292. Various forces contributed to my victory, but I believe the work of volunteers and the personalized letters were the most effective.

Ray Humphreys, a senior staff member of the Republican National Congressional Committee on Capitol Hill in Washington who spent his life helping Republican candidates for Congress, first entered my life one dark evening a few days after the primary vote. We met in Mt. Sterling where a heavy storm had knocked out electricity for the night. Humphreys and I got acquainted in a candlelit storefront. At the time, I was visiting county seats, taking soundings in preparation for my campaign for election.

Humphreys had an aggressive personality. He spoke forcefully about the steps I must take without delay. He told me there was no time to waste, and that I must strengthen my volunteer corps far beyond the one that helped me in the primary and train them. He declared I must shed newspaper responsibilities to devote my full time to getting elected. He convinced me to organize a gathering ten days later in Pittsfield. He would arrange for Representative John Kyl, a Republican who had just won a special election in Iowa, to be the speaker. He wanted the audience to include Republican precinct committeemen of Pike County and other local people who were prospective volunteers.

He did most of the talking. When we departed, any feeling of complacency arising from the primary election victory had vanished. My friendship with Humphreys would deepen until his death from a long illness years later.

About fifty people gathered in Pittsfield Community Center for supper and a stirring speech by Kyl. His main point: votes are gained one at a time. Attending were precinct committeemen, most of them wearing neckties bearing the likeness of Illinois governor Stratton. Among others was a young Jacksonville banker, Fred Hosford, who would soon carry my campaign flag in Brown County. Hosford brought with him Bill Carl, a young Jacksonville businessman who two years later agreed to be chairman of the districtwide Findley for Congress Committee. It began my lifelong friendship with Carl and Kyl. Kyl's was especially rewarding during my first few years in Congress.

Although I made my living in the newspaper business, I viewed television as the second-best way to influence voters. The best way was the retail approach recommended by Kyl, personally securing votes one at a time.

After Labor Day, I began buying one-minute prime-time spots on the two Quincy television stations, the only ones viewed by most of the district. They cost about sixty dollars each. Videotaping was not yet available. Spots on film were costly and difficult to arrange. I decided to do each spot in person. Fortunately, the stations were only a block apart. Using an alley, I spent an evening or two each week literally running from one station to the other to present my messages live. I typed prompting words in large type on a letter-size sheet, and then taped it just below the camera lens. When I spoke I took care to keep my eyes close to the lens and never exceed the one-minute limit.

Lucille was a loyal campaigner, and one evening in Quincy her influence was multiplied. Three Pittsfield neighbors, all Democrats, volunteered to help her pass out literature on my behalf. Before they scattered into different parts of Quincy, they decided on their own to simplify their messages by identifying themselves as Mrs. Findley. When I later heard of the adventure, I was relieved to know they were not under oath at the time.

In my speeches, I almost always quoted Lincoln and seldom mentioned foreign policy except to extol Dwight Eisenhower's wise leadership as president. An exception came in May when I made headlines by warning against U.S. military involvement in Vietnam. A newspaper clipping quoted me saying, "We should first determine whether the local population really wishes to resist Communist takeover. If not, we should forget them." This was two years before Eisenhower's successor, President Kennedy, sent twelve thousand military advisers to South Vietnam. They were soon converted into a combat force, the first major step into our Vietnam folly.

My Democratic opponent, Montgomery Carrott, was a well-known car dealer in Quincy. We had two joint appearances on the NBC station in Quincy, each occurring just before the famous televised debates between Vice President Richard Nixon, Republican candidate for president, and his Democratic opponent, Senator John F. Kennedy.

During one of the television appearances, I expressed outrage when Carrott accused me of declaring that the "the family farm is a thing of the past." I did not realize at the time that his misquote would rebound to my advantage. A few days later, Carrott published the same charge in paid advertising in fifteen newspapers. Each advertisement quoted a different farmer as making the same word-for-word criticism of my candidacy. In paid advertising in the next issue of the same newspapers, I included this response: "When

I noticed that each farmer used precisely the same words—all 189 of them—I began to wonder if the farmers so quoted were fully informed about the advertising. Each farmer I talked to denied he had authorized the quotation about me. One farmer even started our conversation by saying, 'The first I knew about this ad was when I read it in the paper.'"

My published response disturbed Carrott so deeply that he unwittingly helped my candidacy in a paid tirade that must have amused most readers. In a one-third-page advertisement in the *Quincy Herald-Whig,* he linked the misquoted farmers with the patriots who signed the Declaration of Independence. Carrott's message: "My opponent has not only insulted me, he has also insulted the intelligence of every voter in the 20th district, as well as signers of the Declaration of Independence. . . . He seems to feel that each statement should have been written by the person concerned—an insult to those fine statesmen who signed the Declaration of Independence." Everywhere I went in Adams County, Carrott's printed tirade produced laughter. The absurdity became my opponent's campaign legacy.

On October 28, a few days before the election, Vice President Nixon made a brief appearance at the Quincy airport. Fighting a severe cold, he spoke from an outdoor platform. It was my first meeting with the future president. Before he began, I handed him a card on which I had typed my name, identifying myself as the candidate to succeed Mrs. Simpson, the widow of Representative Sid Simpson. It prompted him to give my candidacy a welcome plug during his remarks.

Inspired by Wide-Awakes during Lincoln's 1860 presidential campaign, my supporters a century later literally lighted the skies before Election Day. One Saturday night, like modern day Wide-Awakes, scores of volunteers paraded down Maine Street holding aloft Findley signs and sturdy poles wrapped with blazing kerosene-soaked rags. They repeated the show seven nights later. It was all in joyous positive spirit. These days, fire marshals tend to frown on such displays. The Findley marches may not have been edifying on campaign issues, but they demonstrated enthusiastic support by a large group of citizens. Everyone participating seemed pleased to be marching.

Fiery demonstrations and fiery advertising helped bring victory. Our expenditures in the campaign were slightly less than $21,000, all paid in full the day before voting.

I spent election night in campaign headquarters in Pittsfield with Lucille, Craig, Diane, my mother, and volunteers who filled the room. By late evening, returns were complete enough to declare me congressman-elect.

The headquarters room was filled with volunteers, all shouting happily. Lucille and our children were excited too, but they could expect big—sometimes disturbing—changes ahead for them. They feared the fun of family life in Pittsfield would be lost in a suburb of Washington, D.C., a metropolitan area of nearly two million people. Getting settled there in midwinter would not be easy.

For me, it was a night of jubilation, an emotion shared by the supporters who crowded campaign headquarters in Pittsfield. An inexperienced young politician in a small country town had managed to win election to Congress. I had trouble grasping the reality, and when I did, tears welled up along with smiles. For the first time in memory, I was able to laugh and weep at the same time.

7

∞∞∞∞∞∞∞∞∞∞∞∞∞∞∞∞∞∞∞∞

Preserving an Heirloom

A braham Lincoln lingered in my thoughts on January 3, 1961, as I took the same oath of office that he took in 1847. The link between us began during early childhood when Lincoln Logs were my favorite toys. A much-thumbed volume, *The Lincoln Library,* dominated our home's small library. Our family of seven seemed to treat anything related to Lincoln with care and sometimes reverence. We rarely left Jacksonville, but visits to New Salem, Lincoln's log cabin home during early manhood, and his later residence in Springfield were high on the family agenda.

One day I watched my older brother, William, then a high school student, produce several plaster castings of Lincoln's profile he had modeled in clay. One of the castings rests in the curio case of my office.

At an early age, I began memorizing parts of Lincoln speeches. My favorite was his farewell to Springfield citizens in February 1861, before riding a train to Washington as president-elect. When I enrolled in Illinois College in 1939 and joined Phi Alpha Literary Society, I found the memory work useful when called upon to provide a declamation or essay. I was pleased to learn Lincoln was an honorary member of the society and had received much of his education from five former students of Illinois College who had become his close friends and neighbors as young citizens of New Salem village northeast of Jacksonville.

While I was assistant editor of Clarence Streit's magazine, *Freedom and Union*, Lincoln quotes appeared frequently in its pages. Streit had a theory he called the Lincoln Law. He argued that each extension of human rights to others has the immediate effect of strengthening the rights of those who undertook the extension.

My acquaintance with Lincoln deepened in 1947 when I became manager and part owner of the *Pike County Republican*, which had deep roots in Lincoln legacy. A decade later, with the 150th anniversary of Lincoln's birth approaching, Bill Bauman, a Pittsfield photographer, and I formed a partnership we hoped would both promote the anniversary and produce financial gain. We arranged for a St. Louis artist to make a model of bookends patterned after the seated Lincoln in the memorial in Washington. The model was beautifully done, and we contracted, as I recall, for the production of about thirty sets of the bookends in plaster. We were amateurs in marketing, however, and sales were slim. The profit was slightly under zero. In my office are three treasured sets, still useful and attractive.

In early November 1960, a few days after I became congressman-elect, I began a tour of the 20th congressional district to express my gratitude to voters, especially to those who had volunteered in my campaign. On the tour, I followed a set routine. I tried always to visit the office of the local editor before making any other calls. A newspaper owner myself—on a small scale—I learned to pay close attention to the people who decide what goes into a newspaper.

In Quincy, the largest city of the congressional district, I visited the newsroom of the *Quincy Herald-Whig*. When I entered, Arthur Higgins, editor in chief, called out, "Findley, I hope you did not neglect to send a letter of appreciation to Abraham Lincoln." The newsroom staff howled its appreciation. I replied, "He was by far my most influential supporter." I did not exaggerate. During the two years leading to Election Day 1960, I believe I quoted Lincoln in every speech I made. In the years that followed, I found that, time after time, his legacy provided guidance, comfort, inspiration, and support.

When I reached Capitol Hill, I encountered Representative Fred Schwengel, a Republican from Iowa similarly devoted to the Lincoln heritage. He was already established as the preeminent Lincoln fan in Congress. He carried in his wallet slips of paper on which Lincoln statements appeared in small type. They helped him quote Lincoln any time, accurately, at length, on almost any topic. He gloried in correcting someone's misquotation. Relaxing one day in the cloakroom that adjoined the House floor, I heard a colleague say irreverently but with a chuckle, "Fred is so wrapped up with Lincoln that he won't be satisfied until he goes to the theater some night and gets shot."

Civil rights bills dominated the early years of my work on Capitol Hill. On one occasion, I offended Republican leader Gerald Ford by sending a form letter to my Republican colleagues, urging them to vote for the open housing civil rights bill. I cited the tradition of Abraham Lincoln, founder of the Republican Party. Enough Republicans voted yes to assure passage. Ford voted no, but subsequently supported and voted for all other civil rights measures. He was offended because I "went public" in appealing to fellow Republicans to vote for a civil rights bill our leader opposed. He kept a copy of my letter to Republicans in a desk drawer and pulled it out one day when I arrived to ask a favor. After lecturing me briefly and calmly, he granted my request. It was not unusual for members of both parties occasionally to vote contrary to the preference of leadership. What was exceptional was making a big public fuss about it. If you will pardon a brief diversion, a man sitting on the edge of a lake spoke of making a fuss. He heard a man in deep water shout, "Help! I can't swim," to which the spectator responded, "I can't swim either, but I don't go around making a big fuss about it."

Another Lincoln-fan colleague was Paul Simon, an Illinois Democrat and, like me, a weekly newspaper publisher. He was elected to the U.S. House of Representatives in 1974, later to the Senate, and in 1976 was briefly a candidate for the Democratic nomination for president. Years earlier, while a crusading state legislator, Simon wrote an excellent book about Abraham Lincoln's service in the Illinois House of Representatives.

In 1970, the mandated readjustment of congressional district lines seemed likely to place Simon and me in the same district. If that happened, I mused, Simon and I would engage in a series of debates, a junior-size echo of the debates Lincoln had with Stephen A. Douglas in 1858. If paired against Simon, I knew I would have a high risk of defeat, but I was confident any debates would be civilized, fun, and, hopefully, edifying. Subsequent redrawing of district lines veered in a different direction, so no debates with Simon occurred.

In Congress, Simon and I got along well personally, and I often checked to see how he voted on a pending issue on the House floor before casting my own vote. Although we sometimes disagreed, I always welcomed his viewpoint. We frequently supported each other's initiatives. In 1975, when a vote was about to occur on the House floor on my resolution to advance the federation of democracies, Simon argued for approval.

Lincoln's statements seemed to fit almost every controversial issue that confronted the Congresses in which I served. During debates on Vietnam, I quoted him frequently as I made speeches and introduced resolutions calling for an end to the conflict. Today, forty years later, as I call for termination of our war in Afghanistan, I again quote Lincoln's protests and warnings against war initiated by presidents without congressional approval.

As I helped draft the War Powers Resolution when the Vietnam War was winding down, Lincoln's written warning against presidential wars seemed to be written with our current challenge in mind. In a letter to William Herndon, his law partner, dated February 15, 1848, Lincoln provided a powerful and timeless argument against preemptive wars initiated by any one person, even the U.S. president.

Allow the president to invade a neighboring nation whenever he shall deem it necessary to repel an invasion and you allow him to do so whenever he may choose to say he deems it necessary for such purpose, and you allow him to make war at pleasure. Study to see if you can fix any limit to his use of power in this respect. . . . If today he should choose to say that it is necessary to invade Canada to prevent the British from invading us, how would you stop him? You may say, "I see no probability of the British invading us." But he will say to you, "Be silent. I see it, if you don't."

The provision of the Constitution giving the war-making power to Congress was dictated, as I understand it, by the following reason: Kings had always been involving and impoverishing their people in wars, pretending generally if not always that the good of the people was the object. This our convention understood to be the most oppressive of all kingly oppressions, and they resolved to so frame the Constitution that no one man should hold the power of bringing this oppression upon us. But [President Polk's] view destroys the whole matter and places our president where kings have always stood.

Lincoln's warning is as pertinent today, when our country is bogged down in wars in Iraq and Afghanistan, as when he expressed it in 1848 as a member of Congress.

Legislation I introduced directed the architect of the Capitol to place in the marble floor of Statuary Hall, an early chamber for the House of Representatives, a brass engraved plate that marked the exact location of Lincoln's desk when he served a term as a Whig member of Congress. I helped mortar the plate in position. It is now a regular stop for tourists being guided through the Capitol building.

During my last five years in Congress, a sofa that was in Lincoln's Springfield law office served as the centerpiece of my office. It is now in my office at home. Its horsehair upholstery is in shreds, evidence that it had much use during Lincoln's twenty-four-year career as a lawyer, perhaps because his sons often played robustly in his office. Lincoln had two Springfield carpenters make the sofa in

1837, his first year as a lawyer. I purchased the sofa and the documents from the Pennsylvania Historical Society in February 1978 for $6,000. I had helped the society sell furniture to the National Park Service for display in the Lincoln Home. The sofa will soon be displayed permanently in the Habtoor Leadership Center on the Illinois College campus.

In the 1970s, the Abraham Lincoln legacy kept showing up prominently in my work on Capitol Hill. The most enduring episode related to the future of the Lincoln home in Springfield, a city that became part of my district in 1963. Nicolay, who later coauthored with John Hay a ten-volume Lincoln biography, once described the Lincoln home, quite accurately, as "the precious heirloom of the republic."

In 1955, six years before my Capitol Hill years began, William E. Skadden, a Springfield citizen, addressed the annual meeting of the Pittsfield Chamber of Commerce and presented slides showing that homes of former presidents, except for Lincoln, had been preserved and the environs of each developed to encourage public visitation. I was in the audience as Skadden's slides and commentary provided a distressing view of the Lincoln home and its neighborhood. A two-story souvenir shop was located across the street. Another one functioned two doors north of the Lincoln home. The state of Illinois owned only the Lincoln Home itself and the small lot on which it was situated. The city of Springfield owned several vacant lots. The rest of the four-block neighborhood surrounding the home was private property, and a mess. The neighborhood was badly decaying in all directions. A plan for restoration and preservation was urgently needed.

When I reached Capitol Hill, federal involvement seemed unlikely, partly because Illinois Governor Otto Kerner publicly predicted no governor would let the state of Illinois lose control of the home. The Springfield Junior League proposed restoration of the area surrounding the home to its appearance during Lincoln's time, but no solid steps forward ensued.

In December 1966 I talked with Governor-Elect Richard Ogilvie and Springfield's veteran mayor, Nelson Howarth, about the possibility of National Park Service involvement. To my surprise, both were strongly supportive. A few weeks later, a fire severely damaged a residence just north of the Lincoln home. The blaze focused community attention on the need for a comprehensive preservation plan for the neighborhood.

On February 12, 1969, during a dinner program organized by the Abraham Lincoln Association, I announced I would introduce a bill in the U.S. House of Representatives that would make the Lincoln home and environs a part of the National Park System. I also called for a drive for private funds to advance the project.

The bill had smooth sailing on Capitol Hill. All of the twenty-three other Illinois House Members, including several who had served in the Illinois legislature, cosponsored the bill. Illinois Senators Everett Dirksen and Charles Percy were supportive. Governor Ogilvie announced his support, despite a negative recommendation by State Historian William K. Alderfer.

Representative Julia Hansen, chairman of the subcommittee that deals with funding of Department of the Interior projects, visited the Lincoln site and announced her support. A National Park Service team spent four days studying the home and its environs. The following week the Springfield city council endorsed my bill after rejecting a private firm's proposal to establish a wax museum near the Lincoln home. Two months later, state and civic leaders met with Park Service officials in Springfield to discuss prospects. On September 19, word arrived that my bill had received administration endorsement, provided that a marvelous, unexpected amendment would be added, authorizing a federal appropriation of $5.8 million, a step already approved by the Bureau of Management and Budget. Full funding by the federal government was beyond my wildest dreams. Yet there it was in black and white.

With the funding amendment joyfully attached, my bill was soon approved without controversy by the House of Representatives.

Charles Percy guided it quickly through the Senate. President Nixon, without even a nudge from me, decided to visit Springfield on August 18, 1971, for the sole purpose of signing my bill and speaking at a public ceremony in Representatives Hall in the refurbished Old State House where Lincoln delivered his famous House Divided Speech.

Early steps on the Lincoln Home legislation began in 1969. All legislative aspects of the Lincoln Home National Historic Site deed were accomplished in record time, just over a year. The process of restoration and preservation of the four-block area has required thirty-nine years. The residence itself has been strengthened and protected. An unobtrusive but handsome and efficient visitor center, designed by Springfield architect Wally Henderson, was erected on Seventh Street, a block from the residence. Except for a church, located at the northwest corner, the entire area surrounding the home is under the supervision and control of the National Park Service. The neighborhood has been restored, including the move of several structures to their locations in the Lincoln era.

In the early years of Park Service takeover, I had the joy of working closely with Park Service Officer Albert W. Banton Jr., first superintendent of the site. On retirement after a long and distinguished career, he gave me his Park Service uniform hat, which I proudly display in my office. On my office wall is a photograph showing Nixon, seated in Representatives Hall of the Old State House, signing my bill. Another exhibit displays the pen the president used in writing his last name. He gave Ogilvie the pen used to sign his first name.

This legislation was personally very satisfying and ranks near the top of the varied experiences I had in Congress. It is the one success certain to survive the march of years.

Today, visitors find the neighborhood, not just the house, as it existed in 1861. No one can walk east on Jackson Street, look up and down Eighth Street, and tour the residence without a marvelous, tingling feeling of closeness to Lincoln. It is a joy that more than a half-million people experience each year. Millions more will be inspired in years to come. The republic's "precious heirloom" is in good hands.

With the restoration of the Lincoln home environs well underway, my attention turned to another aspect of the Lincoln heritage. As I read biographies of Lincoln, I noted the authors kept repeating misconceptions about his brief congressional service. All full biographies and the one book devoted to his work as a member of Congress presented this period of his life as a failure. It was not. As a one-term member of Congress he became an influential Whig spokesman, speaking nationally in the upcoming presidential campaign. On the House floor, he matched wits successfully with famous politicians of the day. Had he decided to seek reelection, all signs indicated he would be successful.

Inspired by the biography of Lincoln's service in the Illinois legislature written by my colleague, Paul Simon, I decided to try my hand at a volume that would accurately present the career of Congressman Abraham Lincoln. It was an interesting writing experience, my only one with a major Madison Avenue publishing house. Major publishers like to have at least one Lincoln book in their inventory, and at the time Crown had none. When I explained that Lincoln's two years in office were a major, successful part of his political life, despite the tendency of biographers to treat it as a failure, Crown offered me a contract.

Charles Cooney, skilled in the archives of the Library of Congress, provided yeoman service in research, assembling data, and identifying unpublished illustrations. The end result, A. Lincoln: The Crucible of Congress, was published in 1979, three years after the project began. At my request, colleague Paul Simon edited every word of my manuscript and wrote an introduction. He told me he took my text to bed night after night. His recommendations were very helpful. Because I leaned heavily on federal employees—my congressional staff and the experts at the Library of Congress—I sent the $7,000 advance I received from Crown to the U.S. Treasury.

Crown sold out its printing of seventy-five hundred copies and did not reprint.

I was elated when Prof. David Herbert Donald, a Pulitzer Prize–winning Lincoln biographer, publicly described my book as "indispensable" and "the best account of an important period in Lincoln's life." Lincoln specialist Michael Burkheimer's anthology *100 Essential Lincoln Books*, published by Cumberland House Press, includes *A. Lincoln: The Crucible of Congress*.

Its appearance in bookstores prompted notices in both *Time* and *Newsweek* magazines. Both reported what I considered a minor aspect of his congressional term: his collection of $3,252 for mileage to and from Washington, more than the shortest distance would merit. His excess of $676.80 and the mileage excesses of several other House members were reported in the *New York Tribune* by the renowned editor Horace Greeley, who had just finished his one-year career as a member of Congress. Lincoln may have found consolation in the fact that mileage was paid on the "usual traveled route," not necessarily the shortest distance. *Newsweek* published Greeley's commentary accompanying the mileage data: "Let no man jump to the conclusion that this excess has been charged and received contrary to law . . . The members are all honorable men. If any irreverent infidel should doubt it, we can silence him by referring him to the prefix to their names in the newspaper." Members of Congress, then and now, customarily find the prefix "honorable" before their names, whether they deserve it or not. Even though Lincoln was accused of overpayment, he must have admired Greeley's wit. He made no public response to the newspaper's disclosure.[1]

The Lincoln legacy was a focus in my early years on Capitol Hill, but not the major one. I was heavily engaged in farm-related legislation and already active in budget and foreign policy controversies.

Late in 1961, I learned sobering political news. The latest U.S. census forced Illinois to reduce its U.S. House delegation in the next Congress by one member. After much jockeying, the Illinois legislature met the challenge by placing me and much of my former district into a new, enlarged one that included a major part of the area long represented by popular Democrat Representative Peter F. Mack.

After surmounting a big hurdle in my first congressional campaign, a more challenging contest lay just months ahead.

8

◇◇◇◇◇◇◇◇◇◇◇◇◇◇◇◇◇◇◇◇◇◇

Battling a Veteran

In redistricting, I lost several rural counties in the north part of my district. The new 20th District included several counties as new territory for me, including Sangamon County, with Springfield as the seat of government for both the county and state. It also included Macoupin, a large county that included Peter Mack's hometown. The new district had a population of 445,000, a big increase from 299,000 in the old.

Every ten years, redistricting is the duty of the state legislatures after the latest census is complete. The total population needs to be divided into 435 districts—the legislated limit on the membership of the U.S. House of Representatives—with population of each as equal as possible. Population increases mean a gain in congressional seats for some states, losses for others. When I first served in Congress, New York had the largest population. Today, California outstrips it by a two-to-one ratio. Illinois population has not quite kept pace with national growth, resulting in a shrinking Illinois delegation on Capitol Hill throughout most decades. The redrawing of district lines to accommodate changes nationally is often contentious.

My opponent Mack had represented Sangamon County for fourteen years, and was well-known for his leadership on the Interstate Commerce Committee. He once flew a small plane around the world on a "peace mission" and sponsored annual trips to Washington for disadvantaged children. He had many friends and few critics. This meant that I had to establish quickly a large and favorable personal acquaintance and an army of additional volunteers throughout Lincoln's hometown as well as several other counties, mostly Democratic, beyond my old district.

The addition of Sangamon County, although a partisan challenge, brought several assets. It had a large population of Republicans well experienced in political campaigns who were eager to have a Republican represent them in the U.S. House of Representatives. They were led by J. David Jones, one of the finest political leaders in my experience. Always kind, thoughtful, and never demanding, he was chairman of the Sangamon County Republican Central Committee, later a state representative and Republican district committeeman. Barbara Greening was his leader of women's affairs. In every respect they were high class. On several occasions Barbara and her husband, attorney Alfred Greening, provided overnight housing for me in their Williamsville home.

In early years after law school, Alfred Greening and Robert Cronson were the "gatekeepers and watchdogs" stationed in the reception room of Illinois Secretary of State Charles Carpentier's office suite in the state capitol building. Thanks to their watchful examination of people, papers, money, and calls that went in and out of the secretary of state's office, Carpentier emerged from long years in that often controversial office without the slightest hint of corruption or mismanagement. Cronson and Greening were passionate about defeating Mack. I never learned why but rejoiced in their commitment. They took a close and continuing interest in all my campaign activities, even to designing yard signs and hand-out literature.

Springfield had a large African American population, well led by fine people like Eulalia Corbin. One day, J. David Jones, who lived next door to the Corbins in his youth, learned of a showdown that occurred one evening when an African American stranger from South Carolina visited the Corbins. He was invited to have supper and spend the night with them. During the meal, the guest mentioned that he was a Democrat. This disclosure prompted the head of the Corbin household to inform him firmly that he was welcome to finish the meal, but no Democrat would ever be permitted to spend the night in the Corbin house. Jones said the episode illustrated the intense loyalty to the Republican Party that once prevailed throughout the nation's African American community. All that changed, Jones said, when Democrat Franklin D. Roosevelt became president in 1933. Jones and the Corbins worked hard to win African Americans back into the Republican Party, an endeavor I strongly supported.

Most political observers gave Mack the edge in the campaign because of his seniority in Congress, popularity districtwide, and the district's usual partisan balance that favored Democrats. He was undefeated in seven campaigns, while I was a novice experienced in only one, a win that some experts considered easy. The Republican Congressional Campaign Committee in Washington recognized my uphill battle by dispatching Ray Humphreys to organize a council of war.

Kenneth Stark, a banker-farmer in Pike County, accepted leadership of day-to-day campaign activities. Reading through the brittle pages of three large scrapbooks devoted to my 1962 campaign against Mack brings to mind its controversy, fireworks, buffalo burgers, fly-in at Springfield airport, and President John F. Kennedy's visit to Springfield on Mack's behalf.

Stark had business interests to supervise, but he managed to commit nearly full-time to organizing my campaign. He was experienced in the politics of agriculture, finance, and the Republican Party. He mastered most of the challenges in politics, but an exception occurred the day he invited all 202 Republican precinct committeemen in Sangamon County to a sit-down breakfast meeting with me in Springfield's Leland Hotel. Only twelve appeared at the appointed hour. Stark had neglected to request confirmation from those who planned to attend. An urgent appeal to Republican employees in nearby state offices by John Caldwell, a senior assistant to Secretary of State Charles Carpentier, soon had many of the empty seats filled, but Stark was desolate. Later that day, he handed me his handwritten resignation as campaign chairman. I told him the breakfast disappointment was just a tiny passing blip on the radar screen and asked him to stay on the job. He agreed to do so.

I expanded a mailing list of members of my Congressional Advisory Council. In addition to an occasional newsletter, I sent each a membership card with a calendar on the back. It was similar to earlier mailings to the council. On the face of the calendar, I quoted favorite bits of Lincoln wisdom accompanied by a photo of myself. Two examples: "Important principles may and must be inflexible" and "Let reverence for the laws . . . become the political religion of the nation."

Campaign contributions were handled informally. We lived by the honor code. It would be several years before the Federal Elections Commission and its reporting requirements came into being. Until then, there were no certificates to sign, no dollar limits, and no public quarterly reports. Democratic Party leaders in at least one Springfield precinct were especially resourceful. Pints of whiskey wrapped in a ballot marked for the Democratic ticket and accompanied by a five-dollar bill were distributed.

I preferred to be uninformed about who gave how much, but an insurance company official I met on a Springfield street one day handed me a bundle of currency that he said totaled two thousand dollars and came from people in the insurance industry. I handed it, uncounted, to Stark, knowing he would make proper use of it.

Bill Carl, a young Jacksonville businessman, agreed to chair my districtwide campaign. Thus began a long and ever-growing friendship that lasted until his death in 2009. No one could have a better, more loyal friend. Although quiet and unassuming, he was a master at disarming critics, and Carl Cleaners, which he and his brother Ted owned in downtown Jacksonville, became a center where complaints about my activities were heard and usually resolved. Stark and Carl always had the good advice of my congressional staff leaders. Chief among them were Dr. Don Norton, who left his professorship at Western Illinois University in 1967 to head my district staff, and attorneys Stephen Jones and Robert Wichser who, fresh from law schools, took turns heading my Capitol Hill staff. All provided skilled counsel and leadership.

Carl recruited and trained volunteers. He established two Findley leaders in each county, giving one the goal of recruiting a volunteer leader in every precinct, the other the task of passing the collection plate to meet financial demands. In effect, volunteers became a districtwide political organization to benefit my candidacy only, and the system caused some resentment and criticism among Republican precinct committeemen. They didn't like a Republican organization devoted to one candidate. Soon after my nomination in April 1960, George W. Wilson, Pike County's Republican chairman, and his deputy, Hugh Kerr, stopped at our residence in Pittsfield on different days to urge me to disband the Findley volunteers. I tried to explain why I could not do so, stating that I would need volunteers in the upcoming general election campaign and beyond. Volunteers, I added, focused on my personal needs in the campaign while precinct committeemen had partywide responsibilities. Most Republican leaders, I believe, recognized that my organization brought new people into the Republican mainstream. I cannot recall even one occasion when a volunteer attempted to influence my position on any issue or sought a job or personal favor for anyone.

Carl and his team always succeeded in making volunteer activity enjoyable, and this helped keep the volunteer ranks surprisingly well filled. Carl's team never achieved full coverage of every precinct of the district, but more than half were fully staffed by volunteers. Carl kept trying to fill the gaps.

Findley buffalo barbecues became the rage in the campaign against Mack. At the initial offering at the county fairgrounds in New Berlin one day in October, more than two thousand people paid a dollar each for a barbecue sandwich. The turnout was so great the volunteers averted a supply crisis by mixing a modest amount of plain beef with the buffalo meat. At the barbecue in Macomb only one person went hungry. Lucille was about to try a sandwich when Don Morgan, my McDonough County finance chairman, in a playful mood told her—inaccurately—that the butchers had a terrible time getting the buffalo hair separated from the meat. Lucille laid down the sandwich and to this day has not tasted buffalo meat.

Over the years, a variety of popular events were arranged by volunteers. I enjoyed every one of them. The annual Findley Trail Ride became so popular it attained institutional standing. The first ride was organized in Pike County in 1965 by a committee of horse lovers led by attorney Harlington Wood Jr. of Springfield, who had served in the Eisenhower administration as U.S. district attorney. When Wood was appointed U.S. federal judge by President Nixon, Al Mavis, a real estate developer, took the reins. He led all rides until afflicted with a fatal infection. The final ride was headed by Dick Lisenbee, a Bluffs farmer. It attracted over five hundred riders. Horses were more numerous in central Illinois than a century earlier when they powered farming and most transportation.

Each year, the ride was based in a different county seat. A platoon of volunteer trail bosses handled details, ably assisted by my district leader, Norton. George Hamilton Sr. and his food crew in Franklin catered three meals a day. Everett Vestal of Roodhouse was the designated fiddler for square dancing. Each ride got abundant publicity, all of it noncontroversial.

In the ride in Hancock County, riders gave me a handsome made-to-order saddle decorated with my name and congressional seal. On another trail ride, Boe Woosley of Winchester, a trail boss and artist, gave me a portrait in leather. The saddle and portrait are displayed in my office. When I attended Woosley's funeral years after the rides ended, his family displayed trail ride memorabilia near the casket.

The rides were advertised as nonpolitical family outings, but, not surprisingly, they displayed Findley posters. As evidence of their bipartisan character, Democrat Bill Hungate, a colleague in

Congress and later a federal judge, entertained the trail-riders on two different occasions with jokes and exuberant self-accompanied songs. A favorite performer was druggist and campaign volunteer Lloyd Coffman of Roodhouse, a superb humorist and impersonator of Mark Twain.

On other rides, diplomats from foreign countries were featured speakers, and most of them braved time in the saddle. The most colorful were diplomat Vladimir Mechulayev of the Soviet Embassy in Washington and his wife Valentina, who joined the ride in 1973. At the time, because U.S. diplomats faced severe restrictions on travel while in Moscow, I had trouble securing U.S. State Department permission for the Soviet couple to visit mid-America for the trail ride. They wowed the audience Saturday night by appearing in colorful costumes on stage where they made brief statements. Daughter Diane fulfilled her usual duty, handing them Super Duper Pooper Scoops she had decorated. When we visited Judge Hungate's home in St. Louis several years before his death in 2007, we found his Super Duper Pooper Scoop prominently displayed.

Memorable was the intrafamily experience of attorney Bob O'Shea of Springfield when he was the Democratic candidate opposing my reelection in 1972. One evening, his niece, an avid rider on Findley Trail Rides, asked, "Uncle Bob, what will happen to the Findley Trail Rides if you win?"

For fifteen consecutive years the trail rides brought pleasure to people of varied occupations. On a September weekend each year, they mixed together in two days of trailblazing on both horseback and wagon. The Saturday ride covered about ten miles. After a church service in the saddle on Sunday morning, an abbreviated ride ended with fried chicken served early enough for the patrons to load up and get home before dark. Grover Smith, an engineer for a telephone company, organized the tractor-pulled wagons. They were occupied by dozens of people like Lucille who preferred playing bridge while sitting on a bale of hay to being astride a horse. When Grover died, his wife Kathy and son George took over as wagon masters. The rides became a source of pride for volunteer trail bosses who made them smooth and safe. Hardly a week goes by without someone stopping me to recite fond memories of trail rides past. Trail bosses, the men who organized and patrolled each ride, were in a special class, and the rides were a special joy for our daughter, Diane. Each year she proudly carried Old Glory as she rode at the head of the lineup. Several recent obituaries listed trail boss leadership among the deceased's life accomplishments. The rides came to an end only because they became dangerously large and the cost of liability insurance rose sharply.

Wood, organizer of the first ride, came into my life in 1961, when he arranged for me, newly elected to Congress, to use his U.S. attorney office in Quincy as a place to meet constituents. From that year until his death, he was a friend and adviser on many issues.

During the first ride, Wood, a skilled horseman, coached me on how to relax posterior muscles so I could survive two days in the saddle once a year. At six feet four, he matched the stature of Lincoln, his lifelong hero and inspiration. He earned the title of peacemaker through his masterful work as head of the Civil Division of the U.S. Department of Justice during the Nixon administration. He recognized and protected the right of citizens to protest against the Vietnam War but insisted on policies that prevented bloodshed.

In October 1971, 170 volunteers organized an air trip from Springfield to Washington for a weekend of tours and speeches. Those responding filled two chartered airliners. Addressing the gathering Friday night, Senator Goldwater quipped that in contrast to the big fly-in crowd from my district, he had only one visitor during the past three weeks from his Arizona constituency.

When Madison County was added to my district, the campaign featured train riders in addition to horse fans. One Saturday in October 1972, over one hundred volunteers, including my eighty-year-old mother, boarded a chartered train in Springfield that took them to Alton and neighboring communities, where they spent a few hours spreading the word door-to-door about my work in Congress.

Annual Findley Corn Roasts in Sangamon County retained popularity. For a dollar, visitors got ham, beans, and unlimited ears of sweet corn freshly dipped in warm butter.

The success of these events helped motivate citizens to get involved as campaign volunteers and stay involved. I believe most of them saw my campaign activities as a fun-filled way to advance good government. The last two words may sound pretentious, but I believe them accurate. While not always agreeing with everything I did or said, they seemed convinced I was trying to improve life in America. Disagreement on a specific issue or two did not seem to dim their ardor for my continued service on Capitol Hill. For example, several were deeply opposed to abortion but did not challenge my position that the issue is too complex and intimate to be solved by sweeping constitutional prohibitions. Dairy farmers were steadfast, even though they knew I opposed the federal regulatory, price-fixing programs for their industry.

All farmers were not of one mind. Most produced several different commodities. Their efforts yielded corn and wheat, as well as dairy products and soybeans. They liked my general approach to agricultural issues, even if they occasionally took issue with my positions.

One autumn, Lloyd Gordon, an implement dealer in Riggston and a friend since high school days, arranged a gathering of soybean growers in a large barn on his property. They had one thing in common. They were upset with local market prices and my opposition to a proposed government program of price supports. When I arrived, he warned that the barn was jammed with several hundred farmers. When I entered, no one smiled, much less clapped. The barn was as quiet as an empty church. Not a single "hi Paul" or a cough. I began my remarks by saying the scene in the barn reminded me of one of Lincoln's favorite stories. It was about a convicted murderer being dragged to the gallows. Nearly trampled by people rushing to get a good position as spectators of the hanging, the prisoner called out, "No point rushing. The fun won't start until I get there."

The joke got a few grins, but my later discussion of bean pricing brought no applause. I warned them government pricing, in the long run, would get soybeans in the same oversupply problems that plagued corn and wheat, commodities heavily influenced by government enticements. Later, many soybean producers remained loyal as volunteers and voters. I believe most of them decided how to vote on Election Day on a variety of issues, some of them totally unrelated to agriculture.

Volunteers augmented the work of party regulars, the Republican precinct committeemen and women who form the backbone of party endeavors. Through the years, most of the elected party officials provided solid support and, in many cases, close friendship. Some volunteers may have simply liked me personally, while others enjoyed contacts with the bright and aggressive people who were my congressional staff leaders. Others volunteers enjoyed politics as a competitive sport and perhaps helped me simply because I stuck to my convictions. Still others may have just enjoyed the excitement of working with the organization's diverse assortment of pleasant, energized citizens.

For me, excitement on Capitol Hill seemed never ending. The House included a variety of fascinating personalities, one of them the powerful but aging Clarence Cannon of Missouri. He was treated with great deference because he chaired the powerful Committee on Appropriations, which initiated all funding for the federal government. He rarely spoke on the House floor, but when he did he had a large, attentive audience. No one, however, had the slightest idea what he said, because he mumbled all his words so softly. Even the shorthand experts who try to capture every word uttered during official proceedings were completely frustrated. After he spoke, the official reporters had nothing to report, so the *Congressional Record* for the day routinely published these words: "Remarks of the gentleman from Missouri, Mr. Cannon, will appear later in the Extension of Remarks." They never did.

Sometimes, private conversations at the rear of the chamber were more interesting than speeches for the printed record. One day, Lee H. Hamilton of Indiana, one of the most respected—and respectful—members, had an unusual experience. Bella Abzug of New York, briefly a presidential hopeful, confronted him. Hamilton told me, "She almost pushed me against the wall. She was outraged because I declined to cosponsor one of her proposals. She cursed me close-up in the foulest language I ever heard in my life, then left. About twenty minutes later she returned to ask a favor, this time using the most gentle and courteous words imaginable. All this within a half-hour."

Every day posed a new challenge or two. From my first day in Congress I ignored the advice venerable House Speaker Sam Rayburn traditionally gave new arrivals: "To get along, go along." In other words, he advised, be quiet for a few years and don't make waves.

I had a good reason to reject the advice. I had little assurance of reelection and recognized that my first term might be my last. If so, I wanted to make the most of that term, and make the biggest waves possible for worthy causes. I had a role, for example, in defeating the Kennedy plan to establish government management of the production and marketing of feed grains.

9

Ignoring the Speaker's Advice

When we arrived in Congress, Republican John B. Anderson of Rockford and I were the only newcomers from Illinois. He and I joined a group of Republican colleagues called the Conservative Club. Both of us hewed to the conservative line in our speeches and voting in the early years. Because of his conservatism, Anderson was appointed to the Rules Committee but later achieved national prominence as a liberal, campaigning unsuccessfully for president, first as a Republican and then as an independent.

Throughout my career, I stuck to conservative principles in fiscal matters but became an advocate of social services, racial equality, and other human rights issues. One year, Americans for Constitutional Action, a conservative lobby, gave me a midrange score of 55 percent. The same year a liberal group, Americans for Democratic Action, graded me 46. This led Republican colleague John Ashbrook of Ohio, noted for conservatism, to quip that I was a "middle-of-the-road extremist."

When Ralph Nader, the consumer advocate, had Nader's Raiders swarming over Capitol Hill one year, his organization produced a separate leaflet summarizing the record of each House member. The text describing my record began with one word: "bewildering." In fiscal policy and budgeting I was solidly with conservatives, but on social issues, civil rights, and aid to underprivileged I was, to Nader, a liberal. In later years, he and I became personal friends and allies on many causes, especially the plight of Palestinians and abuse of presidential war powers. Perhaps my voting record seemed bewildering to Nader because the variety of major issues I confronted was itself bewildering.

I found myself constantly on the move. Throughout my career in Congress, I commuted to my home district at least twice a month. In the early years, until Ozark Airlines started a direct flight from Springfield to Washington's Dulles Airport, I usually parked my campaign van at Lambert Field in St. Louis.

For Lucille and our children, our new life was confusing and often distressing. We occupied a rented house in Northern Virginia during my first year in Congress, but resided in our home in Pittsfield for the second, as I knew my career in Washington would swiftly end if I failed to keep home-district fences well mended. Opportunities for constructive effort on Capitol Hill had to be balanced with my quest for reelection. Strangely, the two goals were separate but intermingled. Attainment was difficult, requiring periodic adjustment of time and place. After victory on Election Day 1962, we returned to Falls Church and purchased our rented house.

The move to Falls Church required Lucille and our children to leave good friends and a happy life in a small town. Diane's unique correspondence with famous men eased the pain of leaving Pittsfield. When I sent a birthday card to Albert Schweitzer in 1965, Diane, age eleven, tucked in her own message to the world-famous medical missionary. He responded from his hospital in Gabon, Africa, "I enjoyed the letter of your daughter Diane. She invited me to come to your home and tell her about my hospital and the animals. Alas, I do not travel any more. More than 550 in-patients and a great number of out-patients need much attention. . . . I feel privileged to work at my age and guide my hospital. We are six doctors and 15 European nurses." Perhaps inspired by that exchange, Diane autographed a small school portrait a month later with this message, "I like Ike." At her request, I delivered it to former president Dwight Eisenhower when I met him later that day in Gettysburg. Two days later, she received in the mail a portrait of Eisenhower autographed "with affectionate regards." In an accompanying letter, he said her message gave him "great lift" and signed off "I like Diane."

On the legislative front, in my first term I invited two other weekly newspaper publishers in the Republican freshman class, Ohio Republicans Charles Mosher and John Ashbrook, to join me in introducing legislation to rescind long-standing postal policy under which newspapers were distributed free of cost throughout the county of publication. The policy benefited weekly publications mainly, because most dailies made limited use of the postal service for delivery of their publications.

Free-in-county newspaper distribution had started as a device to advance literacy in frontier America. Our legislation let us present ourselves as authentic conservatives. Our bill increased government revenue by ending the subsidy of our own private enterprises. Most editors, uncomfortable about receiving a government subsidy, applauded. One approved our legislation but suggested we also abolish the franking privilege that lets members of Congress use postal services without charge. None of our intrepid trio acted on this suggestion.

In the spring of 1961, I joined other first-term Republican congressmen in a visit with former President Dwight Eisenhower at his retirement farm near Gettysburg, Pennsylvania. Happenstance produced national news coverage of Ike's and my views on farm policy. An Associated Press reporter heard me tell the former president I wanted to get the government out of the grain business. Ike responded, "Brother, so do I." I was pleased my conversation with Eisenhower made national news so early in my career. It was doubly gratifying because his stated views matched my own. It was a promising start as I climbed the legislative hill.

That same month I became a member of the Agriculture Committee, thanks to House Republican leader Charles Halleck of Indiana. He recommended that assignment to Speaker Rayburn along with other Republican committee assignments. The House approved them in a single resolution.

The committee assignment made sense for me and for Illinois, which by many standards is the leading agricultural state in the nation. For several years I was the only Illinois member of the House or Senate serving on a principal committee dealing with farmers. Believing that vitality of our nation's agriculture is best advanced by a system in which farmers respond as directly as possible to the needs and preferences of consumers, I set out to be a voice for farmer freedom. I did my best to protect the right of the individual farmers to make their own decisions on what crops to plant and when.

The committee assignment gave me frequent opportunity to speak out and make positive headlines throughout Illinois, where farming, even in Chicago, was recognized as a major economic activity. I quickly became acquainted with committee Democrats as well as Republicans.

Four Republicans in the freshman class were appointed to the Agriculture Committee. When straws were drawn to determine priority in seating, I won first and Bob Dole of Kansas, later a presidential candidate, second. This made me the senior new Republican with Dole as my seatmate. We continued as seatmates for four years. He is one of the funniest people I ever met. He quipped that he was sentenced, not appointed, to the Agriculture Committee.

Agriculture Committee meetings often produced bipartisan humor. One spring day in 1961, Chairman Harold Cooley called on committee members, one after another, to ask questions of the witness, former governor Orville Freeman of Minnesota, newly appointed as Agriculture Secretary. Cooley asked members to ask only brief questions, nothing more. When Paul Rogers of Missouri took his turn, he expounded for at least twenty minutes without posing a question. Bob Dole interrupted with these words, "Mr. Chairman, please ask the gentleman to repeat his question." All laughed except Rogers.

Texan Bob Poage, destined to become committee chairman and known for shouting whenever he spoke into a microphone, was often the target of humor. Democrat Graham Purcell told me, "Poage is the only man I ever knew who got infuriated at the sound of his own voice." Another committee Democrat, Dawson Mathis of Georgia, made a humorous introduction of Poage to a luncheon audience: "Some people say they would rather listen to Bob Poage talk than eat. I understand what they mean now that I have listened to Bob eat lunch."

One day, Clark Thompson, a senior Democratic member from Texas, announced he would not be present at the committee meeting scheduled for the following Thursday. He explained: "There will be a testimonial dinner in my honor back home. It is special. It is the first one I haven't had to organize and pay for myself, and I don't want to miss it."

My first legislative success touched both foreign policy and agriculture. Five months after John F. Kennedy became president, he signed into law a bill that extended the Food for Peace Program under which U.S. grain is delivered to food-deficit countries and paid for with local currency that cannot be spent outside the host country. My colleagues called it funny money. Under my amendment, U.S. citizens visiting such countries could help the U.S. federal budget by using U.S.-owned funny money they could purchase at the U.S. embassy. Embassies holding this restricted currency were in Ceylon, Israel, Egypt, Pakistan, Tunisia, and Guinea. Prior to my amendment, this currency could be used only for local operating expenses of U.S. diplomatic missions. The "tourist dollar" authority quickly became popular, as individual tourists, companies, and foundations doing business in these countries began using funny money for local spending. Within three years, it produced a gain of three million dollars for the U.S. budget—not earthshaking, but a step toward fiscal sanity. I smiled at the knowledge that my amendment quickly saved the U.S. Treasury a bundle.

The Kennedy administration, popular on most fronts, favored greater government manipulation of how much grain individual farmers could produce and when. These restrictions worried many farmers. Freeman carried the flag for the president as secretary of agriculture. I called him "Awful Orville," a nickname that gained popularity when a "phantom acres" scandal, as I called it, came to light. Freeman's department paid for the temporary retirement of twenty million acres from row-crop production but could identify only fifteen million acres. In statements on the House floor, I estimated that this mismanagement cost taxpayers $150 million that one year alone.

My pleas for freedom in farming and against government corruption appeared frequently in the *Congressional Record*. Freeman's supply management plan would destroy the right of each farmer to plant and market whatever grain he wished. If administration plans prevailed, I warned, the government, not the private sector, would emerge as the main buyer and seller of commodities, and ultimately decide what each farmer could grow.

An amendment I offered on the House floor handed the Kennedy administration its first major legislative setback. Approval of my motion sent a major bill to authorize government control of feed grains production back to the Agriculture Committee. During debate, I warned that the bill would put corn growers in a "straitjacket." I declared it "a prismatic menace to farmers, a menace any way you look at it."

My amendment to send the bill back to committee was approved by the scant margin of 10 votes, 215 to 205. Vivid in my memory is grim-faced Freeman standing on the House floor a few minutes after the vote count was announced. His arms were folded as he glared at Representative Neal Smith, a prominent Democrat from Iowa, who was explaining why he voted for my amendment. Smith's vote probably influenced several other Democrats to vote yes, enough to provide the ten-vote margin. My opponent for reelection, Representative Peter Mack, voted no, a decision that proved to be a major point to my advantage in the upcoming campaign. I was smiling and chuckling audibly, not trying to conceal my pleasure at this important victory for the right of farmers to make their own planting decisions.

In the wake of this victory, I was interviewed for radio and print media about what my amendment achieved. I didn't deserve all the publicity, but I loved it. Actually, any amendment to recommit a bill on the House floor is controlled by minority party leadership, not by any other member. Credit for the victory should go to the other 214 members who supported my motion. House Republican leader Charles Halleck, who decided who should recommit the bill, could have offered the motion himself. He did me a favor. He was confident that this role would win me favorable publicity helpful in my campaign against Mack later that year. It did, because major farm groups, including the Farm Bureau, loudly praised me for killing the bill.

With the bill back in committee, I helped fashion a compromise that removed the "grain supply management" provisions. One of my amendments set future government price supports below average market prices, a move away from government management of commodity prices.

When the new version reached the House floor, I offered an amendment that would have prohibited funding under the bill of any recreational facilities that permitted racial segregation. It was rejected, 142 to 106, in a teller vote, a procedure in which names of those voting are not recorded. It was 1961, when the mood of the House majority was not favorable to civil rights legislation. Kennedy signed the compromise bill.

Later that year, I praised Halleck before a receptive farm audience in his Indiana district. I paid tribute to him for skillfully killing Kennedy's initial farm bill, comparing Halleck's leadership to a coach's behavior in a nip-and-tuck basketball game, a metaphor that resonated with Hoosier fans.

In early 1962, the Illinois Farm Bureau, then headed by William Kuhfuss, decided to offer the organization's mailing list to the Findley-for-Congress Committee for use in a campaign appeal to farmers. He told the media my legislative work supported Farm Bureau objectives. Until then, the organization had refused any direct involvement in political campaigns. It was a one-time break with tradition, and Representative Mack fumed.

Over my years in Congress, I won approval on several occasions for a $20,000 limit on aggregate direct government payments to any single farmer, but many producers found ways to circumvent it. None of the major farm organizations, including the Farm Bureau, now champion limitations. Today, almost all major grain and cotton producers receive substantial annual payments from the U.S. Treasury, many in excess of a half-million dollars a year. My goal was to end farmer dependency on U.S. Treasury checks and thereby establish a closer, more efficient relationship between consumer needs and producers of food commodities. Large-scale farmers, not the small ones, were chief beneficiaries of those checks.

My campaigns against direct government payments to farmers sometimes brought hostile mail. A Texas farmer, outraged at my efforts to curb large direct government payments to cotton growers, wrote me several anonymous warnings: "How would you like your wife to have her car explode when she starts it up to take your children to school some morning? We've made arrangements." It was typed on what seemed to be an old typewriter with distinctive flaws on certain keys. Two other letters arrived, each containing similar threats, apparently from the same typewriter. The FBI traced the letters to a typewriter owned by an elderly cotton grower. The letters stopped coming, no charges were filed—I never learned why—and our car was not bombed.

When opportunity arose after U.S. combat in the Vietnam War ended, I was a salesman for farm produce, focusing on new uses for soybeans, a commodity then considered useful only for producing mash for animal feed and vegetable oil. In 1973, after packing a small suitcase full of soybean goodies prepared by University of Illinois scientists, I visited the Soviet Union on a side trip from nearby Norway where parliamentarians from NATO countries were convened. The U.S. embassy staff in Moscow used the soybean items to prepare a dinner for U.S. and Soviet officials. Dinner guests pronounced the meal delicious. Although only a small step forward, I believe it helped introduce Soviet leaders to the food benefits of soybeans.

During my years on Capitol Hill, I helped organize three International Soybean Fairs. The final and most successful one was sponsored in 1979 by the American Soybean Association in the Cannon Building on Capitol Hill. Attendance exceeded a thousand guests. Its main goal was to promote acceptance of soybeans as a food, not a feed. With newly arrived Ambassador Chai Zemin of China as special guest, the event drew ambassadors from thirty-five countries and diplomats from seventy-nine others. Chai's embassy staff served ten different soybean food items popular in China. The College of Agriculture at the University of Illinois sponsored an exhibit that included a soy product I considered as tasty as ice cream. In brief remarks as chairman, I noted that soybeans were produced the previous year on sixty million U.S. acres. The event got wide newspaper and television coverage.

My first public initiative to advance my dream of a federation of democracies while in Congress occurred when I addressed an Honors Day convocation at Carthage College in Hancock County. I said federation "would be the most impressive possible action to meet the Communist threat and might usher in a millennium of peace." I urged the United States to "take the lead in sponsoring a convention of delegates to take up the proposal." On Capitol Hill I was identifying like-minded colleagues who would support specific legislation soon to be introduced.

My first term in Congress featured several legislative successes, along with soybean promotion, but it also featured a political battle royal with Representative Peter Mack, who represented the district adjacent to mine. My contest with Mack was one of the few in the nation pitting two members of Congress against each other. Both Mack and I publicly deplored the redistricting, and most political commentators forecast a close struggle. So did I. In the Republican primary I had received 1,761 more votes than Mack received in the Democratic primary, but that small vote sample in each party could not foretell the voting in the general election. Sangamon County Republican chairman J. David Jones reminded me, "The first duty of a would-be statesman is getting elected." Although I was determined not to neglect legislative challenges, I knew I could not neglect the reelection campaign.

One day in 1962, personal oversight yielded headlines any politician would dread. It had a direct bearing on my election-day fortunes. With the one hundredth anniversary of the drafting of Lincoln's Emancipation Proclamation approaching, I was invited to participate in a ceremony commemorating that event at Lincoln's tomb in Springfield. The National Park Service asked me to deliver to ceremony officials the precious inkwell Lincoln used in signing the document. I agreed knowing that anything connected with Lincoln always produced good publicity.

Arriving at Lambert Field Airport in St. Louis with a small box containing the inkwell in hand, I stopped at a pay phone booth to call Lucille, who was waiting for me at our Pittsfield home. Before making the call, I placed the box on a shelf in the booth. When I hung up, I forgot to retrieve it. Partway to the parking garage, I realized my oversight and raced back. The box was gone. Frantic, I called the airport lost-and-found, vainly examined waste bins throughout the airport—even on the tarmac—and had nightmares about how Representative Mack would portray me as hopelessly irresponsible. I also called the police and the main television stations in St. Louis, asking that they broadcast news about the inkwell. Deeply shaken, I drove my campaign van to Pittsfield. Late that evening, a teenage youth who routinely checked airport pay phones for loose change brought the boxed inkwell home, showed it to his father, and went to bed. When his father learned on the eleven o'clock news of my mishap, he called police with news about his son's acquisition. Lucille awakened me at 1:30 A.M., after receiving a welcome call from a St. Louis officer. Police arranged delivery of the inkwell to Springfield in time for the ceremony at the Lincoln Tomb. How could I be so lucky? The odds against retrieval were surely at least a million to one.

When the ceremony was over, I was content to leave the ink-well in the custody of Park Service officials for its return trip to Washington.

Mack was an experienced, successful politician. He had reason to be optimistic, and hit hard, especially in paid advertising in newspapers. In a half-page message, the Mack for Congress Committee bemoaned my negative voting record in large, easily read type: "Findley voted against the space program, Social Security, rural electrification, programs for the aged and blind, unemployment compensation, college aid, healthcare, education, welfare, educational television, and higher minimum wages." It was fairly accurate. I had voted against almost all of them, because they proposed new authority in Washington and that entailed increased spending at the federal level that I described as budget-busters.

One evening, after a day packed with campaign events in Springfield, I drove to Jacksonville to spend the night at the residence of John Carl, father of Bill, my campaign manager. He had invited me to stay overnight whenever I wished. The lodging was not only free, it usually had a rewarding bonus: a chance to chat with the senior Carl, a wise immigrant from Greece. After I related a verbal assault earlier in the day from Mack, I asked Carl how I should respond. He reached back to ancient Greece, saying, "Walking with a student through the marketplace in Athens one day, Socrates fell down when bumped by an ox. Helping Socrates to his feet, his student asked, 'Why don't you kick the ox back?' Socrates replied, 'I probably would if I were an ox.'" I got the point and ignored Mack—for a few days.

Later I forgot the Socratic advice and made headlines by charging Mack with voting on both sides of dozens of issues. I suggested he be called "Two-Way Mack." I was quoted in newspapers the next morning as asking, "I wonder how many pairs of pants 'Two-Way Mack' has ripped jumping from one side of the fence to the other?" Mack made no response. Perhaps he too had heard Socrates's counsel.

Mack received friendly headlines when President Kennedy visited Springfield to urge his reelection. I had a good rejoinder. In October, former President Dwight Eisenhower issued a statement saying, "Congressman Paul Findley votes for the principles that make America great. . . . His effectiveness on farm legislation and NATO problems have been widely noted in America and overseas." Ike liked my suggestions about getting the federal government out of the grain business but was especially pleased when I established the Republican Committee on NATO and the Atlantic Community in 1962.

After polls closed on election night, Lucille and I stopped in the storefront in Springfield that served as districtwide headquarters. The campaign had been long and bruising, but I had received broad and diverse support. For example, a large number of students at Principia College, the only Christian Science college in the world, left the campus near Elsah and canvassed door-to-door in both Springfield and Quincy. My team of volunteers was also augmented by enthusiastic party regulars in Springfield, who saw my candidacy as the first serious challenge to Democrat Mack in years.

In the last days before voting, veteran Republican State Senator Bill Horsley privately advised me, "Don't shake the bag." In other words, don't risk raising any controversial new issues. I did not, but I reminded myself that Mack had a large, loyal following and few critics. I was the underdog, and I was braced for bad news. I told Lucille my first term in Congress might well be my last.

To my surprise, I won reelection by 100,558 to 89,522 votes, a solid margin. Ike's endorsement and volunteer enthusiasm, especially among farmers, made the difference.

Early in my second term, I brought to Kennedy's office an armload of letters from Illinois farmers protesting U.S. government sales of wheat to the Soviet Union at discounted prices. Like the authors of the letters, I questioned the wisdom and fairness of giving price breaks to a hostile government. I did not expect to talk with the president on short notice, but I believed personal delivery would enhance the prospect of the mail being called to his personal attention. I learned later that my strategy led to attention during presidential doodling.

When Kennedy was assassinated in November, the entire nation came to a sudden halt. By then I had gained great respect for the president and expected him to exert good leadership through both his first and a second term. My personal contacts with him were few but cherished. I chatted briefly with him at three different receptions in the White House and have a group photograph in which both of us appear. During the Cuban Missile Crisis, I exchanged a few words with him, reporting the results of a constituent survey that showed broad public support if he decided to use military force against the regime of Fidel Castro. I opposed acts of war unless Castro struck first, and, fortunately, Kennedy did not order such acts.

After his death, *The Washington Post* published a half-page reproduction of his last doodle, in which he sketched boats and wrote a few words about poverty. Among other words entered were "Findley" and "wheat"—evidence to me that Kennedy's secretary called his attention to mail I had left with her. When Vice President Johnson became president, the wheat sale was approved.

In July 1964, without my knowledge, a group of constituents proposed my name for higher office. Led by Cass County banker A. C. Hart, the group included attorney Richard Mills of Virginia, Illinois, later a federal judge; M. D. King of Pittsfield and Lewis Herndon of Springfield, both in the milling business; and volunteer leader and homemaker Marge Glesne of Beardstown. During a news conference, they suggested that Senator Barry Goldwater, certain to be nominated by Republicans for the presidency, select me as his running mate. The proposal made a few regional headlines but had no chance of success. The nominating convention was only eleven days ahead. The committee did not know the Arizona senator had already settled on Representative William Miller, a Republican from New York and chairman of the Republican National Committee, as candidate for vice president. The proposal was a thoughtful initiative, heady stuff for a second-term congressman from the cornfields.

One day, Western Illinois University professor Don Marshall, on leave for a year to head my Washington staff, came to my private office distraught. He closed the door and informed me that he had fired a new hire because she turned out to be part of a prostitute ring on Capitol Hill. He said she provided services during lunch hour at a small hotel nearby. He had investigated when other members of my staff became curious about her always-precise midday timetable. At Marshall's request, the police checked out her name and found her a suspect. Marshall had confidently hired her because her sister held a prominent position in the Senate. Recalling the episode years later, Marijo Gorney, one of my best secretaries, chuckled as she recited my remarkably understated admonition to Marshall; "Don, you need to check references a little more carefully."

Reflecting on the new administration headed by Lyndon Johnson, I sensed big changes ahead, not all of them good. He had great public sympathy as he assumed the presidency, and I surmised rightly that he would send more troops to defend South Vietnam and, at the same time, direct Agriculture Secretary Freeman to press for government control of agriculture. I did not anticipate his surprising, and I believed mistaken, decision to favor Communist countries with discounted prices for U.S. grain. I had found Kennedy up front and conservative in foreign policy issues. I had little confidence in Johnson. He impressed me as a wheeler-dealer and not always forthright.

In August 1964, a war measure that later proved to have immense importance was given superficial examination before being swiftly approved by the House and Senate. It became known as the Tonkin Gulf Resolution. Our government was deepening its involvement in the Vietnam War, and Johnson asked for prompt approval of the resolution. It alleged that U.S. military craft had been assaulted by enemy forces in Vietnam's Tonkin Gulf and authorized the president to use all necessary measures to resist aggression in the region. It confirmed my fears about Johnson.

To expedite proceedings, the House agreed to suspend normal procedure by limiting debate time to one hour and prohibiting amendments. Troubled by the resolution's possible conveyance of broad authority to the president, I asked Gerald Ford, newly elected to succeed Charles Halleck as Republican leader, to grant me one minute of the thirty-minute debate time he controlled. He declined, saying all time was already committed to other members. I told him I wanted assurance from the Democratic leaders that the resolution could not be construed as a declaration of war. Ford replied, "Don't worry. This is not a declaration of war. This is just a pat on the back by the Congress, showing support for the president in a moment of crisis."

Ford's assurance did not allay my fears, but I took no further actions at the time. Like all others in the House, I voted yes. I should have voted no and explained my concern in remarks in the *Record*. It is a vote and a failure I deeply regret. I had not explored deeply the war powers issue, but that is not a sufficient excuse. I had ample reason to doubt Ford's reassurance. The House vote was 414 for the resolution, zero against. In the Senate, only two members voted no.

Johnson kept a copy of the resolution in his jacket pocket. Whenever challenged on his authority to proceed with an immense and costly increase in U.S. forces in Vietnam, he would pull the copy from his pocket and read from it, citing it as the equivalent of a declaration of war. Years later, an investigation proved that the alleged assault on U.S. military vessels had not occurred. The resolution was a pretext for war based on false information. That resonates today, in the wake of the 2003 false declarations by then President George W. Bush that were a prelude to our trillion-dollar bloody military disaster in Iraq.

Shortly after the Tonkin Resolution vote in 1964, one of my amendments kept the House of Representatives in a rare all-night session just before Christmas. It would amend an appropriation bill that would prohibit sales of grain to Communist countries on low-interest, long-term credit. When first offered, my amendment failed on a 133 to 133 tie vote. To the consternation of Department of Agriculture officials seated in the House gallery, it was reconsidered in a parliamentary maneuver and approved. I noted that all countries aiding our enemy in Vietnam were Communist. I asked, "Why should we give a credit card to Communists on discount terms?" It was an appealing argument, so potent that a majority maintained support of my amendment through a long night. A compromise was approved on Christmas Eve. After specifying by a vote of 218 to 169 that credit could be extended to a Communist country only with the personal signature of the president on each such transaction, weary members headed for home and the Christmas tree. In the end, Johnson got what he wanted, and the Communist countries got what they wanted: purchases of grain at discounted terms. The all-night ordeal ended in a whimper. My amendment had strong bipartisan appeal, but fatigue and Christmas won out. On any other day, I believe it would have prevailed.

My campaign in 1966 for a fourth term was more relaxed. It was midterm, devoid of the customary hustle and high voltage of a presidential vote. My team of volunteers took no chances, and I had the considerable advantage of being an incumbent. On Election Day 1966, I won a fourth term by defeating Democrat Lester Collins, a former mayor of Springfield, 119,194 to 98,256. It was a 20,000-vote increase in margin from the previous election.

Before and after winning reelection, I continued my campaign against rewarding Communist countries with bargain grain prices. My amendment to prohibit the Export-Import Bank from cut-rate grain sales to Communist countries was rejected in House proceedings, 151 to 119, but my amendment to the Food for Peace program was approved by the House 366 to 23. It became law when President Johnson signed the bill it amended. It required that grain shipped under discounted terms be marked to show that the discounts came to foreign consumers through the generosity of the American people. Another amendment I offered required that benefiting countries must make improvements in local food production. It was approved on a voice vote.

I studied House rules and learned the ropes of procedure and deal-making. I was often on my feet making points of order to the presiding officer. I personally wrote my amendments and explained them carefully in private conversations as well as in statements in committee and on the House floor. My personal acquaintance with the House parliamentarian and his staff paid off.

Part III

VIETNAM DISSEMBLING

10

The French Connection

There was never a time in Congress when I focused exclusively on one issue. Farm issues, usually several at a time, always needed attention. Important issues often needed careful tending for several years, sometimes decades. Early in my career, I was a member of the Education and Labor Committee, and another time on the Government Operations Committee. I got knee-deep in foreign policy long before becoming a member of the Foreign Affairs Committee, where I divided my time among war, trade, human rights, diplomatic relations, and famine.

William Dawson of Chicago, the first African American to chair a major committee, in this case Government Operations, once told me, "If you think you have problems, just imagine what it's like to be black all over." He was noncontroversial, in sharp contrast to the behavior of a later African American chairman, Adam Clayton Powell of New York, who was eccentric and unorthodox at times. While a committee member I found him fair in every respect. One day I watched him seek a parking space, but finding none, he parked his car in the center of busy South Capitol Street. When I checked late in the day, it was still parked there.

Starting my fourth year in Congress, I found myself waist-deep in challenges related to the North Atlantic Treaty Organization (NATO). The Republican Committee on NATO and the Atlantic Community that I organized in the House of Representatives in

1962 had issued statements deploring what we described as U.S. responsibility for the organization's growing problems, especially the discord with France.

In one, I noted with alarm the declining sense of unity and cohesion among several community nations, not just brittleness with France. I declared the Federal Republic of Germany needed improved understanding, as it was still emerging from postwar military occupation. I also recommended cordial initiatives with France.

In 1964, calling for understanding of French grievances, I knew I would be criticized. Passions were high. President Lyndon B. Johnson was so upset with France's decision to withdraw its forces from the integrated NATO structure that he prohibited serving of French wines in the White House. When I spoke up for France, some members of Congress thought I had lost my bearings. Some spoke of Charles de Gaulle as a pompous fool. One seriously proposed renaming French fries as "freedom fries." I communicated with French diplomatic officials both here and in Paris, spoke out on the floor of the Congress to explain de Gaulle's position, and tried to serve as a bridge between the two longtime allies.

My concern was not a sudden impulse. The cohesion of the North Atlantic Community—indeed its permanent political union—had been a personal cause since college days. President Charles de Gaulle had been my hero since my military service in World War II, when he led Free French resistance to the Hitler-directed regime in Vichy headed by French Marshal Pétain. More than anyone else, de Gaulle symbolized the pride and spirit of France.

I admired the French general's unflinching independent leadership of Free French forces when the Pétain regime took orders from German generals during much of the war. To me, France was a country of immense importance to the United States, and de Gaulle embodied French pride, dignity, and hope. I tried to convey to my colleagues an understanding of the grievances that prompted de Gaulle's hostility to anything that would risk France becoming a fireplug sprayed by a dog. Our unofficial Republican committee assembled a panel of experts for a project called Atlantic Studies that included a detailed critique of the alliance's military structure.

My interest was sparked by U.S. anti–de Gaulle outrage that streamed from the White House to village coffee shops throughout America. It arose from de Gaulle's decision to withdraw all French forces from the NATO integrated command and to remove alliance headquarters and other facilities from French soil. U.S. critics, including President Johnson, condemned him as an ingrate, ignoring America's role in defending France in two world wars. Most Americans did not seem to understand the nature of French grievances or the alliance structure. They believed de Gaulle had cut all ties with NATO. They mistakenly thought France was reverting to neutrality. But without a moment's break, France remained an active member of the alliance. When de Gaulle addressed a joint session of Congress in 1959, he tried to make it clear that France would always be a supporter of the alliance. When I first arrived in Congress, senior French diplomatic officials kept reminding me that France was this country's oldest ally. De Gaulle himself once wrote, "France is the cape of the continent, England an island, America another world." He saw France as being on the front line of the Cold War, while England was protected by the Channel and the United States was psychologically and physically a world apart. In less than a century, France had been invaded three times by German forces, the last time suffering the shame of occupation. In the late 1940s, France came close to having a Communist prime minister. Several members of the Communist Party were still in public office. De Gaulle was less concerned about the threat of Communism, although he did not discount it, than the imperial ambitions of Russia. He almost always referred to the Soviet Union by the misnomer Russia.

De Gaulle and most French citizens believed the United States, without consulting the French government, had twice placed France in serious military jeopardy from the Soviet Union. In 1956, de Gaulle considered the U.S.-dominated NATO command indifferent to France's plight when the Soviets, in an aftermath of the Suez crisis, threatened to bomb both Paris and London. In October 1962, when the United States and the Soviet Union faced off over the issue of Soviet missiles in Cuba, President Kennedy called NATO head-quarters to full alert on French soil without first notifying Paris. De Gaulle's suspicions were aroused by similar events in both the Kennedy and Johnson years.

NATO's Standing Committee consisted of the United States, Britain, and France, but when nuclear matters were discussed, Paris authorities were excluded. Because of Communist influence in France, U.S. authorities may have feared theft of nuclear secrets, but such thefts occurred in Britain, not in France. The United States helped Britain develop nuclear weapons but refused to do the same for France. Moreover, the supreme commander of NATO was always an American. IBERLANT (Iberian Atlantic Command), intended from the beginning of the alliance to be headed by a French admiral, was never activated.

As a member of Congress, I believed it my duty to explain the French position to my colleagues and, as best I could, to the American people. No one else seemed willing to tackle the job. This required correcting misinformation, a process that would narrow differences. I felt the French had legitimate complaints against the U.S. government. Some of my colleagues, with a smile, began to address me as *bon Charles*.

De Gaulle was not always right, nor was he always wrong. He could be an irritating personality, but always a great leader. U.S. officials, I believed, would be wise to listen carefully to French complaints. With the advantage of hindsight, we know now that de Gaulle was more right than wrong on Vietnam and on economic policy. France was justified in developing nuclear weapons, and these weapons remain today an effective deterrent to assault on NATO states.

In recent years, NATO has changed for the worse, in my opinion. Its military reach has extended to Afghanistan with generally bad results in alliance cohesion. Those who hoped NATO would progress into a fully integrated government find that prospect gone. During his presidency, de Gaulle believed the European community should remain a "community of states." On occasion, he spoke favorably about a NATO-wide federation as a desirable goal, but he insisted it should not be attempted without a strong "federator," meaning a person, ideally a head of government, who enjoyed alliance-wide respect and commitment. I believe his assessment was timely and accurate.

Several men prominent in de Gaulle's government strongly supported an Atlantic federation that included the United States and Canada, as well as France. So did Eisenhower when he reached reflective years in retirement. Although de Gaulle never, to my knowledge, cited Eisenhower as having the ability to serve as the federator, I believe he was the one person—perhaps the only person of his day—who could have filled that role. Unfortunately, he did not embrace the federation goal publicly while in office. During one of my private chats with him, on July 21, 1967, he reviewed missed opportunities while in the White House, including steps to bring the United States into the European community. He told me, "I always hoped, and expected, that NATO would go beyond military affairs. I was always for the European Common Market [forerunner of the European Union] but always hoped that it would include all of NATO, not just the original six states." He then made a profound summation: "We tend to deal with urgent challenges and leave the important ones for tomorrow." That truism could wisely be emblazoned permanently on the wall of every chamber where government decisions are made.

Today I see no one on the international scene likely to become the federator. As president, Truman carried the text of Alfred Lord Tennyson's poem "Locksley Hall" in his billfold, poetry that contemplated a world parliament. After introducing Winston Churchill at Westminster College in 1946, Truman listened as the former British prime minister spoke confidently of federation, forecasting common citizenship would eventually bring the people of the British

Commonwealth and the United States together permanently. Truman subsequently helped establish NATO, but he made no effort to strengthen it into a federation.

This was the atmosphere as I formulated an unprecedented plan. Sensing the gravity of the French decisions on NATO, I proposed that my Republican colleagues in the House sponsor a Republican mission to get facts firsthand in Paris. Representative Melvin Laird, chairman of the House Republican Conference and later a secretary of defense for President Nixon, and House Republican leader Gerald Ford, destined to succeed Nixon as president, liked my proposal and won majority approval of other Republicans. When they asked me to chair the mission, I of course accepted.

It would be low budget with costs paid directly from conference funds, not by taxpayers. Joining me in the delegation would be Alexander Pirnie of New York, a veteran member of the Armed Services Committee; Hastings Keith of Massachusetts; and James Martin of Alabama. John A. Mathews, a retired army officer and part-time member of my congressional staff, was coordinator. It would be my first attempt to strengthen NATO, of which France was and still is a key member.

Mathews made a list of 103 congressional leaders, diplomats, and military officials, active and retired, each of whom received a letter in which I outlined the purpose of the trip and asked for suggestions. More than one-half of them responded before our departure for Paris. Almost all responses were warm and heartening.

However, in a letter dated June 7, former President Harry S. Truman recommended that our group "reconsider" the trip and leave NATO's problems to the executive branch. The text read as follows:

Dear Congressman Findley: I have read your letter of June 1, in which you seek my suggestions concerning your announced mission to Europe for the purpose of assessing our relations with France and our problems of NATO. What you are about to do is fraught with gravity in a sensitive and specialized field—that could result in adding to the burdens of the Administration and embarrassment to our nation. Under our system, the President is responsible for the conduct of foreign policy. The "facts" you seek are very likely already in his possession. My advice, therefore, to you is to reconsider. Sincerely yours, Harry Truman.

It was the only letter I received from Truman, a man whose service as president I greatly admired. I was not daunted by his theme nor surprised, as I already had learned that presidents prefer that members of Congress stick to foreign policy review and stay away from initiatives on their own. I was impressed that Truman took the time to read my letter and compose a thoughtful response. It reinforced my determination to conduct the mission with care to avoid the "gravity" the former president cited.

Senator Barry Goldwater wrote: "I am in complete agreement with you on this, and you have my support. I think you should do more and more of it." Widely syndicated columnist Drew Pearson wrote: "I heartily approve this idea." New York Governor Nelson Rockefeller, long a supporter of federation, sent his "best wishes."

We took as gifts several small busts of Abraham Lincoln. Ambassador Robert Strausz-Hupe, director of the University of Pennsylvania Foreign Policy Institute, provided advance preparation and wise counsel on several occasions. In consultation with U.S. State Department officials, he suggested an agenda, and when our group approved it, he made a special advance trip to Paris to arrange appointments.

A few days after the letters were mailed, I was seated on the House floor when James Harvey, a Republican colleague from Michigan who later became a federal judge, rushed from the adjacent Speaker's Gallery and handed me a small sheet of yellow paper. With a worried look, Harvey said, "You won't believe what Dirksen just said about your Paris trip." It was a three-paragraph news item torn from UPI dispatches that emerged from one of the media printing machines in the gallery, dispatches that help members keep up on breaking news. According to the dispatch, Senate Republican leader Everett Dirksen responded with the question, "Are you kidding?" when asked by a reporter in the Senate Press Gallery what he thought about "Findley's foreign policy mission to Paris." According to the UPI, Dirksen said, "That's cute," when another reporter explained that the group would explore U.S. difficulties with France. Dirksen then "ruminated out loud" about the legality of the trip, saying he did not know if it would violate the Logan Act, legislation that prohibits private citizens from engaging in foreign policy negotiations.

When I read the dispatch, I was appalled. After all, Dirksen and I were fellow Republicans, and he was the spokesman for the entire Republican delegation in Congress from Illinois. His name was near the top of the list of people who were sent my information letter. A few months earlier he had complimented me on my relationship with news media. I had announced that the trip was purely fact-finding and that the State Department had no objection. Earlier that day, I had conducted a news conference explaining the mission's purpose. There were no critical questions from media, and everything seemed well-organized until Harvey handed me the UPI dispatch.

The next day Springfield's *State Journal-Register* published a report from Washington headlined, "Findley's Fact-finding Plan Founders." I called Dirksen's office. He was not present, but his secretary told me that my letter of explanation had been the top item on the senator's desk for at least two days. She said he obviously had not read it. Dirksen telephoned me later. He was apologetic but disinclined to make a corrective public statement, saying, "It would be like warmed over soup." He must have had second thoughts about soup, because the next day he told media that his exchange with reporters about my trip was "jovial" and should not have been reported. He added that he saw no objection to the trip. The Associated Press offered this summation two days later: "[Dirksen] says he was only kidding when he ridiculed a House GOP plan to investigate U.S.-French relations."

This was hardly the salutary kickoff for the trip I wanted. I undertook damage control. Aware of Dirksen's antics, Eisenhower,

NATO's first supreme commander, welcomed our group to a pre-trip huddle at his Gettysburg office. Former Vice President Richard Nixon did the same in his Manhattan office.

In a column published the day our mission landed in Paris, syndicated columnists Rowland Evans and Robert Novak reported a controversy over the mission within House Republican ranks when Frances Bolton, a senior Republican on the House Foreign Affairs Committee, urged House Republicans to include at least one member of the committee in the mission delegation. Evans and Novak concluded: "The Findley mission . . . is far more entangled in Republican Party politics than international diplomacy." Actually, Bolton's comment made no waves. E. Ross Adair, senior Republican on the Foreign Affairs Committee, had agreed to participate but withdrew because of a schedule conflict.

In Paris, our nine-day agenda proceeded without major hitches. We met top military commanders and civilian officials of NATO and France. Included were Maurice Couve de Murville, foreign minister of France, and Maurice Schumann, a future foreign minister who served during World War II as the radio voice of Free France, broadcasting from London. Thus began my close friendship with Schumann that continued until his death years later. He was one of several French officials who were outspoken advocates of the federation of NATO states that Clarence Streit proposed. Officials interviewed included Manlio Brosio, secretary-general of NATO; French General Pierre Gallois; French Minister of Defense Pierre Messmer; General Lyman L. Lemnitzer, supreme commander of NATO; and General André Beaufre, director of the French Institute of Strategic Studies. U.S. Ambassador to France Charles E. Bohlen was cordial and helpful.

Our discussions revealed that in French eyes, NATO had kept a leader-follower relationship, with the United States always the leader, and Britain often given preference to the disadvantage of France. Several French officials asserted that their country had been consigned to subordination rather than integration, citing evidence that the Johnson administration withheld information and decisions on nuclear matters from France, claiming that Communists had infiltrated the French bureaucracy. The French rejoinder: Klaus Fuchs, a British spy, had been caught stealing nuclear secrets for the Soviet Union, but no similar infraction had occurred in France. France was proceeding with its own nuclear weapons development. Our group explained, as best we could, the prevalence of misinformation about French intentions within Congress and throughout the country.

Although de Gaulle did not grant our request for a personal interview, he sent our group a cryptic message in which he focused on the U.S. role in Vietnam. It was reported by Colonel Deue Chesnais, one of his aides, who attended a dinner party hosted in our honor by General Gallois, a specialist in nuclear strategic planning. France's colonial rule in French Indochina, now known as Vietnam, had come to an end several years earlier. When our visit to Paris occurred, the buildup of U.S. military forces in Vietnam was well underway. As Chesnais reported de Gaulle's message, I copied the words on a card that I have carefully preserved: "I hope you can win a victory in Vietnam. I do not believe you can. If you continue your present 'success' in five years you will be involved in ten places. Then the American people will become tired and return to isolation. In saying that, please remember that neither I nor the French people dislike the American people." It was a stark—and accurate—forecast of the costly failure that lay ahead for the United States in Vietnam.

Before returning to Washington, we laid a wreath at the Tomb of the Unknown Soldier. Hastings Keith pleased onlookers by speaking words of tribute in French with a New England accent. On June 22, Gallois sent a message: "If we want to build something together, we have to be perfectly frank and know exactly what is common to us and what divides us." He also expressed concern over U.S. news media reports that "My country is going to bankruptcy because of atomic expenditures." This, he wrote, "does not respond to reality."

Our small team worked in harmony in preparing for the trip, following the agenda in Paris, and writing the final report. We concluded that France would not soon, if ever, agree to participation in the NATO integrated command structure, but would remain in the alliance and loyally support NATO decisions through national control of its own independent nuclear and nonnuclear military resources. Our recommendations:

In the interest of advancing alliance spirit and comity NATO should be reorganized as a true partnership of equals.

Top command of integrated forces should rotate annually from nation to nation. Before undertaking any military actions, member states should consult candidly and promptly with each other.

To illustrate how little has changed, today's NATO-led forces in Afghanistan operate apart from U.S. military forces in that country. All U.S. forces function under direct U.S. command.

Our mission must have avoided the dangers Truman cited, because several of the nation's leading media commentators gave our report good marks. Dirksen's ridicule was forgotten, and *Newsweek* identified me as one of five "bright young men" in the House. The *Newsweek* article continued: "In June [Findley] caused a stir by leading a four-member delegation [all Republicans] to explore U.S.-French differences over NATO. The idea provoked chuckles from the diplomatic set, but the Findley report turned out to be a balanced appraisal." Hours after the *Newsweek* article was published, I attended a birthday party honoring Dirksen. Guest Richard Nixon, noting that the other four members cited in *Newsweek* were Democrats, asked with a warm smile, "What are you doing with all those liberals?" It was a friendly question.

David Lawrence, editor of *U.S. News and World Report,* devoted a full page of commentary to the work of our mission. It received favorable comment by syndicated columnists Fulton Lewis Jr., Paul Harvey, Roscoe Drummond, C. L. Sulzberger, and Charles Bartlett.

Among those who responded warmly by mail were former British Prime Minister Anthony Eden; former French Foreign Minister Maurice Schumann; General Matthew B. Ridgway, a hero of the Korean War; General James M. Gavin; and Admiral Arleigh Burke. Looking back, the Dirksen episode was high comedy with the senator ultimately stubbing his own toe. I had to chuckle, remembering he relished his reputation as chief comedian when meeting reporters in the press gallery.

The text of our report on the Paris mission filled over three pages in the June 30, 1965, *Congressional Record*. Soon after, Republican House leader Ford appointed me to the U.S. delegation then called NATO Parliamentarians, later renamed the Atlantic Assembly, and praised my work on NATO in a handwritten note. But the *Illinois State Register* editorialized, "In the past year Findley has appeared to spend more time trying to appease and alibi for France's imperial President Charles de Gaulle than in concerning himself with the interests of [Findley's] district." Despite this assessment, the Paris experience deepened my commitment to the federation goal. It reinforced my conviction that nation states cannot meet the needs of the modern era. A growing number of vexing problems are beyond the capacity of any nation state to solve, and that reality should impel the nations experienced in democracy and the preservation of individual liberty to disenthrall themselves from the limitations inherent in alliances and bind themselves permanently together. By year's end a bipartisan group of more than one hundred House members cosponsored my Atlantic Union resolution. The total gave me hope it might advance in the legislative process.

The report on the Paris mission did not end my involvement with France. In my work as a delegate to the Atlantic Assembly, I visited Paris several times, renewing friendships with parliamentarians and other officials I met in 1965. Our daughter Diane, then sixteen, accompanied me on one of my trips to Paris. She spent one full day at the embassy as the guest of the ambassador's family, while I attended NATO activities. During the afternoon, she joined the ambassador's daughter on a stroll in a nearby park. When a flasher displayed his nude body by opening his trench coat, the girls laughed but scampered back to the embassy as fast as they could.

To my surprise, my endeavors in French relations prompted Dennis Embrey, one of the youthful pages who handled calls and errands for Republicans during sessions of the House of Representatives, to give me a copy of *Is Paris Burning?* by Larry Collins and Dominique Lapierre, a gripping account of the last days of German occupation of the French capital in World War II.

When French president Georges Pompidou was invited to address a joint meeting of Congress, Israeli partisans who objected to a French sale of warplanes to Arab states put up a fuss. To underscore the protest, Representative Lester Wolff announced he would signal his protest by rising from his seat in the House of Representatives chamber and walking out when Pompidou started to speak. I thought such behavior was a cheap slap at a distinguished guest and secured the cooperation of my highly respected colleague, Representative Lee H. Hamilton, in countering Wolff's scheme. When Wolff, as expected, rose from his seat as Pompidou began to speak, I was positioned—thanks to Hamilton's cooperation—to occupy the empty seat the moment Wolff vacated it. This meant there was no empty seat on which cameras could focus.

During my visits with Eisenhower at Gettysburg, de Gaulle was an occasional topic. One day Ike told me the French leader could be irritating but he always held him in high esteem for his loyalty to France. When Ike died, de Gaulle came to the funeral in Washington, arriving at Dulles Airport. I waited there with my assistant, Stephen Jones, hoping at least to get a glimpse of the French leader. The State Department had not included us in the official reception party, but, as it turned out, Jones and I were the only ones there. Due to a misunderstanding, the official committee members were expecting the French president to arrive at a later hour.

Attired splendidly in the dress uniform of a French general, he tarried only long enough to say "merci bien" in response to my greeting. A moment later, he was in a Citroën that whisked him away to the French ambassador's residence. As the limousine pulled away from the curb, I thought of the contrast in personalities of the French general just arrived and the U.S. general he had come to honor. De Gaulle was unsmiling, brusque, hurried.

Whenever I met Eisenhower, from a brief encounter in 1952 to our last meeting in his Gettysburg office, his handshake was warm and firm, his smile broad, and his words of greeting conveyed sincerity. Due mainly to my work in NATO, the general and I became close friends. In 1968, Eisenhower asked me for guidance on how his granddaughter, Anne, a college student, could get a summer job on Capitol Hill. Imagine a five-star general of the armies asking a lowly, former navy lieutenant, junior grade, for guidance on anything! By nightfall, Anne had a summer job on my Capitol Hill staff.

De Gaulle could be forgiven for thinking that this was just one more intentional slight of *la belle France* by the U.S. government. Although brief, his greeting remained memorable. Any Frenchman who survived the infamy of the Vichy regime and the years of anti-French bias in U.S.-British councils of government had good reason to be sensitive and cool. For me, it was a thrilling moment. I had just pressed the hand of a hero who came to Washington to commemorate the passing of another hero.

11

Civil Rights and Lobbyists

My most controversial civil rights vote supported enactment of the 1964 bill that barred racial discrimination on most housing transactions, a measure that was unpopular in my constituency and with Republican leader Gerald Ford. Prior to the vote, I dissented from Ford's publicized opposition by sending a form letter to all Republicans in the House urging their support. In it, I cited the leadership of Abraham Lincoln against racism and reminded my colleagues that Republicans are members of the political party that Lincoln brought to national success. My vote—and perhaps my letter to Republican colleagues—helped defeat an amendment that would reduce the bill to a simple statement of sentiment, not enforceable law. The act was approved, 259 to 157.

Although unpopular within much of my constituency, I consider my votes for this and other civil rights legislation the proudest of my career. My district included Springfield, Lincoln's hometown, where terrible race riots had occurred in 1909. Immediately after the riots, the National Association for the Advancement of Colored People (NAACP), the first major civil rights group, was organized there. Ford's vote against the open housing measure was his only dissent in the series. He voted in favor of all other civil rights bills. Perhaps he noted the national appeal of federal action to improve interracial relations.

The next year, 1965, Ford showed he bore no grudge against me by letting me select Frank Mitchell, a fifteen-year-old-student living in Springfield, for appointment as the first African American page in the history of the U.S. House of Representatives. Mitchell did a fine as job as page and went on to a successful career in television journalism. He told me years later that he experienced no racial discrimination in any form from members of Congress or other pages during his work on Capitol Hill. Mitchell said he always tried to carry himself with "dignity and respect." He added, "I hope I made it easier for the next [black] guy coming along." He said page duty helped expand his horizons. "It's just been an amazing life." Asked for advice to a younger generation of African Americans, he said, "It is important to stay connected with people you meet. They can build huge bridges for you later on."[2]

In 1973, in another sign of racial harmony on the Hill, Speaker Carl Albert recognized me during a legislative session in the House chamber so I could note the retirement that day of Ernest Petinaud, the popular African American maitre d' of the House of Representatives dining room. When I began to speak, most of the House members were in the chamber. I first mentioned that Petinaud's first day as member of the dining room staff was March 4, 1925, when Calvin Coolidge began his elected term as president. Then I added,

Well known is Ernest's friendly, affable, kind, considerate public life. Little known is his equally splendid private life. His mother was an invalid for twenty-five years. Until her death in 1936, he devoted his life to her well-being. Two years later, he became happily married. One of his hobbies has been writing cards for handicapped people in his beautiful hand. Under the rules of the House of Representatives, I cannot mention people in the gallery, but on this occasion how splendid it would be if all of us would rise and show our affection for Mr. and Mrs. Petinaud.

As I spoke those last words, my colleagues rose and turned to applaud the Petinauds as they stood at front row seats in the gallery. The applause continued for more than fifteen minutes. Then, all settled back to listen as members took turns in expressing their tribute in words. Majority Leader Thomas P. "Tip" O'Neill said, "In my twenty-one years in Congress this is the greatest honor that I have seen an individual receive from this body." The next four pages of the *Congressional Record* published similar sentiments as others took turns at a microphone. Republican leader John Rhodes said, "Ernest can remember the name of every member and former member and even the wife of almost every member, past and present." Charles Bennett of Florida added, "To know him is to love him." It was an hour of unashamed emotion.

My friendship with the Petinauds deepened in the days that followed. One evening Lucille and I were guests for dinner in their residence, enjoying a meal that Mrs. Petinaud prepared and served, then examining mementoes of their eventful life. Lucille cherishes a gift of perfume from Mrs. Petinaud.

During the evening, Petinaud related a unique experience with Richard Nixon when the future president was a member of the House. Nixon asked him to organize a dinner party at the Nixon residence the following Friday. Petinaud said he regretfully could not, because this would mean leaving his ill wife at home alone. When Nixon offered to send a registered nurse to care for his wife during the party, Petinaud agreed to the assignment. Nixon provided nursing care at his personal expense not just the one night, but until Mrs. Petinaud's health was fully restored, more than a week later.

In 1976, African American Melvin Cobb addressed his high school graduating classmates as salutatorian with the Findleys and my staff in the cheering section. Seven years before, Cobb was one of four young men that staff leader Bob Wichser, his wife, Pat, and Madelyn Evans, another staff member, tutored in the evenings on Capitol Hill. The boys' neighborhoods were devastated by the 1968 rioting and burning in the inner city that followed the assassination of Rev. Martin Luther King Jr. The quartet dwindled to Cobb alone. He became a dependable, efficient part-time employee in my office.

Civil rights remained a major endeavor. In 1977, one of my earliest legislative proposals finally became law. It had nothing to do with race, but it qualified as a major act in advancing civil rights. Signed by President Jimmy Carter in the White House Rose Garden while I stood behind him, it raised to seventy the age below which no one can, with a few exceptions, be denied employment solely because of age. It reflected my long-held belief that some people are young at seventy, while others are old at forty.

I call it my bill despite the fact that Representative Claude Pepper of Florida is listed as chief sponsor, and myself as cosponsor. A year before, Pepper opposed my bill. When it suddenly attained popularity, he changed his mind. I was delighted with his decision, as his support assured prompt enactment. At the time, at eighty-plus, he chaired a special committee on aging. After Carter signed the bill, I thanked him for signing a "significant advance in civil rights." Before leaving the White House grounds, I asked Carter to trade pens with me. I gave him a nice Cross pen and received in exchange the common ballpoint pen he used to sign the bill. "I got the better of this bargain," the president said. Carter's pen is displayed on my office wall below a picture taken of the president and a group of my colleagues at the bill signing.

I took up consumer and taxpayer rights when sugar legislation came before the Agriculture Committee. Controversy over sugar quotas started in the main hearing room of the committee in 1965, when veteran Chairman Harold Cooley banged his gavel and stopped my interrogation of a professional lobbyist. He was testifying on behalf of the quota system under which favored foreign countries are accorded a specific portion of U.S. sugar imports. Cooley ruled me out of order when I asked the lobbyist how much his foreign client paid for his services.

I did not challenge his ruling, but it prompted me to dig deeper into the role of lobbyists in sugar prices at the grocery store. I learned that import quotas kept U.S. consumer prices at about seven cents a pound, contrasted with world prices at two and one-half cents. Other facts about sugar lobbyists and their clients were troubling. Some clients were unsavory leaders of Central American countries. As I dug up information, I placed it in the *Congressional Record*. I estimated that the quota system cost U.S. consumers at least $700 million a year, with $280 million of that amount handed to nonproducing individuals and foreign governments. Lobbyists had reaped $350,000 in fees from sugar interests in the prior year alone. This data fed the media's appetite for exotic themes and kept my reform efforts in the headlines. Compared with the billions of dollars spent by lobbyists today, these sugar lobby sums seem almost paltry.

My assault on sugar quotas strained relations with Representative Page Belcher of Oklahoma, a senior Republican on the Agriculture Committee, as well as with Chairman Cooley. Belcher viewed my endeavors as a veiled accusation that supporters of quotas, possibly including himself, were taking bribes from lobbyists. I suspected Cooley and a few others but never accused any individuals of misdeeds, certainly not Belcher.

Belcher once gave me this advice: "Never introduce a bill, because it might become law." It was terrible advice, reflecting his overriding wish to avoid controversy and thus help achieve reelection dreams. Though I never followed that advice, I did adopt his policy on constituent mail. In his congressional office, each incoming letter was logged. He kept a close watch to assure prompt response to each. When I adopted a similar office procedure, I discovered that my office manager met the challenge of voluminous incoming mail by stuffing a lot of it unanswered in a drawer. She was quickly on the street, job hunting.

The bill to extend sugar quotas swept through the Agriculture Committee without amendment. It seemed headed for routine consideration on the floor until the Rules Committee decided to permit

House action on two amendments I proposed to offer. One would prohibit a quota to any country that hired a lobbyist, and the other would impose a tax on quotas, enabling the Treasury Department to recover some of the bill's cost to consumers. During floor deliberations my amendments failed by narrow margins. The legislation was approved without amendment in both the House and Senate. *Newsweek*'s summation: "[Findley] won acclaim with a brilliant marshaling of facts and questions about what highly paid lobbyists for foreign governments—many of them ex-U.S. officials—really do for their money. Battling the congressional establishment he came closer than anyone could have predicted in winning passage of reform legislation."

The following May, *Reader's Digest* published my article entitled, "Sugar: A Sticky Mess in Congress." It summarized the penalty consumers pay for the quota system and my case for reform. In it, I declared:

> The only valid purpose of the Sugar Act is to protect our high-cost domestic sugar industry. That purpose could be achieved without a complicated program. We should abolish the Sugar Act altogether and substitute a straightforward tariff of, say, two cents a pound. In one stroke that would provide the domestic industry with the protection it needs, give all foreign producers fair and equal access to the U.S. market, and bring millions of dollars into the U.S. Treasury instead of doling millions out. It would reduce the shelf price of sugar and wipe out influence peddling, favoritism, and other abuses.

Writing the article was more complicated than preparing a major thesis in college. The experience impressed me with the thoroughness of *Digest* editing. Each word was examined to eliminate any possibility of exaggeration. My article, moreover, may have been a factor in ending Chairman Cooley's career. In it I reported that

Cooley protected a lobbyist from answering a question I raised. He lost his next bid for reelection.

On another agricultural front in 1966, I accused the administration of dumping government corn inventories on the market as a device to force farmers to comply with so-called voluntary federal programs to control crop planting. I suggested publicly that Agriculture Secretary Orville Freeman cancel partisan speeches and go on a listening tour of farm areas. On another occasion I called for his dismissal from office. For such behavior, Freeman called me the "hatchet man of the Republican Party."

In October 1966, when Freeman visited Springfield on behalf of Richard Wolfe, my Democratic opponent that year, I entered the hotel banquet room uninvited where he was holding a news conference. I immediately stuck out my hand and welcomed Freeman "to the greatest agricultural district in America." It was an unplanned, impulsive decision I made while walking by the hotel where I knew the breakfast was scheduled. I meant no offense or discourtesy. In fact, I thought Freeman might chuckle at the gesture of welcome. Instead, it ruined his whole day.

By nightfall, still fuming, he wrote a letter chastising me for my appearance that morning. He wrote that I remained "only long enough to get [my] picture taken and then ran out!" Notwithstanding this appraisal, I defeated Wolfe on Election Day, 101,964 to 61,877, a healthy margin. Years later, Freeman and I found common ground on other issues and communicated cordially. Both of us buried the hatchet, if it ever really existed.

Five years later, I wanted to retrieve my membership on the Agriculture Committee and retain my seat on Foreign Affairs. To do that I needed the cooperation of Representative Belcher, who had become the senior Republican on the Agriculture Committee.

Belcher was still upset with me and kept delaying a decision. One day, I handed him a signed, undated letter resigning from the Agriculture Committee. I told him that, if he cleared the way for my return to the committee, he could subsequently activate my signed resignation any time he wished. He cleared my appointment, never activated my letter, and did not mention the subject again.

I did not change committees with an eye on the next election. My successful mission in Paris whetted my interest in foreign policy. So did my drive for a federation of democracies. Another factor was my belief that the House of Representatives should exert greatest interest in war and peace policies. I wanted to be on the front line in accomplishing that advance.

Any concern of farmers on my committee was allayed by Belcher's cooperation in letting me return.

Late in 1966, I closed a three-month campaign to force the Pentagon to cancel a controversial $73 million contract to buy fault-prone West German 20-millimeter cannons. They would replace the 50-caliber machine guns on U.S. personnel carriers and landing craft despite official data that showed them with an unacceptable malfunction rate. I called the issue a "gun gap," a term inspired by the "missile gap" charge that helped Kennedy win the presidency. I kept readers of the *Congressional Record* up to date on the "gun gap" issue. I first learned of the scandal from Charles Nicodemus, a star investigative reporter for the *Chicago Daily News*. The army purchase was intertwined in the internal politics of a U.S. obligation to maintain troops in West Germany, a continuing, costly investment that began in the aftermath of World War II. The Bonn government was obligated to provide the Pentagon with a specified value in German manufacturer arms to help offset the cost of stationing U.S. troops in Germany. Provisions of the cannons would help meet that obligation.

My "gun gap" campaign got strong editorial endorsement and news coverage in the *New York Times* and other major media, even a personal appearance on NBC's *Today Show*. On October 3, 1966, the *Times* editorialized, "The army compiled a long 'white paper' to rebut and refute the criticism, but, as Findley has pointed out, it contains self-contradictions, half-truths, or prevarications and does not answer some of the main criticisms. Most important: why, six years after an urgent need was stated for a gun superior to the Russian model, is the government purchasing a gun that is technologically unsatisfactory?" The Associated Press quoted me as saying, "We are limping along with a weapon from World War II while the Russians have larger and better equipment." The upshot: the contract for the German cannon was reduced to a small purchase, a stopgap to meet the "gun gap."

Adding variety to my life, an excise tax on wheat products was pending before the Rules committee. Similar to a flat sales tax, it stirred controversy because it would be passed on to consumers in the form of increased prices. It was a consumer issue, because it added to the price of bread and gave producers of wheat an undeserved bad name. It prompted two actions on my part. At several grocery stores in my constituency, I passed out cards with nickels attached. They dramatized the fact that farmers got only five cents of the fifty cents consumers paid for a loaf of bread. I also testified before the House Rules Committee, arguing that the excise tax on wheat processors was actually a bread tax. A U.S. Chamber of Commerce newsletter reported the scene: "Holding aloft an expensive mink fur piece [actually Lucille's mink stole], Findley reminded committee members that Congress recently wiped out a 10 percent excise tax on furs and other luxury goods. Next the Illinois congressman lifted into view an ordinary loaf of bread. What the pending legislation will do, Findley said with caustic irony, is restore the 10 percent tax removed from mink fur and put it on every loaf of bread sold in the nation." Despite my show-and-tell, the Rules Committee forwarded a rule to the House floor that prohibited amendments. The tax passed the House and Senate.

On other legislative issues, I joined Illinois colleagues John B. Anderson, Robert McClory, and Donald Rumsfeld in recommending committee and House proceedings be covered by television and radio. Our proposal was approved the next January.

I opposed President Johnson's recommendation to lengthen the terms of House members from two to four years, arguing that it would be "a step backward" in representative government, restricting the ability of the public to make timely changes in those holding elective office.

During the year, I continued my efforts to reduce direct federal payments to farmers, contending they are wasteful and a costly barrier between producer and marketplace. I placed in the *Congressional Record* the names of all persons who received more than five thousand dollars in government payments from the sugar program during the previous year. Mark Andrews, a Republican colleague with a beet sugar business in South Dakota, was among those listed. He did not welcome the publicity.

In 1976, my article "Let's Plug the Billion-Dollar Farm Drain" appeared in *Reader's Digest*. In it, I deplored the trend toward direct government payments to farmers that provided little help to struggling small farmers but enriched big operations. Now, thirty-three years later, the farm drain on taxpayers is twenty times larger. Direct payments to farmers now exceed twenty billion dollars annually. These payments have no social merit. They are not people-related. They are based entirely on commodity production, not the financial status of the individual farmer. A far better program would establish a minimum net income for a full-time, commercial farmer. Each farmer above that level would get nothing from the U.S. Treasury.

In the twenty-five years since I left Congress, most of the legislation in agricultural policy that I helped establish has disappeared. A lonely surviving victory is the termination of the federal subsidy to the growers of tung nut oil, once a major ingredient in the manufacture of paint. When my bill became law, government warehouses had a five-year inventory of the oil, with marketing prospects diminishing each year. Its production is now subject to market disciplines, where, in my opinion, the pricing of all commodities should occur.

All farm organizations, including the Farm Bureau, now sing the praises of government payments. I am upset with Congress for letting these expensive donation programs continue. They are disgraceful. Although I don't recommend it, the government could

CIVIL RIGHTS AND LOBBYISTS

manage the disbursement more efficiently simply by writing a $20,000 check annually to each of the one million full-time farmers. After my endeavors on the road to farm-policy sanity, the scene is far worse than ever before. I believe even a small band of resolute members from rural America could turn the tide, but I see no such move even on the distant horizon.

When I first joined the Agriculture Committee, a wise senior Republican member, Clifford McIntire, told me, "If you mail a one-hundred-dollar Treasury check each month to almost any farmer, by the third month he will be convinced he can't live without it."

12

∞∞∞∞∞∞∞∞∞∞∞∞∞∞∞∞∞∞∞

Trading with the Enemy

In 1967, I had my wish—membership on the Foreign Affairs Committee. It was not a sharp turn in my life, because I had already been hard at work at foreign affairs, as well as agriculture. But membership put me in the center of momentous change. In June, a fateful and costly turn for the worse occurred in U.S. Middle East policy, but it was so effectively hidden by government cover-up I did not comprehend its devastating impact until years later.

Meanwhile, I found myself deep in an often lonely battle to turn back a foolish change in U.S. policy in Eastern Europe. I was troubled by America's losing war in Vietnam and astounded at President Johnson's determination to launch a new, ill-considered friendship plan among Warsaw Pact countries near the Soviet western border.

I pressed initiatives against trading with the enemy, because I believed that blocking them served the best interests of the United States. My amendments were intended to counter two dangerous movements that I saw emerging institutionally within our government. The first was the increasing impotence of the House of Representatives in foreign affairs. The House had meekly and unnecessarily yielded much of its influence to the Senate.

Under the Constitution, Senators had the exclusive right to pass judgment on treaties and nominations of ambassadors and other senior officials. All of these were important, but I once reminded

my House colleagues of an earlier era when House members Daniel
Webster, Henry Clay, and John C. Calhoun were actively involved
in American foreign policy. As recently as the end of World War
II, President Harry Truman included a House group in the delegation that helped form and design the United Nations Charter. But
recent House Foreign Affairs chairmen had been willing to take a
backseat and a "ho-hum" view. Political scientists would argue that
the House, as the body closest to the people, was primarily concerned with domestic policy and could point out that revenue bills
had to originate in the House. These objections, however, actually
supported my position. There is nothing more domestic in its impact
than the death of a young man or woman in uniform in battle outside the United States. World War I and World War II were authorized by both houses of Congress.

The Korean War, the Vietnam War, and the current wars in
Iraq and Afghanistan were not even the subject of war declarations.
Over one hundred thousand U.S. men and women have died in
these undeclared wars. The House had to pass bills to finance these
wars, extend the draft, set its terms, pay ambassadorial salaries,
and authorize spending for our embassies abroad as well as for the
Department of State.

The House of Representatives is a branch of government coequal
with the Senate. If pocketbook issues are reflected in House elections, so are issues reflecting war and foreign policy. Most voters,
especially those who pay little attention to government, wrongly
assume that the House of Representatives matches the Senate in foreign policy influence. As a reflection of this, voters penalize House
members in the majority when foreign military endeavors prove
costly and disappointing. In 1942, Democrats nearly lost control
of the House of Representatives because the American people were
unhappy about the string of military losses in the Far East. In 1966
they lost nearly fifty House seats, largely because of dissatisfaction
with the war in Vietnam. Republicans lost control of the House in
the 2006 election because of dissatisfaction with the war in Iraq.

Years ago, through neglect, the House lost its proper, legitimate role in foreign policy. Beginning in 1962, I sought to help the House retrieve that influence through speeches, objections to unanimous consent requests, amendments—each in opposition to what I considered wrong and harmful foreign policies—and legislation. Situated in the minority all twenty-two years, my endeavors were often seen as negative—against positions of the majority—but these initiatives were actually building blocks for new policies, new programs, and new vision. I sought a simple but elusive goal: reestablishing the House influence on foreign policy as equal to the Senate, as intended by Constitution framers.

In an October major foreign policy address in New York, President Johnson outlined a proposal to "build bridges" to Eastern European Communist countries except Albania, whose near-total isolation may have made it seem irrelevant to the president. His proposal could not have come at a worse time, nor have been more misguided.

Johnson was motivated partly by the fact that his foreign policy had become sterile and mired in the Vietnam War, causing other areas of the world that deserved urgent attention to be neglected. These included the Middle East, the growing estrangement between the Soviet Union and China, the throwing-off of colonialism in Africa, and our difficult relations with Canada and Mexico. One of the most neglected but important issues was NATO and our relations with continental European powers, none more important than Germany and France.

The United States was fighting in Vietnam, according to Johnson, to prevent expansion of Communist China into the Southeast Asia "rice bowl." President Eisenhower's administration had popularized the domino theory whereby if one domino—Vietnam, for example—"fell" to the Communists, Cambodia, Laos, Thailand, and others might topple, and the Communists would gain great military and political advantage in the Cold War.

I was perplexed and concerned to read that the president wanted to extend discounted credit and other forms of aid to several members of the Warsaw Pact—the Soviet Union's answer to NATO—at the very time a war against Communism had already claimed over ten thousand American lives, contributed to inflation, and provoked racial violence in America. His proposal came barely fifteen years after the end of the fighting in Korea, though no peace treaty there had been signed. And, most important, there was growing evidence that the very countries we were now proceeding to assist financially, despite their increasingly bankrupt Communist system, were aiding our enemy in Vietnam in various guises. Their ships carried military supplies to Vietnam, which meant harm to our men and women fighting there. Their political leadership had publicly argued the justness of the North Vietnam cause and urged Hanoi to continue war measures against our forces. These same countries had turned their back to us when we had asked for assistance in resolving the Vietnam conflict. Worse, Hungary, while secretly helping Hanoi, led us to believe it was assisting our efforts to find a peaceful settlement. Moreover, these countries, though they claimed poverty, had "sweetheart deals" through which they actually extended credit on attractive terms to North Vietnam.

In his address, Johnson proposed favorable credit to the friends of our enemy. A more misguided policy would be hard to imagine. What was being proposed was not trade, but U.S.-subsidized credit. Most East European currency was worthless and not accepted as a means of exchange on international markets. Every time we aided their financial resources through easy credit terms on purchases, we enhanced their capacity to aid North Vietnam. Expanded credit enabled each country to expand its already major economic aid to our enemy in Hanoi.

I knew the president's program, if adopted, would end up strengthening Soviet control in Eastern Europe at a time when local citizens were maneuvering to loosen it or break free. As America lessened pressure on Eastern Europe, Moscow would fill the vacuum this created. This would leave East Germany, an artificial rump state still not widely recognized by the international community, Poland,

Hungary, Czechoslovakia, and Bulgaria solidly in the Soviet bloc symbolized by the Warsaw Pact.

Although many citizens in Poland, Hungary, and Czechoslovakia were pro-Western, their governments were firmly rooted in the Warsaw Pact and compliant allies of the Soviet Union. Beginning in 1965, I routinely offered and the House passed a series of "Findley Amendments" to the Food for Peace program, the Export-Import Bank ("Ex-Im Bank"), and foreign aid authorization bills. My amendments restricted benefits of federal government spending and assistance programs from East European nations who traded with North Vietnam. Most of my amendments were ultimately signed into law. With American men and women dying in Vietnam, majorities of House members, Republican and Democrat, kept voting for "Findley Amendments."

My involvement in East European affairs through these amendments, which were sponsored from my position on the House Agriculture Committee, attracted the attention of the Johnson administration. Two highly competent State Department officials came to my office. They were Walter Stoessel, a deputy assistant secretary of state, and Zbigniew Brzezinski, a Columbia University political scientist and writer who later became President Carter's national security adviser. They tried to explain that my opposition was counterproductive. Stoessel did not have much evidence to support that argument, but Brzezinski later wrote me a lengthy letter that supported his argument with examples from Poland. There he wrote, the opportunity of the Poles to buy American grain on credit had allowed Poland some independence from the Soviet Union. In our interview, Brzezinski outlined Polish developments. He recalled that Stalin once said building Communism in Poland was like "saddling the cow," that the Poles were inherently pro-Western, and that beginning in 1956 with the return to influence of Władysław Gomułka, life was improved in Poland. He explained that Gomułka and Nikita Khrushchev had reached a handshake bargain under which Poland would be a reliable ally in military matters and support

Soviet foreign policy at a time when the lifeline of support to Soviet troops in East Germany ran through Poland. But, Brzezinski continued, Gomułka made a number of internal reforms. The police state and terror, arrests, and the "midnight knocks on the door" had been eliminated, he said, and in 1956 Cardinal Stefan Wyszynski had been released from prison. Catholic churches were opened, much of their property was restored, arrests of priests ceased, and the Communist government even subsidized the Catholic University in Lublin.

I countered with several undeniable facts of my own, based on research from the Legislative Reference Service and via Polish emigré circles and my own staff investigation. One year I had one of the brightest of my student interns, Cheryl Card, spend the entire summer evaluating whether the reforms that Gomułka had placed on the books in the late 1950s still existed either in form or substance. The bottom line was not heartening. Gomułka had become increasingly intolerant of opposition in all areas, students were regularly arrested, and some beaten. No follow-up occurred from the State Department.

There were also signs of turbulent anti-Semitism coming from the Communist Party, and some of the old-line Communists were cheerleaders for the North Vietnamese. More troubling was Gomułka's outspoken criticism of the 1968 revolt in Czechoslovakia. Nevertheless, Johnson proposed favorable trade treatment to Eastern Europe. The United States would extend the attractive trade terms any nation enjoys, most-favored-nation (MFN) treatment, by legislative action to Poland and several other East European countries; reduce trade restrictions on hundreds of items; authorize the Ex-Im Bank to guarantee Italian credit on U.S. machine tools for a joint Soviet-Italian Fiat automobile plant to be built in Russia; and allow the Ex-Im Bank to guarantee the credit of four additional Eastern European countries—Poland, Hungary, Bulgaria, and Czechoslovakia—for purchase of United States' goods and services.

Following the announcement of the initiatives, House Republicans led a drive to curtail the Ex-Im Bank's ability to carry out the president's credit plan. In 1963, the Ex-Im Bank had been barred by statute from guaranteeing credit of Communist nations unless the president made an express finding that it would be in the national interest. Upon becoming president, Johnson made two such findings, both in 1964, and as a result, the Ex-Im Bank was allowed to guarantee credit of Yugoslavia and Romania for purchase of goods and services from U.S. businessmen and guarantee loans made by U.S. commercial banks to these countries. The Soviet Union and four other Warsaw Pact countries could receive credit guarantees, but only for purchase of agricultural goods. That exception opened the door to big boosts in their foreign exchange position.

With the president's October 7 announcement, however, Poland, Hungary, Bulgaria, and Czechoslovakia became eligible also for guarantees previously available only to Yugoslavia and Romania. It was this action that House Republicans decided must be reversed. Our means for doing so was amending a fiscal 1967 supplemental appropriations bill that contained provisions affecting the Ex-Im Bank. Southern Democrats joined with Republicans in attaching to the bill an amendment that clearly prohibited the bank from guaranteeing the credit of any Communist nation.

This amendment was sponsored by a senior colleague, Representative Frank Bow of Ohio, and me. It won near unanimous Republican support. Eighty-five Republicans supported it with eight against. Eighty-two Democrats, fifty-three from the South, voted for the amendment, one hundred thirteen against.

However, the Senate softened the restriction, and in conference it was modified to include a presidential waiver clause. The president could ignore the restriction if he certified the national interest required it. The House Republican leadership criticized this waiver, but it was accepted in a roll call vote, 129 to 102. Only six Republicans voted to accept it, and seventy-four rejected it. Thirty-two Representatives who voted on October 18 for the House version switched their position and voted to accept the Senate-imposed waiver. If they had voted for the House recommittal motion, the bill would have been rejected.

My campaign against cut-rate terms on U.S. sales of grain to countries trading with the enemy stirred diplomatic fury. Earlier in the year, one of my amendments prohibited grain sales on easy terms to "any nation which sells or furnishes or which permits ships or aircraft under its registry to transport to North Vietnam any equipment, supplies, or commodities so long as North Vietnam is governed by a Communist regime."

In December, this prohibition held up a grain sale to Yugoslavia under the Food for Peace program and stirred a fervent top-level response in the State Department. Yugoslavia requested five hundred thousand tons of surplus grain, mostly wheat, on attractive terms, two years to pay, and low interest rates. In peacetime, I would have supported the sale enthusiastically, but not when the Tito regime in Yugoslavia was supporting the Hanoi regime.

At issue, in my view, were Johnson's halfhearted war measures in Vietnam and Congress's failure to change course in the war. Measured response seemed to be Johnson's operative doctrine. Our forces were not allowed to make a massive response when attacked. Selective Service brought most of our military forces into battle, but our nation was never mobilized. No war bonds were issued. No tax was levied to finance war expenses. No rationing. Nothing was done to put the nation on a war footing. As a proud veteran of World War II, I held strong views about how our government should behave in wartime. First, unless precisely required by treaty obligations, attack, or a war declaration, acts of war should never be undertaken. Once war is constitutionally initiated, the president should mobilize the entire nation and unite all its political, diplomatic, and economic resources behind our military forces. Instead, the Vietnam War was pursued as a sidebar activity. Despite congressional amendments to the contrary, the government tried to pursue in Eastern Europe policies that clearly undercut our military goals in Vietnam.

Applied to Yugoslavia, my amendment provoked high controversy. The December 13, 1966, *New York Times* reported: "The question of whether the Findley amendment prohibits further food sales to Yugoslavia . . . depends on the definition of the term 'nation.'" An editorial rejected my amendment as "short-sighted." A *Washington Post* editorial called it "congressional myopia." Happily for me, the *Illinois State Journal,* the leading newspaper in my district, called my reasoning "sound."

U.S. officials argued that shipments of medical supplies to North Vietnam were from charitable organizations within Yugoslavia, not from the government. I rejected that argument. Another issue concerned the efforts of the State Department to persuade me to look the other way when, in direct violation of the Findley Amendment, they wanted to extend credits to Yugoslavia. Again I rejected that argument in a five-page legal rebuttal prepared for me by Hyde Murray, counsel for Republicans on the Agriculture Committee. Murray was one of my closest friends. We worked closely on all matters relating to agriculture. The rebuttal Murray prepared argued that no shipment from a Communist state like Yugoslavia can occur without the sanction of government officials, so no distinction between private and government actions can be made. A copy of the rebuttal was sent to acting Secretary of State Nicholas Katzenbach. In a lengthy column about the Yugoslavia controversy, columnist Drew Pearson supported the State Department position: "The key policy of trade with European Communist nations was the subject of a knock-down closed-door debate last week between Rep. Paul Findley [R-Ill] and acting Secretary of State Nicholas Katzenbach, who said to Findley, 'In our opinion, Congress was interfering with foreign policy when it adopted your amendment . . . ,' 'I disagree,' shot back Findley. 'If this wheat sale is consummated, I think that the president and the State Department are treading on the prerogatives of Congress which has lots of responsibility in the field of foreign policy."

In the second week of December, the Undersecretary of State Eugene Rostow and Assistant Secretary for Congressional Relations Douglas MacArthur II, nephew of the general, met with House Republican leader Gerald Ford, seeking a way to finesse my amendment. At

Ford's suggestion they went to my congressional office. The House was in session at the time, but I returned to my office to listen to their plea. It was obvious they wanted me to "look the other way" and let the illegal sale with Yugoslavia be consummated. I declined.

During the not-so-private luncheon Pearson mentioned, Katzenbach was cordial at first. He lost that composure when an assistant quietly handed him a copy of my five-page legal brief. It apparently had reached his desk just minutes before he left for the luncheon. He glanced at the brief—proof that I already had made up my mind to fight the sale to Yugoslavia. Katzenbach was furious. I confess I was amused, but I tried hard not to show it. Prior to the invitation to lunch I had said nothing that would lead anyone to believe I would back down. Katzenbach had no basis for believing that a private lunch would win me over. Flush-faced, he did not tarry for coffee. On December 30, 1966, the *Illinois State Journal* quoted me as saying to reporters, "It makes no sense for us to send aid to a country like Yugoslavia that insists on aiding our enemy."

The General Accounting Office chided the White House and the State Department for attempting to make an end run around my amendment. The sale to Yugoslavia did not go through.

A dismal process became routine: restrictive amendments, often introduced by me and imposed by the House were watered down during House-Senate conference committee work. Few gains remained. By then, I was a seasoned warrior, used to reversals. I rarely showed—or felt—anger or frustration. I knew that a determined majority can ultimately prevail in the House. On these amendments, the majority usually stood with the administration, ignoring the fundamental issue—the folly of helping nations that trade with our enemy. Despite the ultimate outcome, the process brought near-unity among House Republicans against policies harmful to the national interest, and it strengthened the role of the House in foreign affairs. For a time, the House had to be taken seriously.

My campaign brought an interesting experience in the House dining room. W. Averell Harriman, the former governor of New

York and President Franklin Roosevelt's wartime ambassador to the Soviet Union who participated in the Yalta conference, took me to lunch because he was upset at the impact of my amendments. My friend and colleague on the International Relations Committee, Representative Jonathan Bingham of New York, who once worked for Harriman, arranged the date.

A man of imposing stature, Harriman had been carrying out diplomatic missions for Democratic presidents for at least thirty years. In 1956, he made a serious effort to win the Democratic nomination for president. He also minced no words. As soon as we sat down together, he told me my "proposal [was] the God damnedest, silliest thing" to come out of the House. He banged the table with his fist and was frankly confrontational and insulting. He said, "Your amendments are helping the Communists, not hurting them." I considered his behavior as an act and found it amusing. Bingham was embarrassed, and Stephen Jones, who was aghast, asked, "Mr. Ambassador, did you use such language when speaking to Marshal Stalin as you use to an elected member of Congress?" And without a pause, Harriman turned his steely gaze on him and said, "You're God damned right I did." At least Harriman had the virtue of speaking directly. He did not convince me, but I heard him out as politely as I could. Bingham later apologized, but I thanked him for this glimpse of one of the great players on the diplomatic stage.

In January 1967, after being approved for membership on the House Foreign Affairs Committee, I launched another protest, this time against Poland. The Johnson administration wanted to shift payment of Polish debts to the United States from U.S. dollars to Polish zlotys, which were of almost no value outside Poland. I contended that this change would amount to an $18 million loss to the U.S. Treasury in the next twelve months alone. In a seventeen-page white paper to the State Department, I complained that Poland was actually engaged in a war-by-proxy against the United States through its economic, military, and moral support for U.S. enemies in North Vietnam. Receiving no satisfactory response from the administration, I offered an amendment to pending legislation that canceled Poland's favored status in trade relations with the United States. To the consternation of Polish diplomats watching proceedings from the gallery, it was approved by the House of Representatives. However, due mainly to the influence of Representative Clement Zablocki, a senior member of the Foreign Affairs Committee with Polish ancestry, privileged trade status was restored in subsequent negotiations by Senate-House conferees. When I offered an amendment to keep Poland and Yugoslavia from receiving government credit at below-market interest rates, the House voted no, 157 to 200. It probably would have sailed through had it applied only to Yugoslavia.

While the Yugoslavia legislative battle was proceeding, I was involved in another highly contentious effort, initially successful but ultimately thwarted. It was the special case of most-favored-nation treatment for Poland and Yugoslavia, the only Communist countries in Eastern Europe enjoying that privilege. This provision meant that tariffs paid on imported goods from Poland and Yugoslavia could not exceed the tariffs paid by the most favored nation, for example, close allies like Britain and Italy. For any other Communist country exporting to the United States, the tariffs were nearly prohibitive.

Yugoslavia received favorable treatment after Tito's dramatic break with Stalin in 1948. Prior to the break, Tito had been as repressive in domestic policies as Soviet leader Stalin. Once he broke with Moscow and insisted that he alone would control events in Yugoslavia, the U.S. government rushed to support him with favorable tariffs. In fairness to Tito, he did liberalize some aspects of society and took an independent line in foreign policy.

The situation was different in Poland. Stalin had liquidated the Polish Communist Party before the war except for a few faithful retainers or those his secret police agents could not find to arrest. Most of the surviving Communists sat out the war in the Soviet Union and came to power riding, in a sense, on Soviet tanks. Gomułka was an exception. He was a genuine Polish nationalist but also a Marxist. During the war he remained in Poland. He believed his country should find its own way in building socialism. For this independent streak, he was placed under house arrest by Stalin, but the Soviet dictator did not dare execute him as he did much of the Eastern European leadership after the break with Yugoslavia. On the other hand, Communists kept their foot on Poland's neck. Gomułka returned to power in Poland when Khrushchev gained control in Moscow. Ten years later, Gomułka had retrenched on almost all fronts. He did not move against the Catholic Church because 95 percent of the Polish population, including many Communists, were practicing Catholics, but he had no trouble harassing students, Jews, and intellectuals. Despite this grim scene, the U.S. government was still allowing exports from Poland into this country under the attractive MFN terms.

I believed it was time to send a message to Gomułka. With few allies, I called the attention of House members to the deteriorating environment in Poland. For many Polish Americans who had friends and relatives in Poland or who were of ethnic Polish origin, it was a difficult time emotionally. I made it clear that my opposition was to government policy not the people.

In the worsening political environment of 1967, the administration feared its Eastern European initiatives would falter on House-passed restrictive amendments, a process that might threaten Poland's MFN status. The Polish diplomatic corps was always a significant professional group, a cut above the rank-and-file Soviet and East European diplomats. The Poles also had political support in this country, and they had a very sophisticated and respected foreign minister, Adam Rapacki, who had a broad European cultural and educational background and had been a prewar socialist. He transferred Stanislaw Pawlak to the Polish Embassy in Washington, where he became, in effect, the field marshal for Poland's efforts to defeat Findley amendments. Pawlak, an experienced diplomat fluent in English, made the rounds on Capitol Hill, including my office.

My staff and I were the target of his wooing. My staff leader, Stephen Jones, was invited to dinner with Leon Rubin, America's largest U.S. importer of Polish ham.

In August, the Foreign Aid Authorization Bill was before the House. I offered an amendment that passed without a roll call vote. Its provisions suspended MFN tariff privilege until the president certified that Poland was no longer supplying war materiel to North Vietnam. It represented a stunning rebuff to the administration's efforts to warm relations in Eastern Europe. In previous years, the act prohibited all forms of aid under the Foreign Assistance Act and other legislation to countries that traded with North Vietnam "so long as the regime in North Vietnam gives support to hostilities in South Vietnam." Existing law barred aid under the Foreign Assistance Act to countries that permitted ships or aircraft under their registry to transport goods to North Vietnam, but it did not affect countries that delivered goods to North Vietnam in the ships and aircraft of other nations.

The new House-voted restrictions were changed in the Senate to permit the president to waive the ban if he determined that doing so would enhance security and promote world peace. Republican Representative H. R. Gross of Iowa, regarded on both sides of the political aisle as a valuable watchdog of the legislative process, won acceptance of an amendment to terminate the president's waiver authority.

When the bill with its new restrictions went to conference, the Senate-House conferees dropped the two House-passed amendments, the one offered by Gross and the other that I offered. When the conference report came back to the House, Gross sponsored a motion to recommit the bill with instructions to restore both his and my amendments. The amendment to restore failed by the tiny margin of four votes. Administration officials kept the ranks of Northern Democrats nearly intact, with only nine of them voting for the motion. One hundred thirty-seven voted with the president. The final compromise bill squeaked through on a roll call vote by a margin of eight votes.

In weeks just ahead, I shifted focus on a related but far greater goal, terminating U.S. involvement in the Vietnam conflict.

13

∞∞∞∞∞∞∞∞∞∞∞∞∞∞∞∞∞∞∞

Agony, No Ecstasy

On the morning of March 26, 1969, a portly man with gray hair was seated in a large black leather upholstered chair like those placed throughout the House of Representatives member offices. This one was situated in a corridor called the Speaker's Lobby, just off the House chamber in the U.S. Capitol. Slumped in the chair was Harold Donohue, a senior representative from Massachusetts.

As he looked at a page of the day's *Congressional Record*, he muttered, "God damn!" He turned to the next page and said, "God damn!" with more emphasis. He fanned slowly through many more pages, all filled with names and hometowns. His expletives stopped. He laid the *Record* in his lap, and, lips pursed, stared blankly ahead. It was a stunning moment for Donohue and for the staff member who stood transfixed as he watched from a distance. The veteran congressman had picked up a copy of the *Record* for a quick look before visiting the speaker's offices. What he saw forced him into a somber reverie that would be repeated countless times in countless places in America in the days immediately ahead.

The *Record* published that day included a massive insertion that I had ordered during the House of Representatives session two days earlier. The issue contained the Roll of Honor, the names and hometowns of the 31,379 U.S. military personnel killed so far in Vietnam. Printed in small type, three columns to a page, the names covered 121 pages. The insertion was a big step in rallying public support for termination of the war.

It was the era of hot-type composition on linotypes, and the task of setting the names in type was more than all the Government Printing Office (GPO) printers and equipment could handle during one night. Delivery of the March 25, 1969, *Record* was delayed by nearly a day.

My request for publication was routine, and it was routinely approved. But it proved so daunting at the GPO that it later prompted a change in House rules that limited the amount of "extraneous material" that a member could routinely insert.

My decision to publish the Roll of Honor arose from a conversation with my assistant Stephen Jones. He reminded me that the June 1942 issue of *Life* magazine published the names of all U.S. military personnel killed in the first six months of World War II, a listing that deeply stirred public sentiment. It occurred to me that publication of the names of war dead in Vietnam would dramatize the enormous cost of the war and, at the same time, honor those who died.

It was a time of national transition, with Richard Nixon inheriting the challenge of Vietnam when he was sworn into the presidency just two months earlier. To me, it would be a good time to honor the war dead. I signed a letter to the secretary of defense asking for the names of all members of the armed forces who had perished in Vietnam.

Two weeks later a telephone call arrived from the director of the Office of Statistic Services in the Pentagon, who asked if I minded if he spoke as a private citizen about my request. I encouraged him to speak frankly. With feeling, he said, "I am concerned about the request for the names. I question whether publication would be in the public interest." He felt free to speak openly, because our families had developed an acquaintance and lived in the same neighborhood in Northern Virginia. I responded, "I am absolutely convinced that the names should be made public."

The box containing the names and hometowns arrived in my congressional office a week later. It contained an immense computer printout that provided exactly the information I had requested. The list was divided by states and military services within each. The next day, at the close of legislative business in the House chamber, I was routinely recognized to speak for thirty minutes and, in conclusion, I received permission to revise and extend my remarks and include extraneous material. When finished, I stepped to the speaker's desk and gave the box to the clerk seated there. Only a few members took notice of what I had said, and none inquired about the material to be inserted. That is, until the next morning.

Almost all individuals interested in politics who reside in Washington read the daily issue of the *Congressional Record*—except on the morning after I inserted my Roll of Honor. There was no distribution that morning. All over the city the same question was asked: "Where is the *Record*?" To numerous phone callers, the GPO announced the missing *Record* would be available later that day. My staff was later peppered with questions: Why had I done it? What did I hope to achieve? How did I get the list of war dead?

That issue of the *Record* elicited strong reaction, most of it warm approval but some of it sharply critical. For months it was used to call out names in antiwar marches, peace vigils, and other demonstrations of public discontent with the war. Legislators in several states became so outraged at the use of the names by the antiwar groups that they persuaded their legislatures to enact laws making it a "criminal offense" to "read the names of the Vietnam military deceased" in "anti-war, anti-draft and anti-police rallies." These laws were declared unconstitutional by courts as violations of the First Amendment of the Constitution. Members of Congress requested hundreds of copies of the *Record* for families and other friends of the deceased who were grateful for the positive recognition publication provided.

In remarks that preceded the Roll of Honor, I urged Richard Nixon, the new president, to withdraw U.S. forces:

If the toll continues at the present level for the next eleven months, it will surpass our losses in World War I. . . . What advantage to the national interest has been secured by the death of the men listed in the following pages? Were sacrifices of this magnitude justified by events and issues in Vietnam? These names should be called to the attention of the administration and the American people, because they establish as no other arrangements of words can possibly do, the true dimensions of the Vietnam War in total overall terms, as well as the most intimate. . . . The publication is thoroughly justified, of course, for another reason. While our combat participation in the war may have been a grievous error from the beginning, as I firmly believe it was, the men who have died in this mistaken conflict nevertheless deserve every recognition and honor. . . . The fact that misguided national leadership, in which I freely acknowledge my share of the blame, erred in sending them to war in no way diminished their heroism, made no easier their sacrifice, and lessened not at all the anguish of their relatives.

On July 22, 1969, I inserted a second Roll of Honor in the *Record*, listing the names and hometowns of nearly three thousand additional victims, those killed in Vietnam since Nixon took office. By October 12, 1972, I introduced additional Rolls of Honor into seven issues of the *Record*. My initial Roll of Honor statement was not my first protest against the Vietnam War, but it was my most influential.

The day before placing it in the *Record*, I offered these remarks on the House floor: "The justification for withdrawal is plain; the United States made a fundamental mistake in committing troops in the first place. A rational corrective action is to withdraw, rather than to compound the original error."

When first elected in 1960, few of my constituents knew much about Vietnam. Possibly a few knew about Laos and its significance, but to most of us in western Illinois, Southeast Asia was as far away as the moon. The U.S. assumption of political responsibility for South Vietnam was in its sixth year, but this had led to only a handful of U.S. casualties. A review of recent Vietnamese history helps explain the complexity of problems confronting me as a member of Congress.

Johnson presided over a massive, fateful deception that misled Congress and the American people. I would have strongly opposed his war in Vietnam as early as 1963, and so would most of my colleagues, had we known two things.

First, as demonstrated conclusively by the Pentagon Papers, the multivolume history of the United States' involvement in Vietnam, almost everyone involved at the senior levels of government in both the Kennedy and Johnson administrations recognized that the task of saving South Vietnam from Communist takeover was probably unattainable. These previously secret documents were released to the public through the *New York Times* by Daniel Ellsberg in 1971.

Second, shortly after Kennedy's assassination, Senator Richard Russell, the most influential member of the Senate and a well-recognized hawk, warned President Johnson in a secret message that Vietnam was a struggle we should avoid, that we could not win, and that it would ultimately be a disaster. Johnson ignored these warnings and kept them secret. For whatever reason, he allowed himself to be persuaded, despite his broad political experience, that the United States should prop up what was increasingly becoming an authoritarian, dictatorial government that enjoyed little public support.

Johnson moved cautiously throughout 1964, but once he was elected to a full term, he began to raise troop levels from thousands to a half million. He tried to fight the war in Vietnam by pretending it did not exist. This compromised his role as commander in chief. He did not want to tell the American people, much less the Congress, the great sacrifices that would be needed to "win." He did not request a war tax or rationing. He pursued a futile "measured response," never releasing the full weight of our military might against the North Vietnamese. As our involvement deepened in lives lost and money spent, public protest became deafening.

In early years, I believed victory could be won but only with the use of massive American military power and at the cost of substantial casualties. I did not view the struggle in Vietnam as a civil war or an internal conflict, but as aggression by international Communism. That probably was the opinion of 90 percent of the American people. My opinion began to change as a result of two incidents: first, when a constituent, Captain Phillip Smith of the U.S. Air Force, was shot down on a military mission near North Vietnam and captured by Chinese Communists; second, when authority for the military draft came up for extension.

My initial response to our military involvement in Vietnam was to support commanders in chief John F. Kennedy and Lyndon B. Johnson. For most of the first six years of my service in Congress, I was a hawk. I believed then that if American military might, financial support, and, most important, the men and women of our armed forces were engaged in a battle, it was the duty of Congress and the nation to support them. Doing so implied acceptance of the underlying premise that we were right to be there in the first place, and that our commitment of resources was correct policy. Admittedly, during the early years I did not pay much attention to the issue. At the time, my committee assignments were agriculture, as well as education and labor, and my interest in foreign affairs focused on NATO and Western Europe and my belief that the Western democracies should be united in a federation.

I responded to the natural tendency to support the president and "our troops," to believe in the high purpose of the White House, and to view our struggle in the "rice paddies of Vietnam" as necessary to stop international Communism. Almost all my colleagues in the House shared this view. It never occurred to me that Johnson would mislead us, events would be fabricated, the deep internal debate within the administration would be shielded from us, and we would be subjected to presidential dishonesty.

It was clear the Americans doing most of the fighting in Vietnam were minority groups and poor whites. Many of them were from the South where patriotism and support for the military were strong and from ethnic/racial areas of Detroit, Chicago, New York, Cleveland, and Buffalo. Many middle- and upper-class white men, some of them serving in Congress, obtained deferments from the draft. Our son Craig was called by the local draft board and packed up to serve. I hated to see him go. I knew he, like many other citizens, had doubts about the war. In addition, I knew the national mood, unlike the one that existed when I enlisted in World War II, was increasingly antiwar. Craig was rejected for service when medical officers learned that recent major bone surgery had weakened his right arm. I admit heaving a sigh of relief.

General Lewis Hershey, a crew-cut, no-nonsense director of Selective Service, made it clear young men engaged in antiwar protests would be drafted. Aside from the basic bias of Selective Service against young men in low-income families, draft boards became in large part the "center of the storm." Most famous was the raid on the Catonsville, Maryland, draft board in 1965 when Catholic priests Philip and Daniel Berrigan—and others associated with them who became known as the "Catonsville Nine"—destroyed draft board records by pouring napalm on them. They were sent to prison.

By 1967, in back rows of the House chamber, in cloakrooms, and on walks over to the Capitol when representatives talked privately in small huddles, there was growing dissatisfaction with our policy. The war was coming home in personal terms. Don Rumsfeld, a young and promising congressman from an affluent section of Cook County, Illinois, was one of the leaders in the effort to defeat reauthorization of the draft. As I talked to Rumsfeld and others, among them Reps. Charles Goodell of New York and Al Quie of Minnesota, I was impressed with their arguments. When the draft came up for renewal in 1967, I voted no, one of the few Republicans to do so. In the wake of that vote, an admiral on active duty congratulated me on my dissenting vote. Conversing with me one day over lunch, one of his statements stuck in my mind. "When generals have a large army," he said, "they usually find a war to fight." He favored a small, all-volunteer army.

The Danish ambassador to the United States told me privately that our position in Vietnam had no support in his country, although it was a NATO ally, had courageously stood against the Germans in World War II, and refused to be intimidated by the Soviet Union, even when the Red Army occupied part of Denmark. He told me frankly that people in Denmark identified more with North Vietnam than the United States. Those were sobering words.

Although I did not go to Vietnam, as many members did, it dominated my life from morning till night. More than two million Americans served in Vietnam, most of them drafted. Besides those killed, hundreds of thousands of others were injured, blighted for life. My door was always open to people protesting the war. Although many were unkempt and dirty, I had deep and growing sympathy for all protestors. I kept searching for initiatives that would help bring the war to an end.

One afternoon, just after a quorum call, I heard Representative James Symington of Missouri speak powerfully for just two minutes in the House of Representatives Chamber. Almost the entire membership was present when this usually quiet Democrat challenged us all. I may not recall his words precisely, but this was his theme: "Look around you. Here we are, some four hundred human beings—almost exactly the number of young Americans who were killed last week in Vietnam. If we were the ones fated for extinction next week, would we sit on our hands and do nothing? What are we doing about the slaughter in Vietnam? Are we powerless? Have we no authority and duty as members of Congress? Will we keep sitting on our hands and do nothing to stop killing another four hundred next week and each week that follows? I ask you to ponder these questions."

The perplexing thing about Vietnam was that truth, logic, and persuasion seemed to be on both sides of any contested point. To take the most elementary example: was South Vietnam, the Republic of Vietnam, a genuine state of internationally recognized sovereignty, or was it simply an artificial military zone that had been created for redeployment purposes following the Geneva Conference of 1954?

Vietnam had historically consisted of three separate and independent kingdoms, which even the French, once they became the established dominant colonial power, recognized in form if not in substance. By 1954, the French military struggle to suppress the "Viet Minh," or Communist insurgents mostly centered in the north, had effectively divided the country. After Communists won the Chinese civil war, they began to supply the Viet Minh with significant military supplies and other aid. The insurgents defeated the French in a village named Dien Bien Phu. It was a political as well as military defeat. The government of Joseph Laniel fell, prompting a meeting in Geneva in the spring of 1954 of the major Western powers, as well as the Soviet Union, China, and the states and parties associated with the conflict in Korea and Southeast Asia.

Nothing came of the deliberations to reunite Korea, but a Vietnam truce was achieved, largely the result of wily manipulations by Soviet Foreign Minister V. M. Molotov and Chinese Foreign Minister Chou En-lai in persuading Pham Van Dong, the Viet Minh representative, to accept what in reality was less than "half a loaf." The Viet Minh controlled Hanoi, much of the coastline, and about a third of the south including Saigon. The rest of the country was contested militarily or in the hands of the recognized government. The latter wanted it drawn as far south as possible, at the Thirteenth Parallel. The French wanted it drawn as far north as possible, at the Eighteenth Parallel. New French Premier Pierre Mendes-France wanted fast action. He told the National Assembly that he would resign if he did not achieve peace in Vietnam within thirty days, a deadline that was fast approaching.

As often is true in international politics, the major consideration in the Geneva Conference was elsewhere. The Soviet Union did not want France to support the European Defense Community (EDC) that would rearm West Germany. The Chinese did not want another conflict with the United States in Asia. The Korean War ended barely a year before. In return for a handshake deal that France would not join the EDC, Molotov agreed to use his muscle, which was considerable, to get the Vietnamese Communists to agree to some type of cease-fire. The Chinese did likewise. Molotov and Chou En-lai told North Vietnam's Pham Van Dong that his movement would win the elections—which were promised for two years hence—and by that time, they contended, the country would drop into their hands like overripened fruit.

An agreement was reached. Vietnam was cut in half. The North would be controlled by the Communists and the South, where the political and military struggle would continue, would be separate. Reunification elections would be held in 1956. In reality, the agreement proved to be a Pyrrhic victory for the free world. By drawing the line further north than the military situation on the ground justified, tens of thousands of Communist sympathizers were legitimately in the south. The United States backed Ngo Dinh Diem, a nationalist, as president, but he proved nearly as dictatorial and arbitrary as the Communists in the north. Food riots in North Vietnam delayed Communist efforts to retake the South until 1960. Then, local Communist insurgents began operations, supplanted by some from the North who entered the southern portion of Vietnam via the famous "Ho Chi Minh Trail" through Laos and Cambodia.

If Kennedy had lived, he might have adopted General James Gavin's advice to set up enclaves along the Vietnamese coast, and then negotiate our way out as a means of converting Ho Chi Minh into a Southeast Asian Tito. That process, Gavin argued, might make Vietnam a buffer against China. Gavin's suggestions would recognize and fortify the basic nationalistic aspirations of Ho Chi Minh. If accepted, his recommendations would, in my opinion, have prevented the awful human carnage over a divided Vietnam, followed by the still worse carnage in Laos, Burma, and Cambodia.

As early as 1965, I testified before the Senate Foreign Relations Committee, urging the Congress to reexamine Vietnam policy. I told the committee that I did not believe the Tonkin Gulf Resolution, enacted the year before, provided the authority for President Johnson's expansion of U.S. forces in Vietnam. On January 12, 1966, I wrote to President Johnson reporting "public concern about the U.S. role as world policeman." On May 18, 1967, I introduced a resolution, House Joint Resolution 586, that would amend the Tonkin Gulf Resolution to provide for the adjudication of the Vietnam dispute by the International Court of Justice, a judicial branch of the United Nations situated at The Hague. On June 13, 1967, I spoke on the House floor: "We face the possibility if not the prospect of [President Johnson] sending another two hundred thousand or three hundred thousand combat forces to South Vietnam. Under what legal authority will the president undertake such an action? Would it be the Gulf of Tonkin Resolution? . . . I question whether the Congress has measured up to its constitutional responsibility in recent years." On July 10, 1967, I spoke again to my colleagues, "No one can reasonably contend that the Tonkin Gulf Resolution of 1964 or President Johnson's electoral victory gave him a mandate to send ground forces without limit into Vietnam." Two weeks later, I repeated the theme: "I do not believe anyone can properly read into this resolution the authority to bring us to the present level of involvement. As President Eisenhower stated last week, 'This resolution provided only limited authority.'"

In August 1967, a bipartisan group of fifty-seven members called for a "full scale" debate on U.S. policy in Vietnam. Joining me at a news conference were Democrat William Hungate of Missouri, and three Republicans, Bradford Morse of Massachusetts, Charles W. Whalen of Ohio, and Barber Conable of New York. The resolution we introduced would direct House and Senate committees to determine immediately "whether further congressional action is desirable in respect to policies in the Southeast Asia area."

The same month, as a new committee member, I introduced House Resolution 869, cosponsored by twenty-one Republicans. It called upon the House Foreign Affairs Committee "to review the implementation of the Gulf of Tonkin Resolution and to consider whether it empowers the president to carry forward military operations of the current scope and magnitude in Southeast Asia, whether it requires modification . . ., and whether alternative legislation is required." On August 23, I delivered a more detailed message on the same theme as a witness before the Senate Foreign Relations Committee, a statement reprinted by the American Lawyers Committee on American Policy Towards Vietnam.

In September, I introduced House Concurrent Resolution 508, a milder resolution that I believed would attract more cosponsors. It simply called upon congressional committees to report "whether further congressional action is desirable in respect to policies in Southeast Asia." Within a few months, 144 House members—more than one-fourth of the total membership—were cosponsors. By introducing these bills I hoped to prod my colleagues to measure up to what I believed to be the House's constitutional responsibilities under war powers. To my disappointment, none led to committee hearings, much less committee recommendations. The experience convinced me that, except for Senator William Fulbright, committee chairmen, like the majority of other members, were content to duck their constitutional responsibility. They did not want to touch the prickly nettle of war powers. They liked to complain about presidential decisions on war-making but preferred to avoid helping make timely policy themselves.

On December 14, 1967, I lamented, "The Congress will adjourn this week without even touching its most important item of business, fundamental policy in Southeast Asia. For this we should be ashamed." On April 1, 1968—I did not intend it as an April Fool's joke—I urged Congress to cancel its usual Easter recess and deal instead on Capitol Hill with Vietnam policy.

The Rolls of Honor were published nearly a year after Robert McNamara, one of the major architects of our Vietnam policy, resigned as secretary of defense. President Johnson realized that

McNamara had come to his wit's end. He had lied when predicting victory on the battlefields long after he privately concluded that the war was not winnable. By eventually publicly criticizing his own failed policy, he bought a form of amnesty to himself. The president chose as his successor Clark Clifford, a Washington, D.C., lawyer of great skill who had navigated the shoals of Washington political intrigue and national government since the early days of the Truman administration. He was a widely respected figure.

In my zeal to get our forces out of Vietnam, I found myself in a legislative tangle with Clifford over his request to give the Pentagon's Chairman of the Joint Chiefs of Staff, Army General Earle Wheeler, an unprecedented third two-year term. I had no issue with Wheeler personally, but he was one of the principal architects of our disastrous war policy. Wheeler was, as I later told the House, one of the authors of a policy that was "morally indefensible and militarily self-defeating." I realized that if I stood up and objected, I would ultimately lose. The objection of one member on the House floor would take any bill off that particular calendar, but I knew that a determined House leadership could achieve the same result by using other motions, like suspension of the rules. However, by objecting, I would gain the right to explain to my colleagues my main complaint about Wheeler, his willingness to follow a military doctrine of gradualism, also described as measured response. When the reading clerk rattled off the bills, I waited until he came to the one extending Wheeler's term and said, "I object." Immediately, a hush fell over the House chamber. Members turned around, some of them startled, some merely curious, and a few angry. An objection to an item on the unanimous consent calendar was a rarity that many members had not before experienced. At the very least, the episode demonstrated that House rules permitted the free speech rights of a lowly member of the minority.

After I spoke, in short order, Les Arends, the Republican whip, approached me. "What the hell is going on?" his attitude seemed to say. But he only glared. Without saying a word, he turned and strode away. He had been in Congress for thirty years, having arrived in the depths of the Depression when Franklin D. Roosevelt was president and only a few dozen House members were Republican. He had been in the leadership for years and undoubtedly had been consulted about extending Wheeler's term. Now the problem was a Republican—worse yet, one from Arends's home state, Illinois. To Arends and a few others, I was a pariah that day. I received few comments for or against my objection.

Back at my office, most of my staff had gone home for the day. The telephone rang and Jones answered it with the usual "Congressman Paul Findley's office." To which the voice on the other end responded, "This is Clark Clifford, may I speak with Mr. Findley, please?" Jones had trouble believing that Clark Clifford would personally place a call to my office. Jones identified himself and said he would find me and ask me to return the call. Clifford said, "May I call you back? The president is on the other line." When I returned to my office a few minutes later, I telephoned Secretary Clifford using the private number he had left. This was my first contact with Clifford, and I found him smooth as silk. He began by telling me the president had asked him to become secretary of defense and that he was conducting a full review of Vietnam policy. Although I had heard those words before, this time they turned out to be true. He added that he personally—he stressed the word "personally"—had asked for the retention of Wheeler because, being new on the job and having only a year to serve, he needed an experienced chairman of the joint chiefs. By then, Johnson had taken himself out of running for another term. Clifford thought Wheeler was the best source of information he could have.

It was a reasonable argument. I responded that I did not have anything against Wheeler personally but believed he was one of the original architects of the war and would tend to be defensive of his past decisions. I said I sensed a major shift of American opinion that favored getting the United States out of the war as quickly as possible, and that a new commander—General Creighton Abrams—would soon be sent to Vietnam. I simply could not stand by silently and accept an unprecedented third term for a man who had a major role in creating a disaster in Vietnam. For those reasons, I said, a new man without preconceived opinions or an investment in his own earlier policy recommendations would be better.

Clifford, of course, held the upper hand. He knew that, despite my objection, he would get Wheeler's services for two more years. He called, I am sure, as a matter of courtesy to let me know his reasons for wanting the extension. It was approved during a motion suspending House rules on May 14.

Clifford remained politically active for a long time after President Johnson left office. When President Carter presided over the Camp David Accords, which included the Egyptian treaty with Israel, I sat in several subcommittee huddles with Clifford, who at that time represented the State Department on agreements for annual grants to Israel.

There would be many turns in Vietnam after President Nixon took office, during which many more Americans died. Heartened by his decision to withdraw twenty-five thousand troops from Vietnam, I introduced the House Resolution 564, with over one hundred cosponsors. It said, in part: "Resolved . . . that the president be supported in his expressed determination to withdraw the remaining forces at the earliest practicable date."

The course of our involvement in Vietnam was significantly altered by Watergate. The scandal quickened the strong tide of public antiwar protest, not just by the hippies and military veterans. Nixon did his best to help the South Vietnamese administration, but its survival, like his own, proved impossible. Responding to this tide, Congress finally used the power of the purse—restricting funds for Vietnam, with the help of my vote—to end U.S. involvement in Vietnam. Under the circumstances, U.S. forces put forth their best efforts. The failure of basic policy is no reflection on those who served.

On May 20 and 21, 1970, I organized and chaired ad hoc hearings in the main Foreign Affairs Committee hearing room for "Student Views toward United States Policy in Southeast Asia." The hearing occurred during Nixon's controversial military incursion into Cambodia, which seemed to be universally viewed as a dangerous widening of the war. With the approval of Committee Chairman Thomas E. Morgan, the committee's veteran chief of staff, Boyd Crawford, arranged for the publication of the hearings as an official committee document, the only time in my congressional career that I was listed as chairman of hearings sanctioned by an official committee. Participating with me were three senior Democrats and two other Republicans. Sixty-three students, representing universities and colleges from coast to coast, were heard during two long days. The full text of the proceedings was later printed and distributed widely. The record included nineteen other statements presented by individuals or groups of students. The hearing room was jammed with war protestors from 9:00 A.M. to after 5:00 P.M. both days. For the most part they were orderly, although most were ill clad. I recall one moment when I instructed two young men to occupy chairs instead of continuing to lie on the floor. Several witnesses had to be told to remove their caps while testifying.

I sought opportunities to hear directly the reasons veterans protested the war. One evening Lucille and I visited an encampment on the lawn of the Great Mall in Washington where protesting veterans were gathered. Several veterans from Illinois were seated together. When a lighted joint was passed from one to another, Lucille might have been offered a puff or two but for an outcry from one of the young men: "Jeez, don't hand it to the congressman's wife." Lucille and I both laughed. We did more listening than talking. It was a misty night and the lawn was soggy from a rain earlier in the day. As we sat there, veterans took turns explaining their opposition. They were serious and thoughtful.

Another day my assistant, Bob Wichser, who worked tirelessly advancing my pro-peace initiatives, drove our station wagon, with Harvey Phelps, a Carlinville weekly newspaper editor, and me as passengers. At one point, we crawled slowly through a crowd of unruly protestors who, noting my member of Congress license plates, tried to upset our vehicle. They stopped pushing when Wichser finally convinced them I too was a war protester.

Cynics claimed that Richard Nixon could have obtained in 1969 the cease-fire he finally obtained in 1973. There is no credible support for that theory. The Vietnamese were still bitterly fighting, with the North Vietnamese holding the upper hand. Instead of ordering an all-out military assault, Nixon worked on an ultimately successful plan to withdraw. He established improved relations with the Soviet Union and the People's Republic of China, so these Communist power centers would stop aiding our enemy and ultimately pressure North Vietnam to the peace table. Nixon ended the draft, a decision that dampened protest, and he stirred support of "the silent majority"—his term for the nonprotesting majority of citizens—by bringing the troops home while trying to strengthen the South Vietnam forces. He simultaneously intensified war measures against North Vietnam and sanctuaries in Cambodia. All of this cost more lives in Vietnam, but the overall situation improved marginally. It was widely believed at that time that U.S. forces had to get out but that withdrawal should occur in a way that did not lead to a sudden collapse of the South Vietnamese government.

Nixon's efforts toward improving relations with China and the Soviet Union were for the most part successful. In May 1972 the Soviet Union decided to proceed with a summit meeting, notwithstanding Nixon's decision to bomb Hanoi and mine Haiphong Harbor. It was clear that Moscow viewed its relationships with the United States as more important than its investment in the Vietnam War. The same was true in China. While more circumspect than the Soviets, China had high-level meetings with the Vietnamese leadership, and records of these meetings show the Chinese wanted the war ended. They did not expect their Vietnamese allies to cut tail and run, but they did expect to achieve a negotiated settlement that would allow the United States forces to withdraw.

The Vietnamese leadership in Hanoi remembered being promised a quick victory in two years by China and the Soviet Union in 1954 if it would accept a piecemeal settlement. Twenty years later the war continued. But the North Vietnamese had to face the near-certainty of a long military stalemate in a costly, bloody "full throated" war. The South Vietnamese army that the U.S. government had been financing and advising did better than expected. Only one provincial capital fell, and the efforts to conquer the country in 1972 through conventional military means failed much like the so-called Tet Uprising of 1969.

In late summer at the Paris Peace Talks, movement toward a negotiated settlement began. By that time, it was clear President Nixon was going to be reelected, China and the Soviet Union were going to improve their relations with the United States, and even North Vietnam had its breaking point. It was time to make a deal. And here, one must credit the Nixon school of *real politik*. His initiative in China is generally credited as his greatest foreign policy achievement. Perhaps equally great was the agreement reached at Paris in January 1973 that momentarily ended the Vietnam War. Acting through Henry Kissinger, Nixon broke the deadlock. Neither side got all it wanted, but each got something. The U.S. gave up getting the North out of the South, and the North gave up getting Thieu out of the presidential palace in the South. Both sides agreed to a "cease-fire in place," which simply meant everybody stopped shooting at each other. There were other specifics, but at the end of the day when all was said and done, the war ended. Would the cease-fire hold indefinitely if political and financial conditions were met? Probably not, as Ho Chi Minh's dream of a united, independent Vietnam was still unfulfilled.

The Nobel Peace Prize went to the Paris-based negotiators of the cease-fire, Kissinger and North Vietnam's Le Doc Tho. It should have gone to Nixon, who conceived and planned each step.

The peace that Nixon negotiated was short-lived. Soon after the Paris deal, Congress, controlled by Democrats and weary of the war, cut funding for U.S. military operations in Vietnam and did not fund the promised humanitarian aid for the North Vietnamese. My vote helped end U.S. military operations in Vietnam.

Like almost all of my colleagues, I did not know the status of the Nixon negotiations in Paris or the details accepted by both sides. My all-consuming objective was withdrawal of U.S. forces and an end to U.S. casualties. My vote helped make the majority when Congress refused to fund the terms of the peace deal Nixon had negotiated.

This refusal prompted the North Vietnamese to resume the war, and due to a series of poor military decisions and miscalculations by South Vietnam President Thieu in abandoning the Central Highlands, Saigon fell in April 1975.

By then, Watergate had washed Nixon out of office. With him gone from the presidency and military funds cut, the new administration headed by former Vice President Gerald Ford was unable to provide further help for the South Vietnamese government.

The result was unification of the two Vietnams under Hanoi rule. The Vietnam War was ultimately lost in Watergate. No one will know whether Nixon's plan with its carrots and sticks would have worked. Records show that the peace constructed at Paris proved to be a fragile stack of cards that could not withstand the political torrent of Watergate. Several million people died in Vietnam, Laos, and Cambodia during that period.

During our evacuation from Saigon, I turned to legislative measures that were intended to make future presidential wars less likely.

Part IV

STRUGGLE AGAINST FOLLY

14

◇◇◇◇◇◇◇◇◇◇◇◇◇◇◇◇◇◇◇

Curbing Presidential Wars

President Johnson cashed the blank check of the Tonkin Gulf Resolution, which had passed without a dissenting vote in the House and only two negatives in the Senate. We now know it was based upon hostilities that did not occur. The resolution retroactively approved reprisal against the alleged attackers, but it did not authorize other war measures.

When our involvement in Vietnam was finally terminated, I was already busy crafting legislation that hopefully would make disasters like Vietnam less likely in the future. That, to me, meant clarifying the relationship between Congress and the president in the exercise of war powers. It was a neglected area, one that had no legislative clarification. Presidents have "bully pulpits," as President Theodore Roosevelt once observed. They can marshal public opinion much easier than any Congress at its best. This placed a special burden on the legislative branch as it attempted to exercise its war-powers responsibilities.

In Vietnam, President Johnson carried forward a massive long-term war without specific approval of Congress. He engaged in deceit on a towering scale. The Tonkin Gulf Resolution was based on a fraud. While not in any respect a declaration of war, Johnson brazenly used it as such. I was a witness of his misbehavior on several occasions.

165

Johnson did not treat the American people as adults who deserved truth and candor. Worst of all, Congress, with the exception of a few members like Senator William Fulbright, failed utterly to challenge Johnson's abuse of presidential authority.

In World War II, the people of the United States viewed Hitler and Tojo as real threats. Vietnam was never so viewed. Not in a hundred years could the Vietnamese pose a serious challenge to U.S. territory. In our zeal to resist what we described as international Communism, we overlooked the powerful, enduring passion of nationalism. Ho Chi Minh accepted affiliation with Communists, but his primary mission was the independence of his country, and the expulsion of colonial rulers.

The Vietnam ordeal sharpened my comprehension of war far beyond the lessons of World War II, where, although serving in the combat zone in the Far Pacific, I was sheltered from most of war's horror and ugliness. I saw few American dead bodies close up and knew none of them personally. When I visited Nagasaki immediately after the Japanese surrender, I saw only vast rubble. No dead bodies were visible in or near what a few weeks earlier was a city of many thousands. To most people, war dead may have been statistics, not the remains of individual human beings. As I looked around the devastation, I thought of the Japanese soldier whose body I found at the bottom of the hill near the officers' quarters. The photo of his family I found nearby was vivid in my memory. I wondered if his family may have lived—and died—at Nagasaki.

In contrast, Vietnam was a searing, heart-wrenching ordeal. I was confronted repeatedly, face to face, by victims of the war. One day I visited more than two thousand young amputees being treated at Valley Forge Army Hospital. Another day I listened over the phone as Kathleen Akin, for years a close neighbor in Pittsfield, sobbed uncontrollably about the death of her eldest son, John, who was killed by a land mine during his first day of duty in Vietnam. Other days, I attended funeral services for constituents killed in Vietnam and viewed remains dressed in uniform in open caskets.

Dozens of times, I spoke at public services dedicating trees planted as living memorials to war dead, sometimes sons of close friends.

War became personal as never before, and I hated it. I believed it a throwback to survival of the fittest in the jungle. Somehow it had to be replaced by the rule of law, the pursuit of equal justice for all human beings. Dismayed by the awful human blight and suffering of innocent people that is common to every war—including World War II, the last "good war"—I accepted the necessity of an international organization strong enough to substitute judicial law enforcement for war.

Although I recognized that the president must be able to order acts of war quickly in severely limited, extreme circumstances, the drafters of the Constitution went to great lengths to make sure that no president, even the most devious, could use war powers as a ready instrument of presidential policy. Indeed, the Constitution establishes clearly that, with the exception of veto overrides, government policy can be established only when the president and both chambers of Congress agree. Although the Senate has the exclusive authority to ratify treaties and approve the president's nomination of justices, judges, ambassadors, and other high government officials, the House of Representatives is coequal with the Senate in respect to all other aspects of foreign policy, including the use of the instruments of war.

Out of remorse over Vietnam and a deep-seated passion against war, on March 26, 1970, I introduced House Joint Resolution 1151, a resolution dealing with presidential war powers. I believe it was the first such bill introduced in the House of Representatives. It became the forerunner of the War Powers Resolution, ultimately enacted over President Nixon's veto. Since the resolution's enactment, all presidents have complied with its provisions, although often disputing its constitutionality. In my argument for the resolution, I stated, "If the [War Powers Resolution] had been in effect in 1962 when the number of U.S. advisers in Vietnam was increased from seven hundred without combat gear to ten thousand equipped for combat,

President Kennedy would have been required to explain his action promptly and in writing to Congress." To me, this suggests that even a cautious Congress might have forced Kennedy to reconsider this fateful first introduction of combat forces in Vietnam.

I contributed two principal provisions in the resolution's final version. The first one required a prompt, detailed, written notification by the president to Congress whenever a decision is made to introduce U.S. forces or to increase such forces substantially in any region where military hostilities are either likely or actually underway. My second contribution appeared in the committee report. It declared the right of Congress, by concurrent resolution, to require the termination of any military operations undertaken by the president without specific congressional authorization.

When Nixon vetoed the resolution, I helped organize the campaign to override it in the House of Representatives. A bipartisan group of about ten members stationed themselves at doors leading to the House Chamber so that during a vote to override, all members arriving while the vote was in progress could be correctly informed about the pending question. On the override resolution, 284 members, including many Republicans, voted yes and 135 voted no. Fourteen did not vote. The veto was overturned.

The War Powers Resolution was the product of sober reflection about Vietnam. Its chief sponsors, myself included, considered it an important step in preventing what we called "presidential wars." The resolution, as enacted, represented a long-needed statutory clarification of the proper relationship of the president and Congress in the exercise of war powers. It would be one of the most important projects of my congressional career. It is noteworthy that in my occasional subsequent encounters and correspondence with Richard Nixon, he did not mention my role in the override of his veto.

In an event connected directly with the termination of the war in Vietnam, my constituent, U.S. Air Force Captain Phillip Smith, was set free after seven and one-half years of captivity in the People's Republic of China. He was captured when his navigation equipment failed during a night flight and he unintentionally flew over Chinese land and was forced to land by Chinese military forces. If Nixon had not opened discussions with Beijing as an element in his campaign to disengage our forces from Vietnam, Smith might have languished in prison for many more years. For several years, Smith was constantly on my mind. I made futile calls to Chinese diplomatic missions in Paris and London and through an embassy in Poland, attempting to rescue him. I also made pleas to President Johnson and President Nixon. When Nixon made his groundbreaking visit to Beijing in 1973, Smith was released and permitted to walk alone across the border into Hong Kong, then a possession of Great Britain. I helped welcome him home during a joyous public dinner in Roodhouse, near his Greene County farm home. It was an emotional event. The guest of honor had been a part of my endeavors and concern for six years.

For most Americans, the most vivid memory of the Vietnam War is the long, black marble memorial on the Mall in Washington. It is magnificent. Did the publication of the names of war dead in the *Congressional Record* in 1973 help inspire the artist who designed it? Perhaps. I walk past the wall at every opportunity. It is, I believe, the greatest war memorial of all time. It honors the war dead by indelibly etching each name in durable marble that will last for centuries. In contrast, the Rolls of Honor that I placed in issues of the *Record* were entered on perishable paper, souvenirs of which are greatly cherished but are now yellowing and becoming brittle. Unlike the marble, they will someday turn to dust. But when printed they served two noble purposes: a prompt, solemn recognition in a modest but majestic way of the individual war dead and a display of names in a way that helped shorten the war and the list of casualties.

Making presidential wars less likely in the future requires constant vigilance. In July 2008, to my astonishment, two former secretaries of state, James Baker and Warren Christopher, called for the replacement of the 1973 War Powers Resolution. By authorizing presidential war-making in several additional instances, their proposal constituted a threat to constitutional restraints on presidential power. With the help of John Remington Graham, an expert on constitutional history and law who resides in Canada, I prepared, in collaboration with Don Fraser, my friend and Democratic former colleague from Minnesota, a critique of the Baker-Christopher proposal for publication. Fraser and I were on the Committee on Foreign Affairs when the 1973 War Powers Resolution was enacted over President Nixon's veto. Fraser served as a Democrat from Minnesota in the House of Representatives from 1963 to 1979, and as mayor of Minneapolis from 1980 to 1993.

The article that Fraser and I drafted was published as an op-ed in the September 21, 2008, issue of the *Los Angeles Times*. This is the text, slightly abbreviated:

> The House Foreign Affairs Committee is conducting hearings on proposals to amend the War Powers Act of 1973. One proposal, House Joint Resolution 53, would wisely tighten restrictions on executive war-making by the president. Another, proposed by a 12-member commission led by two former secretaries of State—Republican James Baker and Democrat Warren Christopher—but not yet introduced as a bill, would dangerously expand the authority of the president to order acts of war without authorization by Congress. Baker and Christopher are scheduled to testify before Congress on Wednesday about their proposal.
>
> The framers of the Constitution . . . meant to prohibit the president from waging war without a declaration of war or specific authorization by Congress, except when necessary to repel attacks on American territory or commerce, its military or citizens. The Baker-Christopher proposal assaults this crucial prohibition.
>
> In recent history, an unauthorized presidential war brought calamity to the United States. Ambiguity in the Gulf of Tonkin Resolution of 1964 was used as a pretext for executive

(left) I won my first electoral victory at fifteen, becoming sophomore class president at Jacksonville High School.

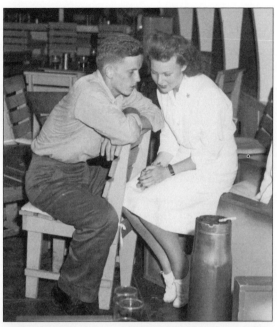

(right) Meeting my future bride, navy flight nurse Lucille Gemme, for the first time in 1944 on Guam.

(below) Directing the Illinois College band in a 1941 concert.

(above) In 1961, ready to drive our 1955 Oldsmobile, with the other three Findleys aboard, to Washington, D.C.

(right) Chatting for the first time with President Dwight D. Eisenhower in January 1961 in the Capitol Hill Club in Washington. We met frequently at Eisenhower's Gettysburg office during the president's retirement years.

Delivering farmer protest mail to President John F. Kenndy's office on October 25, 1962. Secretary Evelyn Lincoln promised to deliver it personally when Kennedy returned from lunch.

Participating in a ceremony at France's Tomb of the Unknown Soldier in Paris, June 1965.

At a press conference after the Republican-sponsored fact-finding mission I chaired in June 1965 in Paris. I am seated between House Republican Conference Chairman Melvin Laird (left) and House Republican Leader Gerald Ford.

In 1965, Frank Mitchell of Springfield, second from left, made history as the first African American page to serve in the U.S. House of Representatives. On the right are House Republican leaders Gerald Ford and Leslie Arends.

(right) Dressed in a new flight suit for the 1969 Findley Fly-In at Springfield, Illinois, airport. It was my first—and only—experience at the controls of a Stearman training biplane.

(left) Asking President Lyndon Johnson, "What about the Palestinians?" during a White House meeting on February 6, 1967, four months before the fateful Israel-Arab Six-Day War. Years later, former U.S. Sen. James G. Abourezk recalled thinking, "There is a guy with guts." *White House Photo*

Greeting a crowd with Nelson Rockefeller on the steps of the Lincoln Home in Springfield during the New York governor's bid for the presidency in 1968.

In 1968, ready to help Capitol Architect George Stewart cement into the marble floor in Statuary Hall of the U.S. Capitol a brass plate marking the location of Lincoln's desk when he served a term in the House of Representatives (1846–1848).

Looking on with Illinois governor Richard Ogilvie on August 18, 1971, as President Nixon, seated at the desk where Abraham Lincoln wrote his First Inaugural Address, signed the bill making the Lincoln Home in Springfield a National Historic Site.

(right) Diane's vision of her father heading for a soybean sales mission to the Soviet Union in November 1973, amid symbols of Egypt, trail rides, and tennis.

(below) Listening in April 1974 as President Salim Rubyai Ali, seated on the sofa in his reception room in Aden, South Yemen, tells a translator he has decided to release my constituent from a prison sentence for espionage. At left is the translator. At far right is Foreign Minister Mohammed Motie.

On December 19, 1974, with Vice President Gerald Ford standing between, Senator Hubert H. Humphrey and I hold plaques commemorating our leadership in the enactment of the Famine Prevention Program.

In the Oval Office on April 24, 1975, seeming to advise President Gerald Ford with vigorous gestures on how to be president. *White House Photo*

With South Korea Ambassador Pyong-choon Hahm, special guest at the September 1976 Findley Trail Ride.

For fourteen consecutive years, I rode a horse once a year, two days at a time, with the other riders—one year over four hundred—who attended the Findley Trail Rides.

Paul Findley

'The Good Life' of a Congressional Recess

The article in The Washington Post of Feb. 9, "Congressional Recess, by Any Other Name . . ." smacks of a bit of jealousy, carrying with it the implication that reporters, too, might enjoy the leisurely life of a "congressional recess" or "district work period"—whatever you choose to call it.

If that is the case, I only wish you could have been with me these seven days to enjoy the good life in Illinois. Enclosed is my daily schedule for this period. As you can see, I had a ball!

Lest you be unfamiliar with Illinois' geography, I can assure you that I did not take my swimming suit and snorkel on my recess—there are no sunny beaches in Illinois at this time of year. Nor did I take my skis. There is still plenty of snow and ice in Illinois (unlike Washington) because it is usually 10 degrees colder in my district than it is here, but we have no mountains.

But I had a ball, nonetheless, and I am certain you would have also. In fact, I hope that you will make plans to join me for a later recess in the 20th

The writer is a Republican representative from Illinois' 20th congressional district.

district. Of course, as a hard-working reporter, you'll be prepared to stay out until midnight driving halfway across Illinois and then getting up early the next morning for a 7:30 a.m. meeting. And I'm certain that you are used to spending all day Saturday and Sunday going from one meeting to another. I assure you, it's the best way I know to meet a lot of wonderful people and learn what is on their minds. It helps me better represent them in Washington, and who knows, it might help you do a better job of reporting for them.

Oh, by the way, if you come with me next time, you'll want to bring along your wash 'n' wear shorts and shirts. In our travels we'll have to move from one motel to another almost every night, but I'm sure you're used to living out of a suitcase. And bring some Dramamine. If you aren't used to so much traveling and excitement, all this "fun" can really get to you.

THURSDAY, FEBRUARY 10

11:20 a.m. Left National, TWA 561
1:15 p.m. Left St. Louis, Ozark 862
1:49 p.m. Arrived in Quincy
2:30 p.m. Visited Channel 7
Visited Herald Whig Newspaper
Visited Channel 10
Met with Joe Ourth, who wants a job
6:30 p.m. McHugh Theater, Administration Building, Quincy College, for Quincy Town Meeting
8:30 p.m. Met Bob Mays at MacHugh Theater following Town Meeting. He presented a proposal on Corps of Engineers assistance in dredging a recreational lake on Quincipel Island
8:45 p.m. Met Doiora Whitney at MacHugh Theater following meeting with Mr. Mays. Committee to Keep Telephone Operators in Quincy
9:00 p.m. Met with approximately 15 constituents on individual problems, policies, and issues
10:00 p.m. Stopped for a Burger Chef and milk shake
10:47 p.m. Left Quincy, Ozark 507
11:12 p.m. Arrived in St. Louis (Mr. Iversen met me at the Ozark ticket counter at airport and drove me to the Bel Air Hilton)

ILLINOIS

Chicago

Champaign

Quincy

Springfield

Jacksonville

20

Alton

St. Louis

FRIDAY, FEBRUARY 11

a.m. Called Betty Kriegshauser, a patient at Barnes Hospital in St. Louis
a.m. Talked by phone with Washington office preparing statement on Ag-Land Fund
p.m. Attended World Food Program discussion session, Bel Air Hilton
5:45 p.m. Dinner—Greater St. Louis World Food Program, Bel Air Hilton
6:45 p.m. Introductions
7:00 p.m. Speech—"Dimensions of the World Food Problem and the Role of the United States"—explained Famine Prevention Program.

SATURDAY, FEBRUARY 12

a.m. Due to fog, drove 166 miles from St. Louis to Champaign, Illinois
noon Annual Awards luncheon, College of Ag., University of Illinois—Awarded with Certificate of Appreciation for contributions to agriculture and its development in Illinois and the world.
p.m. Drove to Springfield, Illinois
5:00 p.m. Tour Illinois Bell Museum, 529 South 7th, Springfield (Dick Kahne)
6:30 p.m. Reception, Abraham Lincoln Assn., Apollo Room, Forum 30
7:30 p.m. Attended Abraham Lincoln Assn. Dinner, Forum 30, Springfield. Following dinner attended a special showing of the Lincoln Home Visitor Center film.

SUNDAY, FEBRUARY 13

a.m. Attended Church
noon Lunch
1:00 p.m. Met with various constituents prior to dedication ceremonies
2:00 p.m. Participated in dedication of Lincoln Home Visitor Center, First Presbyterian Church, 7th & Capitol, Springfield.

3:15 p.m. Attended Ribbon Cutting Ceremony at Visitor Center
p.m. Dinner
7:30 p.m. Springfield Town Meeting, County Farm Bureau Building, 2449 North Dirksen Parkway, Springfield
9:00 p.m. Met with George Cashman, retired Curator of Lincoln Tomb
9:15 p.m. Met with constituents on individual problems, policies and issues

MONDAY, FEBRUARY 14

10:00 a.m. Alpha Jones. Received a book of poetry that she had written.
10:15 a.m. John Kirby. Discussed a highway problem
10:30 a.m. Father Mascari. Discussed plans for a golden age retirement center for rural Americans
10:45 a.m. Dale Rowand and Ken Redfern, Department of Ag. Discussed plans for an International Visitors Day at the State Fair
11:30 a.m. Stopped for a hamburger
11:45 a.m. Drove to Jacksonville
12:15 p.m. Made visits around Jacksonville Square
1:30 p.m. Attended Ribbon Cutting Ceremony at District Service Office of Honorable Jim Reilly, 224 West State, Jacksonville
2:00 p.m. Jacksonville Town Meeting, City Council Chambers. Was made an honorary fireman and an honorary policeman by the city of Jacksonville and received commendation from the City Council and Mayor Hocking for assistance on solving community problems.
3:30 p.m. Met with Don Lakin in mayor's office, regarding Murrayville/Woodson water plant
3:45 p.m. Met with Dr. Fuhrig in mayor's office, regarding Conference of Churches, Great Decisions Series, China slides
4:30 p.m. Stopped at McDonalds for a cheeseburger
4:45 p.m. Drove to Alton
7:00 p.m. Alton Town Meeting, Metropolitan National Bank on Beltline, Community Room, Alton
8:00 p.m. Met with various constituents on individual problems
9:00 p.m. Interview with Southern Illinois University radio on foreign policy

TUESDAY, FEBRUARY 15

10:00 a.m. Met with Mary Heitzig and Mayor Joe Susnig of Jerseyville, regarding city problems with HUD
10:30 a.m. Met with constituent who wants to establish cable TV for Carlinville
noon Lunch with Board of Directors of Alton-Wood River Chamber of Commerce
2:00 p.m. Toured Lock and Dam 26 at Alton
4:00 p.m. Met Harold Rice, President, Alton-Wood River Area Federation of Labor, at the Stratford, Alton
6:30 p.m. Dinner with AFL-CIO union officials
8:00 p.m. Drove to St. Louis

WEDNESDAY, FEBRUARY 16

7:30 a.m. Spoke at Grain and Feed Assn. of Illinois Annual Meeting, Stauffer's Riverfront Towers, St. Louis—"The Future of On-Farm Storage"
9:00 a.m. Discussions with Grain and Feed Assn.
10:50 a.m. Left St. Louis, TWA 482
1:30 p.m. Arrived at National Airport
p.m. Appointments in Washington office

Facing reality, the *Washington Post* on February 22, 1977, published details of my "congressional recess."

(left) In 1977, tooting a trombone with background provided by banjo player Bill Gard at a benefit supper in New Canton, Illinois.

(below) In July 1978, standing behind the president in the Rose Garden as Jimmy Carter signed an employment rights bill for seniors that I cosponsored with Representative Claude Pepper.

As chairman of the 1978 Illinois agricultural mission to the Peoples Republic of China, I received souvenir scarves for mission colleagues from Deputy Minister of Agriculture He Kang.

With Ambassador Han Xu in June 1978 after the diplomat addressed graduates at Illinois College, Jacksonville, Illinois, the first major public audience for a Chinese Communist official.

In 1978, presenting a plaque to clowning Bob Hope after sponsoring a joyous seventy-fifth birthday party for him on the floor of the House of Representatives.

In 1979, the first of several meetings with Egypt's president, Anwar Sadat (left), and his ambassador to Washington, Ashraf Ghorbal.

On February 18, 1980, PLO chief Yasser Arafat wrote: "Thank your daughter Diane for the nice pottery which I keep permanently on my desk. God will always be with you because you are dedicated to a cause of justice." Later that year a bomb destroyed the pottery and Arafat's office but not the PLO chief. In December 1991, Arafat sent me this autographed card with his portrait.

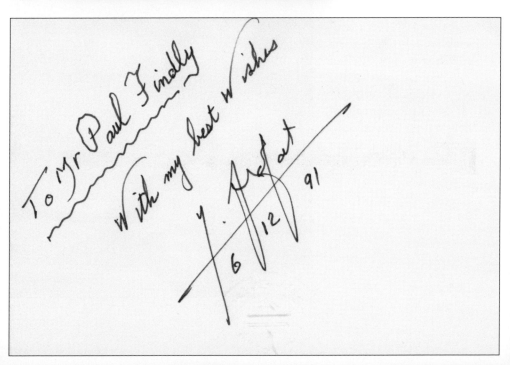

To Mr Paul Findly
With my best wishes
Y. Arafat
6/12/91

(above) In 1980, a special train brought several hundred volunteers from Springfield to Alton where they spent the day campaigning for me.
State Journal-Register

(right) In 1981, as a congressional group left the White House Cabinet room, I (here seated to Reagan's left) told President Reagan that I believed the Palestinians deserved an independent homeland of their own.

Gesturing during a joint lecture in July 1989 with Sheikh Ahmed Deedat before a Muslim audience of over thirteen thousand in Cape Town, South Africa.

While visiting King Abdullah II in Jordan on February 11, 1999, the monarch said that during his student days, his father, King Hussein, handed him a copy of *They Dare to Speak Out,* with the instruction, "Read every word carefully."

(right) Much of my post-Congress career has been spent behind rostrums, although few as fancy as this one.

(below) Handing Dubai philanthropist Khalaf Al Habtoor the honorary doctorate degree during Illinois College commencement exercises on May 16, 2010.

war-making in Vietnam not intended by Congress. That war was unjustifiable from a military or geopolitical standpoint. The resolution retroactively approved the retaliation by President Johnson for an attack on navy ships in the Gulf of Tonkin, and it warned North Vietnam and all interested parties of U.S. readiness to engage in further military operations through the South East Asia Treaty Organization. But it contained no language that actually authorized the president to order acts of war in the future. Johnson nevertheless used it to increase the U.S. commitment in Vietnam to half a million men.

As domestic opposition to the war increased and U.S. forces began to withdraw, Congress passed the War Powers Act of 1973. We were members of the House committee that helped frame this resolution and were engaged in the process until it was passed over the veto of President Nixon. It is a necessary and proper law that forbids a president from waging war without authority from Congress, except to repel attack. It requires the president to provide full details in writing within 48 hours of a decision to order war measures or substantially enlarge military forces in a foreign country. It also requires the president to terminate the use of armed forces undertaken without authorization from Congress within . . . 90 days, unless the country is under attack and Congress cannot physically meet. It authorizes a member of either the House or the Senate to force a vote of disapproval at any time such war-making is underway.

In framing the 1973 resolution, we assumed that enforcement would be attained through vigilance in Congress, with impeachment as the ultimate penalty for any president who willfully violated his authority. It was understood at the time that insignificant use of military force by the president without prior approval of Congress might be tacitly accepted. But the measure signaled that never again would Congress tolerate an overt and aggressive breach of constitutional principle by the president in committing America to a costly war without the approval of Congress.

The War Powers Act has effectively restrained unwarranted and dangerous abuse of military power by presidents. The 1991 Gulf War was authorized by Congress, as were the current hostilities in Afghanistan and Iraq. War measures in both countries remain controversial, but at least they were authorized. Notwithstanding these realities, the Baker-Christopher panel urges scrapping the War Powers Act of 1973 in favor of a so-called War Powers Consultation Act of 2009, which would increase the war powers of the president far beyond the limits allowed by our Constitution. This commission is asking Congress to approve legislation that would enable the president to start a war—or in any way use military force—without even a report to Congress, much less consultation. The proposed legislation has loopholes big enough to allow major military operations by the president alone. Among these loopholes we find that "limited acts of reprisal against terrorists or states that sponsor terrorism" are exempt from reference to Congress. But who identifies "terrorists"? Who defines "terrorism"? Who determines which are "states that sponsor terrorism"? Who defines "limited"? The president alone. Congress is consigned to the role of an uninformed, unconsulted bystander.

Under this exception, the president could, without even a nod to Congress, ignore historic rights of national sovereignty and commit acts of war against any country that he determines is a haven of terrorists. He could, for example, declare Iran a state that sponsors terrorism and carpet-bomb its nuclear facilities. The language is sufficiently ambiguous to enable a willful president to start a major war without constitutional authority, repeating the disaster of Vietnam.

An expansion of presidential war powers proposed by Baker and Christopher would allow "acts to prevent criminal activity abroad." But who defines "criminal activity"? Who decides what "acts to prevent" such activity should be used? Again, the president alone decides. Still another loophole is the exclusion of "covert activities" from approval by Congress. With recent revelations of CIA bombings in Pakistan and the scandals at Abu Ghraib and Guantanamo fresh in mind, it must be obvious that the country needs more oversight, not less.

The War Powers Act of 1973 is basically sound, and it remains an important measure to sustain the rule of law.

Baker and Christopher testified on behalf of their proposal on March 5, 2009, claiming that the 1973 War Powers Resolution "was not working" and was "unconstitutional." Instead of giving their proposal additional consideration, the committee turned its attention to a constructive proposal that retains all the essential provisions of the 1973 Act.

In discussing the Baker-Christopher proposal, Fraser told me, "It stands the Constitution on its head." The House subcommittee let it die without consideration when the Congress adjourned.

As I write in September 2010, a major test of war powers in Congress is nowhere in sight. President Obama, after weeks of deliberation with his national security leaders but with no apparent participation by members of Congress, decided on a major increase in combat forces in Afghanistan. Under the law, the president's decision should be reported immediately in writing to Congress. In the normal course of legislative process, Congress would consider the decision and pass judgment on it.

After trying to make presidential wars less likely, I found myself—of all places—entangled in the future of two presidents, two vice presidents, and their would-be successors.

15

‹‹‹‹‹‹‹‹‹‹‹‹‹‹‹‹‹‹‹‹‹‹‹

Intruding at the Summit

I was the first Republican member of Congress to call for the impeachment of Republican Vice President Spiro Agnew. I did so because of his indictment for corruption when governor of Maryland. Nine days later, in response to a variety of pressures, not just my public call, he resigned as vice president.

Gerald Ford, the Republican leader in the House of Representatives, was nominated to fill the vacancy by President Richard Nixon and Congress approved.

When Nixon resigned in August 1974, Ford became president and nominated Nelson Rockefeller to fill the vacancy in the vice presidency, a nomination quickly approved by Congress.

As the end of the Ford-Rockefeller term approached, Ford surprised Mrs. Ford by deciding to seek election to a full term and, for reasons that escape me, decided against keeping Rockefeller as his running mate. As Ford cast around for a replacement, I unintentionally created a storm by warning him against choosing former Governor John Connolly of Texas, a recent convert to Republican ranks.

Agnew had been a curiosity from the beginning of his career. The only time I recall meeting him was on his official aircraft, Air Force Two, when I was in a group of members of Congress who accompanied him on a short flight to a ceremony. He mingled briefly with others aboard before sequestering himself behind a curtain.

He was trim, neatly garbed, and self-confident. Although my subsequent endeavors for his impeachment may have been a factor in his resignation, in correspondence that occurred years later, he cordially supported my Middle East activities and praised my book, *They Dare to Speak Out.* He rose from executive of Baltimore County, Maryland, to vice president of the United States in just six years. He had the good luck to be the Republican nominee for governor in traditionally Democratic Maryland in 1966. His opponent, George Mahoney, was anathema to many Democrats due to his well-known racism; Agnew was elected because voters disliked Mahoney. As governor, Agnew avidly promoted New York governor Nelson Rockefeller for president. When Rockefeller announced suddenly he would not seek the nomination, a position he reversed six weeks later, Agnew was furious. He felt humiliated, but he had his revenge. His savior turned out to be Richard Nixon.

In 1968, Nixon was the leading candidate for the Republican presidential nomination but did not have the nomination sewed up. Liberals in the Northeast tended to support Governor Rockefeller. Rising in popularity among those on the right was California governor Ronald Reagan. Southerners, as well as border state and mountain state Republicans, were beside themselves in their enthusiasm for Reagan. Good-looking, articulate, and a well-known movie actor, he was a political natural.

Nixon's dream of nomination was threatened by the popularity of Rockefeller on the left and Reagan on the right. In the early weeks of 1968 and at the convention in Miami I canvassed, without luck, other delegates on behalf of the New York governor. Nixon was popular as a centrist candidate with good relations on both right and left. He had an ally in Strom Thurmond of South Carolina, who only four years before was a Democrat. Although he was an avowed segregationist in earlier years, he accepted the job of holding southern delegates in line for Nixon. As a condition of full support, Thurmond elicited a pledge that Nixon would not choose a liberal as his running mate. This ruled out John Lindsay, Nelson

Rockefeller, Mark Hatfield, and Charles Percy. But Nixon kept in mind the future challenge of winning the general election. He would be hard pressed in the South because of the support former Governor George Wallace was getting as an independent candidate.

I was a delegate for Rockefeller at the 1968 nominating convention. The Findleys, well adorned with Rockefeller buttons, had rooms in the hotel considered Nixon headquarters. I viewed Rockefeller as the strongest available candidate because of his executive experience and wide popularity, especially among independents and minorities. I believed he could heal the nation's racial divide. If Rockefeller had been Nixon's running mate in 1960, the Republican ticket probably would have defeated Kennedy and Johnson.

Many conservative Republicans in my district were upset with my endorsement of the New York governor. One evening, I received a telephone call from Quincy, Illinois, during which several constituents took turns berating my position. Midway through one of the presentations, the phone connection went dead. I did not want the group to believe I had hung up on them, but, lacking the phone number of the constituent who originated the call, I had a frantic few minutes before I was able to reconnect the call.

After Nixon won the nomination, he looked for a conservative running mate who would appeal to Southern and border state voters without being a segregationist. Governor Agnew of Maryland fit Nixon's requirements perfectly, and the choice paid off. Nixon-Agnew won the election. As vice president, Agnew was a nonentity until Nixon used him to attack his critics in academia and the media and build support among the "silent majority," a large portion of the citizens Nixon portrayed as being quietly in his corner. Agnew was popular in delivering hard-hitting speeches written by Pat Buchanan.

The prospect of Agnew later gaining the presidency troubled me greatly. He was not "my kind of Republican." I wanted to keep the Republican Party in the progressive center and preferred prospects like Governor Rockefeller and former governors William Scranton and Mark Hatfield.

Early in Nixon's second term as president when Agnew seemed certain to be the next Republican nominee for president, I joined Senator Charles Mathias of Maryland and a few other Republicans to discuss what should be done to avert that unappealing prospect. The consensus of the group seemed to be that a third-party response should be seriously considered. This became moot when Agnew's indictment for corruption occurred and his star plummeted.

A Baltimore investigation initially aimed at Agnew's successor as county executive resulted in subpoenas to numerous engineers and contractors who did business with Maryland's city, county, and state governments. Faced with the prospect of being indicted, they testified that they had been paying off Agnew, even delivering him cash in his vice presidential office in the Old Executive Office Building, next to the White House. Agnew was guilty of receiving tainted money and not reporting the income on his tax returns, but whether it represented a bribe or extortion was at best murky. Giving 5 or 10 percent of the value of a contract to a politician in office appeared to be such a venerable Maryland tradition that one reporter suggested Maryland change its state motto to "Maryland: the white envelope state."

Given these realities, I was troubled by the constitutional challenge Agnew's felonies presented. According to evidence reported in the media, some of the felonies occurred during his service as vice president of the United States, not just as Baltimore county executive or governor of Maryland, and were therefore impeachable.

To me, the felonies charged against Agnew set him apart from others under indictment, because he was a heartbeat away from the presidency. A sitting vice president in the dock in a criminal trial was not an inspiring prospect. If Nixon should die or resign during the trial, it is hard to imagine anything more grotesque than Agnew taking the presidential oath of office while a defendant in a Baltimore courtroom.

I concluded that prompt impeachment and Senate trial for removal of Agnew from office made sense. To clear the constitutional question and avoid an awful, unsettling spectacle should

Nixon leave the presidency for whatever reason, I decided to do what I could to speed Agnew's impeachment. There was an element of urgency. A grand jury had already begun its investigation in Baltimore. I reviewed these issues in remarks in the *Congressional Record* on October 1, 1973. Hoping the move would help his position with the public, Agnew had written to Speaker Carl Albert, asking the House to investigate charges against him. Probably seeing it as a frantic ploy, the speaker refused. In a letter to the speaker and in a speech in the House, I urged Albert to reconsider, citing the urgency to avoid a terrible situation if Nixon suddenly left the presidency. Agnew complicated the scene by publicly announcing that he would not resign as vice president even if indicted. In a statement to the House I said, "Today, in order to focus the attention of the House on the urgency of the matter, I have introduced a privileged resolution, one of inquiry. It directs the attorney general to furnish the House with any facts related to allegations against the vice president." I added that if the House Judiciary Committee took no action, I would offer a privileged motion in the House to discharge the committee of further consideration and bring the matter before the House for a vote. In a letter, I urged Attorney General Elliot Richardson to intercede. He responded promptly in a brief letter, "The case is not sufficient." I did not need to press further. Fortunately, as a part of a plea bargain, Agnew resigned the office of vice president nine days later, on October 10, 1973, and accepted without protest a finding of guilt on a minor felony charge.

On nomination by President Nixon and approval by both houses of Congress, House Republican leader Gerald Ford became vice president a few weeks later. I will add a tiny footnote to this historic process. I strongly supported Ford for vice president, but before votes were cast, he related an unpleasant experience he had with Representative Wayne Hays, a domineering but powerful senior Democrat from Ohio. Hays was upset with me over some of my foreign policy initiatives and tried to keep me from a NATO parliamentary delegation he would soon head in Canada. When Ford nominated me for a place in the delegation, Hays demanded that he select someone else. With his usual upfront candor, Ford told me that, with House approval of his appointment as vice president coming up soon, he did not want to irritate the often-vindictive Hays. Ford said, "I know I was a coward to cooperate with Hays. I tried hard to find a replacement. The truth is I couldn't find another Republican who wanted to serve on the delegation. I finally had to tell Hays he would have to take you after all." I found the episode amusing and assured Ford that his attempt to comply with Hays's edict was an act of prudence, not cowardice.

When the Watergate scandal led to President Nixon's resignation in 1973, my acquaintance with him was in its thirteenth year. I had been in his presence on many occasions. I always enjoyed his company. I never heard him utter words that were profane, anti-Semitic, or even coarse. Perhaps the Nixon on the tapes, whose raw language proved to be a major reason for his downfall, were words of an insecure actor trying to participate comfortably in ugly rants with close aides in the Oval Office, spouting reckless utterances that he assumed would entertain his staff but remain secret. Ultimately, he lost a lot of his middle-class base because of his taped profanity alone. Maybe he was simply more careful in choice of words when with members of Congress or on a public stage, but more free and himself behind closed doors.

In my experience, his personality was complex. Nixon usually seemed furtive and ill at ease. Always controversial, he may have felt the outside world consisted only of enemies. The few times I remember him completely at ease were during visits I had in the privacy of the Oval Office and during the day he visited Springfield, Illinois, to sign my bill that made the Lincoln Home a part of the National Park Service. There, he beamed in total, relaxed happiness when, seated with him in the presidential limousine in Springfield, I handed him a bundle of newspaper clippings. They reported his daughter Julie's smiling, triumphant visit in nearby Jacksonville a few days earlier when she dedicated a new elementary school in memory of President Eisenhower. On other occasions, his broad smile seemed forced.

For several reasons, I was one of the last three Republican House members to announce support for impeachment. I considered that his principal misdeeds arose mainly from ill-considered attempts to protect errant staff members from prosecution, and I questioned whether these warranted a finding of guilt. I was also concerned that a trial in the Senate would put the entire nation—not just Nixon—through protracted turmoil and uncertainty. I knew that he would defend himself vigorously if brought to trial, and our nation might appear leaderless and therefore vulnerable as the prosecution proceeded.

Most important of all, I believed the country needed Nixon's proven talent and vision in foreign policy for the remainder of his term. Although deeply troubled over unlawful missteps that Nixon ordered or condoned, I kept in mind his historic statesmanship in gaining valuable agreements with the Soviet Union regarding nuclear weapons, in opening diplomatic and trade doors to China, and in negotiating a cease-fire in Vietnam. While pained at the grotesque way Nixon sometimes responded to the scandal and at his failure to immediately condemn his campaign committee's burglary of the Democratic headquarters in the Watergate Complex, I concluded that our country would, on balance, be the loser if he was forced from office.

My long acquaintance with him convinced me that he had the steel and vision to tackle Israel's mistreatment of the Palestinians, which already loomed, in my view, as one of our nation's gravest foreign policy problems. My interest in the challenge deepened when I visited the Middle East a few years earlier to rescue a constituent from Aden. I had no hint that Nixon would actually tackle the prickly nettle in the Middle East, but I respected Nixon's competence in dealing with tough foreign leaders, a skill that he honed in Moscow and Beijing. Years after his resignation, to my complete surprise, I learned that on the eve of Watergate, Nixon secretly decided to press Israel for a comprehensive settlement with its Arab neighbors and instructed Secretary of State Henry Kissinger to prepare papers for that major foreign-policy move—a showdown with Israel. The documents for this ultimatum were prepared, but the Watergate scandal interceded. The papers remained unattended in Kissinger's desk drawer. In 1983, Richard Cheney, former chief of staff to Gerald Ford, Nixon's successor in the Oval Office, told me he was completely unaware of the showdown papers Kissinger had prepared. Cheney later emerged as the controversial vice president in the administration of President George W. Bush.

Nixon was unquestionably one of the dominant American politicians of the last half of the twentieth century, and the first president to appreciate the full political implications of the American West, anticipating the fast-growing national political role of California as it became the most populous state in the union. More broadly, he was one of the first American statesmen to fully understand the significance and promise of the Pacific Rim. Until the Nixon years, the United States looked East, rarely West.

His career was advanced in 1952, when he persuaded the California delegation to vote for the Eisenhower-inspired "Fair Play" resolution at the Republican National Convention that, in effect, secured Ike's nomination for president. As vice president, Nixon worked tirelessly as a Republican campaigner, while Eisenhower took an indifferent role as party leader. Nixon took the lead in squelching Senator Joe McCarthy, suffered a heartbreaking narrow defeat for the presidency in 1960, and then a solid defeat as a candidate for governor of California two years later.

Instead of disappearing as a political figure, Nixon narrowly defeated Vice President Hubert Humphrey in the popular vote for the presidency six years later. He ran far ahead in the electoral vote. Four years later, he won reelection by a big margin in both popular and electoral votes.

I watched with dismay the unfolding of the Watergate scandal. The shocking details came to light, piece by piece, through dramatic revelations of a senior bureaucrat identified only as Deep Throat by reporters for the *Washington Post*. In a drama covering long weeks of ugly headlines, they exposed the president of the United States, Richard Nixon, as a conniving, foul-tongued liar who abused the FBI and intelligence personnel in petty partisan missions.

It was a turbulent time in our nation's history, perhaps more so than any other time since the presidency of Abraham Lincoln. America was in the midst of a civil struggle brought about by a sharp change of culture at a generational level, an unpopular and divisive war, racial divisions, war in the Middle East, severe inflation, long lines at gasoline pumps, and uncertainty of the military draft.

Once the House Judiciary Committee voted impeachment with the backing of 40 percent of Republican committee members, it became likely that the House would recommend impeachment and the president would stand trial in the Senate. It was clear that an overwhelming majority of House members favored disciplinary action against Nixon. I concluded that his record of misconduct was too grave to ignore. I was appalled at the mischief he condoned. I concluded that Congress had to act on the scandal.

The problem was to reconcile political and legal demands. Under the Constitution, House members do not determine the president's guilt or innocence, only whether there was sufficient evidence to show "probable cause" to require him to stand trial in the Senate on charges that could remove him from office. There was more than enough evidence, but many House members felt that the evidence, much of it hearsay, circumstantial, and speculative, while admissible for the purposes of impeachment, would be inadmissible at a Senate trial. The odds were at least even that Nixon would be acquitted if tried in the Senate. Quite a number of House members, chiefly Southern Democrats and Midwestern Republicans—myself included—believed that no president should be impeached unless the evidence of guilt was overwhelming and the chances for Senate conviction beyond question. To accept less, we argued, would expose future presidents to impeachment as the equivalent of a no-confidence vote. As an aside, I must note that the impeachment and trial of President Bill Clinton suggest we were right in taking this position. Clinton was impeached in the House in a highly partisan atmosphere and then stood trial in the Senate in calmer circumstances. Every Senate ballot aimed at Clinton's removal from office failed for want of a majority.

In 1974, however, public opinion—some sympathetic and supportive but mostly hostile—had to be factored into the decision on Nixon's impeachment. Clearly, the president had 25 percent of the population behind him, but at least twice that many felt some disciplinary action must be taken. I was deeply shaken. Each day when I arrived at my office and each night when I departed, I passed a lobby filled with television cameras and reporters dealing with the details of the scandal that emerged from the House Judiciary Committee room. Watergate seemed everywhere, day and night. At home, it dominated conversations with Lucille. It even inspired a bit of comic relief. Committee member Representative William Hungate of Missouri, who could be serious as well as funny, lightened the mood by telephone. Using a well-advertised number, Hungate recorded a vocal rendition of his own composition, a hilarious forty seconds titled, "Down by the Old Watergate." The number stayed busy day and night for a few days. All other days seemed somber.

I considered removal of Nixon from office too extreme. But exoneration was not an option. The answer was to give House members an alternative, a middle-ground choice before the vote for impeachment would be considered. The middle ground was censure. It required a stern procedure. When indicted, the accused would stand alone in the well of the House chamber in open public session while the clerk read the approved resolution of censure.

My decision to support censure was made one humid evening in late July 1974 during a discussion with Bryce Harlow, long President Eisenhower's close aide and one of the wisest politicians I've known. When I first met him, he was Eisenhower's chief liaison on Capitol Hill. The act of impeachment was only weeks ahead. We were seated, of all places, on a curbstone near the U.S. Capitol.

Although time was running out in the impeachment proceedings, I felt the stakes were so high for the nation that the censure option must be attempted. At that moment I could not cite even one colleague certain to support me. The morning after our chat, I telephoned Stephen Jones, who had been my chief of staff before opening a law practice in Enid, Oklahoma. I asked him to leave his law practice in Enid long enough to help me mount the campaign for censure. He immediately agreed, came to Capitol Hill, and, working closely with Bob Wichser, my staff leader, found presidential precedents for censure. President Andrew Jackson was censured for failing to release certain documents to Congress. President James Buchanan was censured for his questionable intervention on behalf of certain businessmen. Over the years, several judges and cabinet members were censured by Congress, and in 1954 Senator Joseph R. McCarthy was censured by the Senate.

My first congressional recruit was Republican Delbert Latta of Ohio, a member of the House Rules Committee. Our goal was to secure Rules Committee approval for a motion that, if approved, would substitute censure for impeachment. If the vote for censure failed, we would try to defeat House passage of impeachment or, that failing, hold its passage to a narrow margin.

It was first necessary to secure support from a majority of the Rules Committee. The committee was scheduled to meet on August 13 to decide the procedure it would recommend to the full House of Representatives. I sent a letter on August 2 to all House members, inviting them to cosponsor a resolution urging the Rules Committee to authorize censure as a possible substitute for impeachment. My letter included the full text of the proposed censure option, which stated, in part: "Richard M. Nixon, in his conduct of the office of President—despite great achievements in foreign policy which are highly beneficial to every citizen and indeed to all people of the world—[1] has shown insensitivity to the moral demands, lofty purpose and ideals of the high office which he holds in trust, and [2] has, through gross negligence and mal-administration, failed to prevent his close subordinates and agents from committing acts of grave misconduct, obstruction and impairment of justice, abuse and undue concentration of power, and contravention of the laws governing agencies of the Executive Branch."

It asserted that while the House Judiciary Committee and the courts "clearly established the negligence, mal-administration and moral insensitivity on the part of the President," I questioned whether the evidence was of sufficient magnitude to warrant his removal from office.

In three days, my letter got more than sixty signatures, including prominent southern Democrats, among them Representative G. V. "Sonny" Montgomery of Mississippi, who solicited support among Democrats, and several influential Republicans, including our leader John Rhodes, Republican whip Arends, and several members of the Judiciary Committee. House Republican Conference Chairman John Anderson declined to sign but indicated his approval.

Representative Edward Mezvinsky, an Iowa Democrat, called the censure "a cop-out," but Democratic Party whip John McFall of California announced his support for the censure option, saying, "The whole thing is very sad." Speaker Carl Albert said he would leave the question of permitting a censure vote up to the Rules Committee, but he added, ominously, "I would not vote to censure the president. I would either vote for or against the Impeachment Resolution."

A legal memorandum prepared by Sam Garrison, the able minority counsel for the House Judiciary Committee, helped our cause. Plans were made to release the names of the petition signers. A draft speech urging censure was started, together with an analysis of the evidence against the president for trial purposes. An op-ed was drafted for submission to the *New York Times*. We believed censure had a good chance of committee approval.

Major media began to take our campaign seriously when respected impeachment authority Professor Charles Black of Yale Law School publicly endorsed authorizing the censure option. Latta and I expected to secure more than one hundred names of House members on the petition by the time the Rules Committee met. In requesting House members' support, we emphasized that support would not bind a cosponsor's position if censure failed and votes were actually cast for or against impeachment.

Three days after my letter on censure went to House members, Nixon made a public admission of misconduct that caused me to cancel the censure project. In the House Chamber on August 6, I announced my decision to vote for impeachment, citing Nixon's admission that in June he directed that "the FBI be alerted to coordinate with the CIA to ensure that [an] investigation not expose these sensitive national security matters." Nixon admitted a vital partisan aspect when he stated, "I was aware of the advantages this course of action would have with respect to limiting possible public exposure of involvement by persons connected with [my] reelection committee." It was an undeniable admission of criminal abuse of the FBI and CIA. Nixon had provided "smoking gun" evidence of guilt. I was so stunned I could hardly believe the news.

This was a shock to many others too. In my remarks in the *Congressional Record*, I called on Nixon to resign. Three days later, on August 9, he did. Nixon had been visited a day or so earlier by Senator Barry Goldwater and other senior Republicans who urged resignation. On October 9, Vice President Gerald Ford became the thirty-eighth president of the United States.

I believe the Rules Committee would have approved the censure option and a majority of the House would have approved censure instead of impeachment. This would have permitted Nixon to finish his second term. During those two final presidential years perhaps Nixon might have brought about a comprehensive peace in the Middle East. Certainly censure could have spared the American people and the rest of the world, especially the Palestinians and Israelis, a continuation of costly folly. I say that because I believe the censured president would seek resolute action ending America's long-standing pro-Israel bias, a step that would brighten his otherwise grim page in history.

Some historians and much of the media claim Watergate was a constitutional crisis. It was not. There was hyperventilated news and active criminal investigations, as well as congressional inquiry, but that is the system at work, not a system in crisis. I was present in Washington and a close observer of these stirring events during the entire Watergate-impeachment period. No shutdown of government occurred. There were no troops in the streets of the nation's capital. For almost every citizen, life continued as before. No one had reason for fear. President Nixon challenged his opposition in court, and the courts challenged him in the same way. And when the courts ruled against him, he yielded and ultimately resigned. The system worked, and Nixon helped make it work.

History has been kind to Nixon, even on Watergate. More than thirty years after his resignation, the American people are now able to see the FBI and the CIA in a more accurate light. The revelations of the Church and Pike Committees of the 1970s concerning the CIA and the published memoirs of former FBI senior-level executives displayed dirty linen of the past that gave a certain balance to the exposures of Watergate. The revelations of the past became public under the Freedom of Information Act and the work of the House Committee on Assassinations. When President Nixon and his Chief of Staff Bob Haldeman talked about having the CIA tell the FBI to lay off, it was assumed they were using the CIA as a convenient way to end their criminal troubles.

They probably were, but there were precedents for such presidential abuses. It is now public knowledge that the CIA and FBI were engaged for many years in illegal and unseemly conduct by associating with U.S. gangsters to assassinate Fidel Castro, to sabotage and disrupt the Cuban Republic, to assassinate other foreign leaders, and to conduct illegal wiretaps, "black bag jobs," and illegal mail covers. Fred Thompson, then the minority counsel for the Senate

committee delving into Watergate and later a senator, published his
suspicions of CIA misbehavior.

President Nixon committed wrongs similar to misdeeds by some
of his predecessors, but he was the first president to get caught. President Johnson used the FBI in 1964 for surveillance of the Freedom
Democratic Party during the Democratic convention that year. Of
the seven men indicted for the Watergate break-in, five were either
former employees or former paid contract employees of the CIA.
Whether Nixon's abuses of the CIA and FBI were impeachable may
be questioned. If tried in the Senate, Nixon could have argued that
he was doing what previous presidents had done.

It is an interesting footnote to political history that Nixon's
resignation from office was more helpful to the Republican Party
than Bill Clinton's acquittal in his Senate impeachment trial was to
Democrats. Had the Democratic senators forced Clinton to resign,
Al Gore would have become president. Gore would likely have
been elected to his own four-year term in 2000 and possibly elected
again in 2004. Republican control of Congress would have been cut
short. But, President Clinton was fortunate in his choice of enemies.
Senate Democrats loathed the idea of forcing Clinton out of office,
because it would delight Speaker Newt Gingrich, their Republican
nemesis, as well as Tom DeLay, Gingrich's hatchet-man majority
leader.

The resignations of Agnew and Nixon within a span of a few
months catapulted Gerald Ford to the presidency without an inter-
vening Election Day. His personal electoral experience was limited
to gaining a majority in a Michigan congressional district where
Republicans were dominant. Likable, centrist, orderly, restrained,
and honorable in all respects, he won quick bipartisan congressional support when Nixon nominated him to be vice president after
Agnew resigned. Widely known and respected on Capitol Hill, Ford
had campaigned little beyond his own district except for occasional
trips to help Republican colleagues, like me. He was not flamboyant,
nor was he an inspirational speaker. As he filled out the remainder

of Nixon's second term, he caused storms of protest by granting clemency to private citizen Nixon and to the young men who had dodged conscription for military duty in Vietnam by going abroad. I applauded these decisions, but many vociferous Americans did not. In my view, a trial of Nixon would have run the nation through a painful and exhausting ordeal, as would prosecution of those who ducked the draft. All this would have put off the healing process so badly needed by the nation.

When Ford announced plans to run for a full presidential term in 1976, I knew he had a tough road ahead, even though Jimmy Carter, the Democratic nominee, was not exactly a household name at the time. I was surprised and disappointed when Ford dropped Vice President Nelson Rockefeller as his running mate and deeply concerned when I learned former Texas Governor John Connolly was a prospect. I knew Republican Representatives Paul "Pete" McCloskey, Tom Railsback, and future secretary of defense William Cohen had already publicly stated their opposition to Connolly.

I warned Ford in a letter that selecting Connolly would be a disaster because of Connolly's link to "dirty tricks" in Watergate investigations. "The Democrats have already made Watergate one of their prime campaign issues. Putting Connolly on the ticket would be like pouring gasoline on the fire. By contrast, your reputation for openness and honesty is beyond question. . . . The Republican party has dozens of capable men and women whose integrity, like yours, has remained intact throughout the Watergate era, indeed some whose integrity shines like a beacon in the darkness." I sent a copy of my message to all Republicans in the House of Representatives. Connolly was furious.

A few days later I was at Mayo Clinic in Rochester, Minnesota, where Lucille was recovering from a craniotomy that closed an aneurysm in her brain. It was an anxious time for both of us. She especially appreciated calls from Senator Percy and Shirley Temple Black, a popular movie star in our childhood. Black was briefly my colleague in the House and later chief of protocol at the State

Department. It was during that period that I entered the drama playing out over Connolly.

Connolly biographer James Reston Jr. summarized the unfolding controversy: "On the ABC show, *Issues and Answers*, [Connolly] was asked about the Railsback, Findley, and Cohen remarks, and he picked up on the initials R, F, and C and said they stood for 'Republicans for Cannibalism.' He was seeing his prize go glimmering, and he tried to turn the issue around. It was 'highly questionable,' he said, if he would accept the vice-presidential nomination if Ford offered it to him. At the Mayo Clinic . . . Paul Findley considered this performance and decided . . . to dictate another letter to Ford, infusing his views with greater urgency and poignancy."[3]

My concern about Connolly stemmed partly from publicity that linked him to lobbyists for dairy producers with whom I had a bad experience several years earlier. They contributed one thousand dollars to my campaign one year and several days after the election called to explain how they expected me to vote on dairy issues. I quickly showed them the door. When I learned that Connolly had a close relationship with the same group, I decided to dictate from the clinic a second letter to Ford that Reston mentioned, this time marked "private and confidential." In it, I elaborated on Connolly's relationship with "dirty tricks." In the September 3, 1977, *Washington Post*, columnists Evans and Novak, who somehow secured a copy of my not-so-confidential letter, quoted my charge that "a clandestine operation of Connolly's Democrats for Nixon" tried to falsely smear Democratic candidate Senator George McGovern for choosing "an obscure Greek Communist journalist" as his spokesman for Greek affairs.

In my letter to Ford, I added, "John Connolly's association with this episode, and its link with the 'dirty tricks' uncovered by the Watergate Committee, make him a liability for any position in your administration."

In the September 29, 1977, Washington *Evening Star*, Harvard Professor Nikolaos Stavrou wrote that Jimmy Carter owed his 1976

election to the presidency to two people: me, for writing Ford a letter urging him not to take Connolly as a running mate, and Ford,
"who permitted himself to be convinced by the arguments in that
letter."

I doubt that my correspondence was conclusive in Ford's
decision-making. Many citizens, like the professor, had a high opinion of Connolly's campaign talent. I never met Connolly, but years
later I had a cordial telephone conversation with him, during which
he expressed support for my endeavors in Middle East policy.

My relationship with both Nixon and Agnew ended on a welcome, warm basis. In correspondence during retirement, neither
mentioned my decisions to support their impeachments. Agnew
wrote several letters to me in 1988. In one, dated April 20, he
traces "difficulties" that led to his resignation as vice president to
a confrontation with the American Israel Public Affairs Committee
(AIPAC) and other partisans for Israel over a trip he made to Saudi
Arabia and the Emirates in 1971. He said Nixon asked him to make
the trip to provide "some balance to the teeming of Congressmen
who run to Israel on the slightest pretext." Agnew added that he
rejected persistent demands that he visit Israel on the way home,
because it would "substantially diminish the signal that my visits
were trying to send to Arab countries." Furious pro-Israel partisans, he wrote, "made sure that I would not become president." He
believed these partisans dug up facts about Agnew's corruption as
their way of getting even.

To the best of my knowledge, Nixon never criticized my decision for his impeachment nor my leadership that helped overturn his
veto of the War Powers Resolution. Days after my defeat in November 1982, he wrote, "Your critics . . . would have to admit that you
always called the shots as you saw them even though you knew . . .
the stands you were taking might prove to be unpopular." In a letter handwritten from his New Jersey residence on October 2, 1993,
Nixon thanked me for my condolences on the death of his wife,
Pat, and added: "I often think how much the country lost when you

became defeated when you were trying to be even-handed on the Mideast."

When Nixon resigned the presidency, I was still deeply engaged in stirring, promising events halfway around the world in the People's Republic of China.

16

≈≈≈≈≈≈≈≈≈≈≈≈≈≈

Tugging at China's Door

My work in China policy began fourteen years earlier. In early October 1966, I put the finishing touches on a statement for the *Congressional Record*. In it, I proposed direct relations with the People's Republic of China, beginning with trade in food, as a prelude to normal diplomatic relations. It would prove to be my first major step in what would mature into a long, exciting, constructive journey that helped open the door to a country of immense importance, a nation that had been subjected to long years of pointless and dangerous isolation.

News of my proposal puzzled and upset some constituents who viewed it as being at odds with my concurrent campaign to tighten economic screws on Communist North Vietnam, widely believed to be a puppet of the Beijing regime. I knew Beijing was trying to end the Vietnam War, and I had evidence that the Communist world was not centrally controlled in a close alliance of Moscow and Beijing.

My statement filled more than five pages of the *Record* on October 19 and was supplemented by an eight-page chronology of important events in the history of U.S.-China relations. I warned that U.S. isolation from China carried the high risk of continued misjudgment about each other, deepening hostility, and threat of war. China viewed the U.S. military forces that effectively ringed its coast as provocative. I recommended urgently that the United States adopt policies that would encourage direct, continuing communications on behalf of peaceful relations and mutual benefit. These, I believed, would help allay China's understandable anxiety about U.S. military policy.

I called for a new alliance in the Pacific Far East to help deter China from military adventurism and motivate its officials to enter into mutually constructive trade with its neighbors and America. It would consist of the United States and democratic governments in the Far East. All member states would participate in policy decisions, including security measures. It would be an alliance open to other nations of the area, hopefully including China.

The day my statement appeared, Nixon thanked Stephen Jones, my assistant, for calling it to his attention. They met unexpectedly at the Supreme Court where Nixon had argued a case. Jones had known Nixon since 1964 when working as a researcher in his office in New York City. Nixon, the man who came within a whisker of being president in 1960 and was destined to become the next president, was focused that day on China, as well as his Supreme Court argument. He asked Jones to call my attention to his statement on China that would soon appear in *Foreign Affairs* quarterly. Before returning to my office, Jones stopped at the Library of Congress to request all available books and documents about the U.S. relationship with Communist China.

With the November 1966 general election less than a month away, I divided my time between home-district campaigning and China policy. A constituent, Air Force Captain Phillip Smith, was being held by the Beijing regime as a prisoner of war. He had been shot down by the Chinese when his navigation aids on his fighter jet failed, and he had been captured after he parachuted onto Hainan Island close to the Vietnamese and Chinese coasts.

I had little knowledge of Chinese history but was impressed with Dr. Walter Judd, a much-admired member of Congress from Minnesota who had been a medical missionary in China when the mainland government was governed by Chiang Kai-shek. His allegiance to Chiang continued for many years after Chiang's forces retreated to the island of Formosa, now known as Taiwan, and Communist forces gained full control of the mainland. It was a time when most members of Congress, including me, considered Chiang an important counterforce to any aggressive measures by the mainland government.

When I first met Judd in 1961, he asked me to sign a petition pledging support to Chiang's right to regain control of the mainland. Impressed by Judd's sincerity and the broad, bipartisan support he enjoyed, I signed the petition without question, as did most other members. For me, signing was more a friendly gesture to Judd than to Chiang, although I assumed the Nationalist general headed a formidable anti-Communist constituency and could be a factor in U.S. endeavors in Vietnam.

In the first months after Captain Smith's capture, responding to pleas from his family in Greene County, I tried to learn where he was imprisoned and how he was being treated. I had no inkling that this constituent service would lead me into a quick study of the Communist world, especially the People's Republic of China, and cause me to change my views on how to deal with those in charge. It would entail direct, sometimes controversial involvement in Vietnam policy as well as a search for openings directly to the Beijing regime. It led to personal relationships with Communist officials, enlivened my career on Capitol Hill, produced fierce new challenges from some constituents, and established lasting, personal friendships. One characteristic of the Chinese I did not fully grasp until I left Congress: they do not forget their friends. After leaving Congress, as long as I remained in the Washington area, I received invitations to the Chinese Embassy events, and even today I communicate occasionally with several officials and those who formerly held office.

I was pleased to learn that my article caught the former vice president's attention. I knew it would be controversial among many constituents, and Nixon's implied support was comforting. Several years later, Captain Smith's plight became linked with my endeavors to open trade and diplomacy doors in Beijing and terminate America's bloody experience in Vietnam. In the early years, the China door was largely closed by U.S. policy, and there was little I could do to gain Smith's release.

The Associated Press reported my appeal to President Johnson to seek the release of Smith in negotiations then underway for the return of forty-eight Chinese fishermen held by U.S. authorities. The plea was ignored by Beijing. I appealed to the Chinese government through a letter written in Polish and delivered to the Polish Embassy, the diplomatic mission that handled informal U.S. relations with China. In Paris for parliamentary meetings one winter, I handed a similar appeal, this one in English, to an official at the local Chinese embassy.

Smith was a pawn in a giant international chess game. China and the United States were hostile. Nurtured by myths and false imagery that arose from long years of isolation from each other, both sides feared the aggressive intentions of the other. Smith had little chance to see his home in Greene County, Illinois, again until the United States reached a peaceful, diplomatic breakthrough with China. Bringing about change required public education and a major change in attitude by elected officials in both capitals. It was that simple. It was that complex. The fears of hostility and aggression came partly from long years of pretense over the political influence and military power of the regime on Taiwan and its lobbying in Washington. For the most part, the mainland regime and the United States were total strangers. There was little intercourse between citizens of each country. The countries had no diplomatic or business communication with each other. Isolation breeds fear.

An immediate positive response to my public statement on China was the opportunity to address the Ripon Society, an association of progressive young Republicans at Harvard University. In my remarks to the group on May 7, 1967, I proposed establishment of normal diplomatic relations with the People's Republic of China. The next day *The Harvard Crimson* reported that I was the first

Republican in Congress to recommend this step publicly. In my statement I urged an exchange of diplomatic, cultural, journalistic, and trade missions, but warned that "the two great nations of the Occident and Orient seem to be on a collision course." I suggested that trade relations begin with food sales, and I supported this recommendation with a summary of arguments set forth in my statement in the *Congressional Record*. Lee Huebner, president of the Ripon Society, later a principal speechwriter for President Nixon and still later publisher of the *International Herald Tribune* in Paris, hosted my visit and introduced me to the society. The next morning, Jones and I had the rare treat of breakfast with Professor John K. Fairbank, the eminent China specialist at Harvard, and his wife in their residence.

Wire services reported the gist of my speech, and the *Baltimore Sun*, to my surprise, discussed it favorably in its lead editorial a few days later. It quoted from my remarks at Harvard: "Our present policy has become blind and unrealistic, in fact ostrich-like." The same day, the *State Journal-Register,* the largest daily newspaper in my district, headlined an editorial, "Findley Is Wrong."

My statement drew open hostility from John Birch Society members. When I spoke a few weeks later at an outdoor meeting in Quincy, Illinois, society members attended the meeting and displayed hostile signs on the fringes of the crowd, including these themes: "Trade With China Is Treason" and "Traitors Should Be Executed."

It was not my first encounter with society members, who seemed to be scattered uniformly throughout my far-flung constituency. Most of them were less hostile in their declarations than the poster-bearers in Quincy, but they were firm on basic goals—opposing the United Nations, the federal income tax, and the Federal Reserve Bank. Their billboards often carried this message: "Get the UN out of the U.S., and the U.S. out of the UN." I had occasional discussions with individual members and found them to be doctrinaire and stubborn in viewpoints but not personally hostile. Several members of Congress were openly John Birch Society affiliates, all deeply committed to their cause but amiable in behavior. On several occasions I heard one of my colleagues, Republican Representative Don Bruce of Indiana, repeat with approval the Birch slogan, "Better dead than Red." A few society members, especially several in Quincy, were personally hostile and menacing in countenance and body language. I got the feeling from looking into their cold, glaring eyes that they wanted me to disappear, but I received no physical abuse or threats.

My speech at Harvard and the *Baltimore Sun* editorial caught the attention of China officials. As a result, I became acquainted with personnel of the Chinese embassy.

Thanks to initiatives of the Nixon administration, the door opened wide enough in 1973 to let my constituent, Captain Phillip Smith, come home from almost eight years' captivity in China's prison system. After Nixon's visit, he was permitted to walk across the border into Hong Kong, free at last from his years of confinement. I wish I could have been there to welcome him. After a physical examination and military debriefing, he arrived home to a joyous community-wide welcome in Roodhouse, Illinois. I spoke at a happy community dinner in his honor. He was thin but relaxed and optimistic. After long months seeking his safe return, my handshake with him was an emotional moment for me.

In a letter to me years later, Smith wrote that Nixon's visit to China did not bring his immediate release, but it "brought drastic changes" in prison conditions. "The food improved, the harassment stopped, and the treatment, in general, was more humane. The most important changes that helped me were the steps taken to improve U.S.-China relations. Your initiative in this regard was right on the mark and helped pave the way to fundamental changes . . . that hastened my return to freedom and opened the door to China." He said he lost his freedom while in prison but not his "pride in being an American." He added, "I gained strength I never knew I had."

In June 1975, Senator Charles Percy of Illinois, a close friend who had read my statements about China relations and my experience with Smith, telephoned to invite Lucille and me to join a two-week Senate-sponsored trip to China that would begin two months later. Others on the tour would be Senators Adlai Stevenson III, Jacob Javits, and Claiborne Pell, together with House members Margaret Heckler and Paul "Pete" McCloskey. Spouses were invited, and all accepted. It would be the second U.S. congressional mission since China opened its doors to U.S. officials.

Senate protocol created a challenge for the hosts. Although in the minority, Senator Percy of Illinois had been attempting longer than others to arrange a trip to China. After a discussion, Percy was selected as leader, with Jacob Javits of New York, also a Republican, as co-chair. Years before, Percy was the boy wonder of U.S. industry, heading Bell and Howell at the age of thirty. In my view, Javits was then the most forceful senator, and one of the most effective. Other senators in the delegation to China were Democrats: Claiborne Pell of Rhode Island, a patrician who was laid back; and Adlai Stevenson III of Illinois, former state treasurer, able advocate, and namesake of two forebears of national prominence.

Our visit occurred in the lingering aftermath of the Cultural Revolution, during which the entire country experienced radical, short-term changes. One of its goals was to create general uniformity in salaries and provide experience in menial duties, regardless of career assignments. Vestiges of the revolution were obvious during our visit. While touring a general hospital in Beijing, a surgeon internationally known for his skill in reattaching severed limbs candidly answered our questions. He said his salary was about one hundred dollars a month, and he traveled to and from work on a bicycle. He provided this information freely. At a university we found that faculty members had salaries similar to the surgeon, except for an elderly professor who said an exception in public policy permitted him to retain his pre-revolution salary of about seven hundred dollars a month.

Years later, I learned that during the Cultural Revolution, Han Xu, then high in protocol services who later became ambassador to the United States, was relegated to a janitor's job. Madame Wang, as

I always called her, the third secretary in the Washington embassy during my years there, was dismissed from senior protocol duties and ordered to plant rice on a collective farm. Once the revolution ended, Xu and Wang returned to their former senior positions in the Foreign Ministry. The Cultural Revolution was a rough period for almost all citizens except those in the Communist hierarchy.

A young protocol officer, Mr. Tu, traveled with our group and welcomed opportunities to quote sayings of Chairman Mao. He seemed able to quote one suitable to each change in conversation. The chairman's bits of wisdom were emblazoned in English on large red billboards scattered throughout areas we visited. They were also published in a "Little Red Book" that Mr. Tu distributed to our group. We could not believe one of his declarations. Gays in the military were a frequent topic at the time. When asked about government policies toward homosexual citizens, Mr. Tu said that people with such sexual preferences did not exist in China.

Our most memorable appointment was with Teng Xiaoping, the vice prime minister and regarded as the coming power in China's peaceful economic transition from the radical measures of the Cultural Revolution to a competitive market system. At the time of our tour, he was the acting head of government because Party Chairman Mao and Premiere Chou En-lai were ill. The appointment provided the setting for a frank exchange of views with the man who would soon lead China. Teng was blunt, tough, and severe. At the time, the Peoples Republic of China had inherited the Taiwan regime's Security Council seat in the United Nations, but there was no formal diplomatic relations with the United States. Senator Stevenson, whose father served as the U.S. ambassador to the United Nations during the administration of John F. Kennedy, criticized the U.S. refusal to support the change at the Security Council. While not canvassed on the question, all members of the delegation, I believe, supported the transfer of the "China seat" to the Beijing regime.

When I handed Teng a book of agricultural statistics supplied by the U.S. Department of Agriculture, he responded by sternly criticizing the U.S. government for its decision to sell grain to the Soviet Union, then considered China's most hostile neighbor. I responded that the United States would gladly sell China almost any quantity of grain it desired. When Teng visited Congress in 1979, I gave him a book presenting the life of Abraham Lincoln in photographs. No complaint this time. He smiled and, at my request, autographed the cover of the current *Time* that featured his portrait.

The schedule in China included cities not visited by Western people in more than twenty years. At these stops, thousands of citizens silently lined the streets, often three and four deep, as our caravan passed by. They were as curious about us as we were about them. During a visit to a department store, Lucille found herself completely surrounded by curious Chinese ladies who touched her hair and garments, then peered closely at the contents when she opened her purse. When she visited a shop for a shampoo and hair set, fascinated onlookers followed every move intently. Her red hair made her a curiosity. One of her challenges was disposing of worn hosiery. She tried tying it and leaving it in the hotel wastebasket, but it would reappear the next morning, laundered and neatly folded.

One evening, we were guests in a large auditorium for a colorful program of dancing and singing. Another day, we visited commune farming, where "barefoot doctors" provided basic medical services to people working in rice paddies and other fields. Our schedule included visits to factories, schools, and universities. We attended an official hearing for a couple that wanted a divorce. The wife complained of beatings by her husband. After testimony, the panel told the couple to go back home and attempt domestic tranquility. No doubt it was a show trial for our benefit.

Members of our group took turns offering toasts when our hosts attended our dinners. When my turn came, I quoted this witticism attributed to Stevenson's father, Ambassador Adlai Stevenson II: "Wisdom consists of nine parts silence and one part brevity." The Americans laughed, but the Chinese remained silent. Our interpreter, for some reason, gave up trying to translate the quotation into the Mandarin language.

We were impressed with the cleanliness of China, city and rural areas alike. Strikingly beautiful were the trees, all planted in precise order. Major highways, city streets, and even alleys were lined with trees, often several rows deep. We were told that Chairman Mao had personally ordered the tree planting, the result being cleaner air and significant moderation of temperature extremes in Beijing.

By the time our group exited via train to Hong Kong, I had gained new respect for China and high hopes for a broad, cordial relationship with the United States, especially in trade. Although our tour discovered manufacturing, agriculture, and transportation that lagged far behind the United States, I sensed a passion for progress on all fronts. From the terrible bloodletting of the revolutionary years and continuing human rights abuses the Chinese people emerged graceful, optimistic, and progressive.

As we approached the border, we witnessed a sharp contrast the moment the train entered Hong Kong. We left behind a spotlessly clean Chinese countryside to enter Hong Kong, an unkempt mess filled with garbage and other debris. Signs warned of pickpockets.

After we arrived in Hong Kong, Lucille and I had an unexpected invitation to join another congressional group, this one en route to South Korea and Japan with a final stop at the "other China" on Taiwan. Except for my limited service in Japan with military occupation forces, neither of us had traveled to any of these countries. We accepted the invitation. Our arrival crowded the plane, but we had introductions to local governmental personalities, challenges, and achievements. I was amazed at the confidence, optimism, and progress we found at every turn. It was hard to believe they had left behind a few short years earlier the rigors, hardship, and desolation of war.

Three years later, at the request of Illinois Governor James "Big Jim" Thompson, I chaired an Illinois agricultural trade mission to China. The purpose was goodwill discussion that hopefully would lead to markets in China for Illinois farm products. It was not a Congress-financed trip. Each private organization financed its representative's expenses.

Also in the delegation was a Yorkshire breeding boar, nicknamed "Big Jim" by our group in honor of Governor Thompson. It was the Farm Bureau's gift to the government of China. "Big Jim" survived the air travel in good health and enjoyed successful fatherhood in China for more than a year. He became the most famous hog in China, but parasitic infection caused his untimely death, despite what United Press International (UPI) described as "heroic measures" to keep him alive. When I telephoned Steele with the news that "Big Jim" had died, I had to hurry to assure him that it was the swine "Big Jim" who had gone to hog heaven. The death prompted me to propose an exchange of swine scientists between China and the University of Illinois. He Kang, the deputy minister of agriculture we had met on our tour, accepted the proposal. UPI quoted me: "The exchange is sort of a memorial to Big Jim."

For the tour, the Farm Bureau prepared a supply of small folders that showed pictures and a brief biography of each delegation member. It also displayed a map of China showing Taiwan as a separate country. Our hosts firmly declared the folder could not be used because the error was serious. That evening the delegation joined in altering copies of the brochures in a cut-and-paste exercise that satisfactorily showed Taiwan as a part of China. Imagine the scene: the senior leaders of Illinois agriculture using scissors and paste like kindergarten kids.

We visited labor-intensive communes, rudimentary food production and processing plants, a factory where farm tractors were produced, a brewery, and several urban areas that had been isolated from Western influences for a generation.

One day Steele entered a retail store almost empty of customers and proceeded alone to the top floor where he examined wood carvings. Suddenly he realized the room was packed with curious Chinese. About that time I arrived and crowded my way to his side. I turned toward the crowd and clapped my hands, believing it would be accepted as a friendly greeting. I had noted that at meetings conducted by Chinese, the speakers always joined the audience in hand clapping. Instead, the Chinese silently and quickly opened a wide path for our exit. The open path extended through the Chinese who filled the stairways and were crowded outside. More than a bit embarrassed, I joined Steele in heading down the stairs. He later described my hand-clap as akin to the biblical opening of the Red Sea.

One evening our delegation entertained Chinese officials with a "typical Illinois farm dinner." Farm Bureau's William Allen brought all the makings and cooked the meal of ham, sweet potatoes, and green beans. Our guests joined us in using knife and fork, instead of chopsticks. Dessert was hot apple pie with a slice of cheese on top of each piece. The dinner was a success, with the exception of the cheese slices. Each Chinese guest removed the cheese before eating the pie. None in our group knew that cheese, like several other products, is not an accepted food item.

While our mission did not bring home specific orders for wheat, corn, or soybeans, we heard strong hints that they would soon occur. In April 1978, the Beijing government announced the purchase of 620,000 metric tons of U.S. wheat, 3,555,000 metric tons of corn, and 854,215 metric tons of soybeans—its first direct major purchases of these U.S. commodities. In subsequent years, purchases of similar scale occurred. The wheels of diplomacy often turn slowly, but sometimes with good results. Diplomacy is more like tending a garden than constructing a building. Perhaps we tended the Chinese garden well.

Back home, I found the atmosphere friendly toward China. Han Xu, then deputy chief of the Chinese diplomatic mission in Washington, agreed to speak at Illinois College commencement exercises in Jacksonville. I met him and his small official delegation at the Springfield airport and drove them to the college campus in my well-marked "congressional mobile office."

When we stopped at a gas station in Jacksonville, I could not contain my laughter. Diplomat Han stepped outside my car and shook hands with everyone nearby, urging each to vote for my reelection and citing me as "a great congressman." Chairman Mao would have been astonished. When I was reelected six months later, I sent Han Xu a Certificate of Appreciation for his help in my campaign. His wife, Madame Ge, later told me that the certificate, nicely framed, adorned a wall in their Beijing residence.

At the college, Han presented a message of friendship that was warmly applauded. He declined to accept the honorary doctorate degree customarily provided to a commencement speaker, citing the fact that full diplomatic relations were still in the future. In Springfield the next day for a meeting of the downtown Rotary Club, I presented an abbreviated version of my slide show based on the congressional visit to China. Han Xu provided concluding remarks. The *New York Times* of May 24 carried a half-page report on his visit to Illinois College, Springfield Rotary Club, and Lincoln's Tomb. A large photograph showed Han reaching to rub the nose of a brass likeness of Lincoln's head at the tomb entrance. In Springfield, he toured the Old State House. As I watched, he glanced at a display of Lincoln's speech at Gettysburg, then stepped back and recited it from memory. He had learned it while a student in Shanghai.

Before Han Xu and his wife left Washington for a new assignment in Beijing, Stevenson and I co-chaired a luncheon in his honor in the Capitol building. We kept the guest list short and the entertainment fun-filled. Lucille and I wore Mao jackets. Senator Ed Muskie, later secretary of state and a presidential candidate, hypnotized lobsters, a favorite sport of Maine youngsters. Mike Oksenberg, the China specialist on the National Security Council and in student days a cheerleader at the University of Michigan, led the group in saluting Han by shouting each letter of Han's full name. U.S. Representative Bob Michel, leader of House Republicans and a music major in college, sang original lyrics to the tune of "My Fair Lady." It included these words, "We know you'll soon be leaving for China, but before you close the door, take this advice, sir. Stay sweet and nice, sir, and don't go near the Gang of Four."

Stevenson, a Democrat who had been dropping hints he might be a candidate for president on a third-party ticket, said, "You're all here under false pretenses. My purpose is to announce my selection of a running mate." At this, he nodded my way, and I rushed to his side, raising his arm with mine to applause. The *Alton Telegraph* reported: "It was Stevenson's new third-party ticket balanced by a Republican from Pike County, dressed in attire immortalized by the late chairman of the Chinese Communist Party."[4]

When I called on Han's successor at the Chinese embassy, Ambassador Chai Zemin, for a response, he said with a chuckle: "I cannot hypnotize lobsters. I can't sing. I have no sense of humor. What am I doing here?" It was all in fun, of course, and Stevenson's gesture was the closest I ever came to being a vice presidential nominee. The UPI report closed with these words: "The program had most of the audience as comatose as the lobsters. If [U.S.-China relations] can withstand this type of entertainment, they can survive anything."[5]

Months later, when I introduced Ambassador Chai to a large audience in Quincy, no threatening signs appeared. To the contrary, he, like Han Xu speaking earlier at Illinois College, received warm applause before and after his remarks, a welcome sign of constituent comfort with U.S.-China trade. Quincy, like Jacksonville, is central in the vast rich cropland that produces high yields of wheat, corn, and soybeans, commodities China needs in immense quantities. By then, I believe most citizens had become accustomed to direct relations with Beijing. Taiwan was no longer on the radar screen.

A few days after Election Day 1982, Ambassador Zemin stopped at my office to express his regret at my defeat. He observed, with a grin, "You Americans have a strange way of choosing leaders." The Japanese ambassador called a day later with a word of regret and best wishes in the future.

In 1986, Han Xu returned to Washington as ambassador to the United States. By then, diplomatic relations were fully established, and he revisited Illinois College to accept the honorary doctorate degree he had declined eight years before. Accompanying him were his wife and Miss Wang, third secretary of the embassy. After cancer ended his life in 1994, a group of journalists and former colleagues began a three-year project that produced a splendid biography of the diplomat. I was touched to find the text of my published tribute to Han Xu reprinted on the book cover.

Fred Osborn, a neighbor and retired educator, had an anxious moment in 1985 when he traveled to China with seventeen other tourists. He discovered my name was not widely known throughout the country's officialdom despite my long efforts in China policy. He carried a copy of my book, *They Dare to Speak Out*, for reading on the long trip and had it in his hand while approaching the check-in procedures on landing at Beijing. While the others waited anxiously, an official thumbed through the book, asking, "Is this book anti-Communist?" Osborn assured the officer that it had nothing to do with Communism and was related solely to Israel's U.S. lobby. Other questions followed about me, lobbies, and what the group planned to do in China. Twenty minutes later Osborn and his companions heaved sighs of relief on being cleared for entry.

I tugged at China's door, not through some special understanding of diplomacy or of China itself, but through persistent application of the attitude Ambassador Han Xu called friendship. I found the Chinese people talented, cordial, and isolated. They welcomed me, and I reciprocated. China has since become one of the strongest and most productive nations on earth.

There is always the potential for hostility—even armed conflict—between great powers. The United States must keep channels of communication with China wide open and candid at all times. Just as we found ways in our dealings with Great Britain, France, and Germany to leave behind periods of hostility, we must seek relentlessly the same in our undertakings with the People's Republic of China. It emerged swiftly from the dead-end austerity and rigidity of a Communist economy into an economic giant in the world's competitive marketplace. During this transformation, it made advances in political and cultural improvement with a minimum of bloodshed and turmoil. In the years ahead, all signs indicate the United States should treat China as a friendly partner, not as a threat.

17

◇◇◇◇◇◇◇◇◇◇◇◇◇◇◇◇◇◇◇◇

Combating Scourges

Since 1945, humankind has been threatened by a grave new menace, nuclear warheads. They join famine, tyranny, and war as humankind's mightiest scourges. On Capitol Hill I found myself trying to curb all four. Sixty years later, each scourge has become more threatening than ever.

Today, an enormous world shortage of food looms in the near future. When it comes, it is certain to be the breeding ground for civil strife. During my first years on Capitol Hill, I glimpsed such future travail when shiploads of donated U.S. grain relieved severe famine conditions in India and other countries. I knew donations of grain, while essential in meeting a crisis, did nothing to relieve the conditions that produced it. In 1966, the first steps were taken that led to the Famine Prevention Act, one of the most urgently needed and promising of my legislative projects. When finally enacted in 1975 as Title XII to the Foreign Assistance Act, it authorized long-term agreements enabling U.S. land-grant universities to help famine-threatened countries. It contemplated a program to bring basic education to small-scale farmers, similar to the land-grant extension education program that has benefited food production in the United States for more than a century. Although an agricultural program, it is also foreign policy. When I asked Agriculture Secretary Earl Butz if he would like it administered within his department, he said it belonged in the State Department.

The act had its genesis when Dr. Hadley Read, a senior member of University of Illinois College of Agriculture faculty, sent me galley proofs of his book, *Partners with India*. It reviews the success of the University of Illinois and five other U.S. land-grant universities in helping India establish teaching institutions that focus on food and agricultural needs. They helped end the famine that blighted India in the 1960s.

I had firsthand knowledge of land-grant education. During thirteen years as editor of a country newspaper, I dealt directly with farmers on a daily basis and often with University of Illinois College of Agriculture professionals who brought educational services to farmers in the county where we lived. This enabled me to grasp quickly the message in Read's galley proofs. Continuing education of adult farmers had a major role in converting America's largely agrarian society into a highly industrialized one. It made possible the swift rise in living standards throughout our nation. It helped individual farmers increase per capita food production, a process that freed increasing numbers of the farm population to use their education in non-agrarian pursuits in cities.

Reading the text of Read's book, I was convinced that continuing, basic education could be adapted with good results in other countries. This advance would improve food production, advance personal income, and improve quality of life for farmers and city-dwellers alike. I predicted it could soon banish famine worldwide. The looming specter of serious food shortages would disappear. I based these optimistic assumptions on the remarkable, unique history of food production increases in the United States, thanks in great part to our country's successful experience in emphasizing education of farmers.

I began work on the legislation after becoming a member of the Foreign Affairs Committee in 1967. Two years later, my ideas jelled enough to attract the support of Dan Parker of Parker Pen fame, President Nixon's administrator of the Agency for International Development (AID). Dr. Harold Guither, a nationally known agricultural economist at the University of Illinois, agreed to a short-term assignment—June 1 to August 15, 1975—on my personal congressional staff. He worked exclusively on famine prevention legislation, which underwent over twenty drafts before being introduced late that summer with more than one hundred bipartisan cosponsors.

It proposed a Board for International Food and Agricultural Development (BIFAD) with its seven members appointed by the president. The board would help AID officials make efficient use of U.S. agricultural expertise. The House approved my bill without amendment. It received the largest affirmative vote of any foreign assistance legislation in history. Senator Hubert H. Humphrey of Minnesota, well represented in our discussions by Dr. Dick McCall, secured Senate approval of the House bill, again without amendment. It was signed into law by President Nixon in September 1975.

It required eight years—four Congresses—from galley proofs of Hadley Read's book to Nixon's signature, a typical span for legislation drafted in its entirety on Capitol Hill. Bringing the Lincoln home into the National Park Service took only four years, because it proved a simple and noncontroversial undertaking. After my speech at Harvard on China policy, fourteen years passed before the normalization of diplomatic relations with Beijing.

The legislation permits AID to make multiyear contracts with America's land-grant universities. Under these contracts they gain the authority and resources to help food-deficit countries improve the education of small-scale farmers. I predicted the legislation could be a powerful influence in ending the specter of famine in twenty-five years. Authorization came before the Foreign Affairs Committee and funding was handled by a subcommittee of the House Appropriations Committee.

In my early years on Capitol Hill, seniority alone determined who chaired major committees. That tradition kept Representative Otto Passman of Louisiana as chair of the subcommittee that dealt with foreign aid, a program Passman routinely described as "wasteful give-away." Each year, he brought funding legislation to the House floor with these words, "I rise to request approval of this legislation, but I hope it is rejected." This always provoked laughter. Passman was entertaining in another way: he vigorously twisted his body and arms and even flailed his legs while speaking from the well of the House. This prompted one of my colleagues to observe quietly, "Otto must wear his suits out from the inside." He made no vocal objection and few physical exertions when he brought the bill to fund famine prevention to the House floor.

The bill reflected my conviction that countries backward in basic education of farmers cannot wisely jump into high-tech food production. Steady advances cannot occur in the absence of professional educational outreach that is made available to all, young and old. The emphasis must be on people, not machines. Otherwise, illiteracy will permanently blight society and stymie progress in quality of life.

When I visited Ecuador in 1981 with Peter McPherson, then administrator of AID, the ruling military trio arranged for us to view a film that illustrated the country's "progress" in agriculture. It showed giant planting and harvesting machines, each managed by only one operator, at work in a large field. The machines bypassed small-scale, perhaps illiterate, farmers, nowhere to be seen. It was hardly the progressive step Ecuador needed.

After I spoke to a group of farmers in a remote area of Ecuador, a salesman in the audience came to me to express support for the program I described. He also related a personal experience. He became acquainted with a small-scale farmer whose family had tilled a small plot of land for generations. Early one season, the salesman gave him a supply of feed and fertilizer and during the year helped him make efficient use of it. He also helped him employ prudent soil and water management techniques. That year's production was high. Several years later, he stopped again for a visit and found the farmer had reverted to old habits, with production distressingly low. The farmer needed extension help, someone to show up regularly with wise advice and encouragement.

Famine can be prevented only with prudent long-term programs. Providing humanitarian food relief at a time of famine, boosting national production of specific commodities, and developing new fertilizers and seeds are essential steps, but they are not enough. If small-scale farmers go without basic education, big machines will take over their land and the illiterate people displaced will become a burden on society. We must recognize that, as per capita food production increases, movement of people from farms to urban areas is inevitable. This is actually good news for society if the people making the moves are equipped with basic education. It will enable them to provide services in urban areas that augment the nation's standard of living.

Working on this project nurtured my friendship with two men, Humphrey and Jordan-born Jiryus Oweis, a veteran AID specialist. Two years after the bill became law, I organized a symposium on Capitol Hill on famine prevention attended by ambassadors from over seventy countries. Humphrey pulled himself from his sickbed to address the gathering. Vice President Gerald Ford also spoke. When Humphrey began, he seemed frail, but after a few minutes he spoke with his usual persuasive passion. During his remarks, he recalled his frequent disagreements with me on domestic farm legislation. He directed these touching words my way: "You valiant soldier. You old rascal. Sometimes I think the best friends I've had are the ones I've engaged in political combat." A few days before his death, I received a handwritten message from him: "Keep the universities honest." A great and generous man, I knew these words had no trace of avarice; he wanted me to keep the land-grant universities focused on the central goal of the Famine Prevention Act. When he died a few weeks later, I knew that food abundance had lost a powerful advocate.

In November 1982, my unsuccessful bid for a twelfth term left the Famine Prevention Program without a fervent, experienced champion in either the House or Senate. After leaving Congress, I tried to follow Humphrey's deathbed plea by serving from 1983 to

1994 as a member of BIFAD, appointed by Reagan and reappointed by President George H. W. Bush. I fought with little success to persuade the board to focus on programs bringing basic education to small-scale farmers, the path that Humphrey and I had intended.

From its beginning, the board spent much of its time and resources on collaborative laboratory research projects that were useful but not helpful in educating illiterate farmers. The twenty-five years that I forecast would end the worldwide threat of famine have come and gone. The specter remains.

As I write, I remain optimistic. The Famine Prevention Program remains in public law, and the board still meets, chaired by Dr. Robert Easter, an eminent leader in land-grant education based at the University of Illinois College of Agriculture. He and his colleagues on BIFAD understand what is needed. This reality kindles my hope that succeeding administrations will revitalize the program.

With frightening world food deficits projected in the near future, the Famine Prevention Program is more urgently needed today than when enacted in 1975. The UN Food and Agricultural Organization reported in 2009 that the world's hungry people exceeded one billion, with the percentage of hungry people rising faster than population increases, "a devastating combination for the world's most vulnerable." It estimated that the food crisis "affects one in six people worldwide, almost all undernourished live in developing countries."

Josette Sheeran of the World Food Program, another UN agency, warned, "Today, a record one billion people—mostly women and children—go to bed hungry. . . . Without food, people have only three options: They riot, they migrate, or they die."[6]

Like the specter of famine, nuclear weapons are another scourge that is mounting, not receding. At the end of World War II, only the United States and Great Britain were members of the nuclear weapons club. Today France, Israel, Russia, India, Pakistan, and China have joined. As a member of the House Committee on Foreign Affairs, I heard testimony that forty other nations possessed the materials and technology that would enable them to produce nuclear warhead material on short notice—months, not years.

. In March 1978, I joined Clement Zablocki, chairman of the Foreign Affairs Committee, in sponsoring a "timely warning" amendment to export policy legislation. It sought to secure ninety days' notice before exported materials could be used in assembling nuclear warheads. It was a forerunner of the critical safeguards provision of the Nuclear Non-Proliferation Act. I was a member of the committee that advanced the bill to enactment.[7]

During a private visit years earlier with Eisenhower in his Gettysburg office, the former president made a surprising observation. He said one way to "assure permanent peace in Europe" might be to provide each head of government with a nuclear warhead or two. It was a private comment and one he might not have made in public. He made the statement only a few years after the United States attained the dubious distinction of being the first and, so far, the only nation ever to detonate nuclear explosives as acts of war.

I have reflected on Ike's comment as some world leaders, including President Barack Obama, react with deep concern at the possibility that Iran will attain its own nuclear weapons. Confronted with the reality that a threatening neighbor like Israel possesses a stock of nuclear weapons, Muslim states, including Iran, may someday conclude, however unwisely, that they need a nuclear deterrent against Israel's proclivity for armed aggression. Other states beset with perceived insecurity may reach the same conclusion. The world could quickly be festooned with nuclear warheads. Although that would be the ultimate nightmare for humankind, it may happen if the world fails to establish an international organization able to enforce world law that will surely prohibit possession of nuclear warheads. Survival of the fittest is the law of the jungle.

Despite America's lip-service to nonproliferation of nuclear weapons, our government set the wrong example several times in recent years. It resumed the enhancement of nuclear weapons, and it let languish a program with Russia for major, mutual reduction of nuclear warheads. Happily, Obama is attempting to resurrect that program. Like his predecessors since Kennedy, Obama, however, never mentions Israel's nuclear warheads. They exist, of course, and he injures his own credibility by refusing officially to acknowledge that fact. His refusal is noted worldwide with dismay, if not contempt. Israel refuses to open its nuclear facilities to international inspection and has not signed the Nuclear Non-Proliferation Agreement.

From the moment I witnessed the awesome impact of an atomic bomb in Nagasaki, Japan, in 1945, I committed myself to doing everything I could to eliminate the scourge of nuclear weapons and war. As long as nuclear weapons exist, humanity will be threatened by the possibility that one or more of these warheads will be detonated with horrifying results, whether by tyrannical dictators, deranged individuals, or through accident. America's goal must be the elimination of all nuclear warheads worldwide. Nuclear warheads anywhere are a danger to people everywhere.

Just as menacing to national interest is religious bias in foreign policy. Banishing it has been the major focus of my post-Congress years.

Part V

High Cost of
Religious Bias

18

‹‹‹‹‹‹‹‹‹‹‹‹‹‹‹‹‹‹‹‹‹‹‹‹‹‹‹‹‹‹‹

Middle East Thicket

Midway in my congressional career, I visited the Middle East for the first time. It was a major undertaking in diplomatic relations. Begun in May 1974, episodes followed that covered the remaining eight years of my career on Capitol Hill. On this first visit, I heard complaints about the pro-Israel bias in U.S. foreign policy from Syrian President Hafez El-Assad in Damascus and South Yemen President Salim Rubyai Ali in Aden. They opened my eyes to the abuse of Arab human and property rights by Israel and the complicity of the United States, Israel's only major supporter, in these violations. One thing followed another. I was trapped in the Middle East thicket with no escape possible.

My trip's main goal was to end the abuse of the human rights inflicted on one of my constituents by an Arab government. My mission could be considered an act of desperation over the fate of Ed Franklin, a young man I had never met. He was serving a five-year solitary imprisonment in Aden, capital of the People's Democratic Republic of Yemen, best known as South Yemen. It was closely affiliated with the Soviet Union and considered by the State Department to be the most radical Arab state. A U.S. official told me Mohammed Motie, the foreign minister, got his job by killing more enemies of the regime than anyone else.

Franklin was a teacher posted in Kuwait whose family home was a small village in my home county in Illinois. His mother, Mrs.

Evans Franklin, wrote village news for my newspaper in nearby
Pittsfield. He was returning to Kuwait after a holiday in Ethiopia, a
passenger on an aircraft that had engine trouble and made an emergency landing in Aden. While waiting for repairs, he took snapshots
of the airport and harbor. Police mistook him as a spy for Britain, whose diplomats were sent home in the wake of the June 1967
Arab-Israeli Six-Day War.[8]

The rescue mission was my most substantial effort in constituent
service. It proved to be one of the most productive of the many foreign
trips I would take during my years in Congress and since. Apprehen-
sive about going, I asked Alfred Atherton, assistant secretary of state,
what he would do if I were locked up in Aden. His answer, "Look
for another congressman to come get you out." The response was not
reassuring. I would be on my own when I landed, as the U.S. government had no presence in the country since 1967. Lucille was deeply
concerned over my safety but agreed I could hardly refuse to go.

Dr. John Duke Anthony, a specialist at Johns Hopkins University, was one of the few U.S. citizens who had visited Aden in recent
years. He stopped at my office to relate his experiences. To promote
U.S.-Arab understanding, he later organized the National Council
on U.S-Arab Relations, a group that regularly conducts tours of
Arab countries, specializing in leadership groups.

Before I left Washington for Aden, Secretary of State Henry
Kissinger provided a personal letter that proved useful. In it, he welcomed my "humanitarian mission" and added, "Should the occasion arise, you may wish to inform the officials whom you meet of
our continuing commitment to work for an equitable and lasting
Middle East peace and of our desire to strengthen our ties with the
Arab world." By chance, Aden's Foreign Minister Motie was my
seatmate on the flight from Beirut to Aden. Arriving in Aden late at
night, we were met by a cordial group of officials. I was escorted to
a driver and well-worn Chevrolet assigned to me for the balance of
my stay. My quarters were once the residence of the British air commander for the east-of-Aden region.

After spending three long and anxious days meeting with cabinet officials and touring the desolate, arid countryside with a young protocol officer, I prepared for my final appointment, my last hope for Franklin's freedom. It would occur Saturday evening, a long-sought personal meeting with President Ali. As I had received no hint that Franklin would be released, I was braced for bad news.

As we parked near the entrance to the modest building that served as Ali's reception center, I noticed armed guards standing close to several rifles and other military equipment piled by the door. The president greeted me warmly. He was a tall, handsome man. He did not converse in English. The large, sparsely furnished room had no wall on one side. With Ali were Motie and an interpreter.

Ali opened our discussion by mentioning a border dispute with Saudi Arabia. He said the armaments piled outside the door were captured during a skirmish near the border. He said each bore USA markings, suggesting they were supplied to Saudis by the U.S. government. I told Ali I was unaware of the border conflict but I knew Saudis bought some arms from my country. I promised to give a detailed report to the State Department on my return.

He smiled as I presented gifts. He seemed especially pleased to receive my daughter Diane's pottery and the Arabic edition of the Abraham Lincoln biography. He said, "Lincoln is much revered in this country."

When I began to recite my well-rehearsed plea for Franklin's release, to my surprise, Ali interrupted me in mid-sentence. He said, "I have decided to grant your request. When you want him, you may have him." I felt like jumping with joy. My rescue mission would be a success.

After the appointment with Ali, I went to the British embassy, where I suddenly became choked with emotion arising from Ali's unexpected announcement. Regaining composure, I enjoyed dinner with British diplomats, then excused myself to prepare for departure the next morning. Waiting for me in my quarters was Franklin, together with gifts from Ali and other officials. Franklin was thin and haggard from nearly a year of solitary confinement. He was smiling broadly. He thanked me for coming to his rescue: "I'm glad to be out of prison and eager to head for home." He told me he read the Bible daily and sensed that his family was praying for his release. Among the gifts awaiting me were an antique ceremonial dagger and a beautiful oil painting of rural South Yemen from President Ali, and a mounted lobster from Motie.

The next morning Franklin and I took a flight to Beirut. On landing, U.S. diplomat Richard T. Curtiss arranged a news conference where I introduced Franklin and gave details of my experience in Aden. Years later, Curtiss became my close friend and editor of *Washington Report on Middle East Affairs* bimonthly.

The next morning we boarded a flight to New York City. After landing there, Franklin proceeded to St. Louis airport for a joyous reunion with his family, and I flew south to a happy reunion with my family and resumption of duties on Capitol Hill.

In Congress, I urged in conversation and published remarks that U.S. diplomatic relations with Aden and other Arab states be mended after being severed in the wake of the 1967 war. I cited the example of the British who mended their war-prompted break by quickly reopening their diplomatic mission in Aden.

In the next few years, I had several pleasant and constructive visits with Aden officials, two in Aden, one at the United Nations in New York, and another in Washington when Aden's ambassador, Abdulla Ashtal, at my request, visited the House Middle East subcommittee chaired by Lee H. Hamilton of Indiana. I was senior Republican.

In 1979, upbeat from these meetings, I secured a brief meeting with President Carter. He was alone in a small room off the Oval Office. I reviewed my experiences and urged him to send a diplomatic mission to Aden. Carter responded positively, saying, "I will take care of the matter." Several months later he authorized a mission that stopped overnight in Sana'a, capital of North Yemen, expecting to continue to Aden the next morning. Early in the evening, news arrived in Sana'a of a bloody coup pulled off in Aden by a radical Marxist faction. Ali and Motie were captured and immediately executed.

The next morning, Ambassador Ashtal called me with this message: "The change in leadership in Aden is a local decision of no concern to the outside world. The U.S. mission should continue to Aden as planned." I reported his statement to the State Department, but I was not surprised when the mission was canceled. U.S. diplomatic relations were not established with the region popularly called South Yemen until it was later united with North Yemen.

In the years since, I have often wondered if Ali's decision to free Ed Franklin in 1974 led to Ali's execution. During a reception in 2006 sponsored by Islamic leaders in Sharjah, a part of the United Arab Emirates, I received one man's answer. A guest came to me and identified himself as the Yemen official who prepared the official papers releasing Franklin from prison in 1974. Then, with deep feeling, he said, "Why did you come to Aden? You knew that your visit would lead to trouble for President Ali. He was a good man, and your visit killed him." Shocked by the accusation, I responded, "I had no such thought or indication at any time. My sole purpose was to get my constituent free from an unjust imprisonment." Visibly disturbed, my accuser left the reception. I had a troubling question to ponder: did my visit kill the president of South Yemen?

Four years after I first entered the Yemen world, the much wider Arab community seized my attention. While continuing my activities with Yemen, I began an acquaintance that blossomed into warm friendship with Yasser Arafat, chairman of the executive committee of the Palestine Liberation Organization (PLO) and identified by many people at the time as the world's leading terrorist.

My first two meetings with him were in Damascus in 1978, the first in early January. I was a member of a congressional group visiting Middle East states. Spouses also attended. Knowing that Arafat made his base in Damascus, I secured an appointment before leaving Washington. Two of my colleagues were curious to meet the PLO leader. One was Helen Meyner, a New Jersey Democrat. The other, a Republican, agreed to go only after I promised never to mention his participation publicly. He feared constituents would be upset if they knew he met socially with the man believed to be a terrorist.

Security was tight. Our cars were escorted by heavily armed officers. Arafat, short and much more handsome than his photographs suggest, greeted us with a broad smile from the top of the outside stairway that led to his second-floor apartment. Inside the apartment, for nearly four hours he responded to spirited questions about the PLO organization and what it hoped to achieve. I asked most of the questions. My two colleagues seemed hesitant to speak up, perhaps concerned their questions might later be misinterpreted. My Republican colleague was ill at ease.

Arafat was not. He spoke in halting English and at times looked to a colleague to define a word I used. I asked him the precise terms the PLO demanded of Israel. Was he ready to recognize Israel? He said he could not speak beyond words approved by PLO executive council that had already been published, but he added that the PLO wanted a durable peace that would give all Palestinians security and a decent life. At one point, he declared, "I am a freedom fighter. We are fighting for justice for our people." After the discussion, he hosted a bounteous supper, during which he taught Lucille how to fold pita bread and demonstrated how he arranged his traditional headdress to resemble the shape of pre-1948 Palestine. It was a fascinating evening.

I found Arafat candid and willing to be quoted. His perpetually scruffy beard seemed to belie his genial, courteous manner. He looked like an embattled leader who rarely had time to shave. He was a guerrilla fighter and looked the part. His broad, ready grin and laughter were engaging. Although his hands were small, his handshake was warm and firm. He was a good listener. He had a good sense of humor. He never interrupted questioners. He looked straight in my eyes as we talked. If he was corrupt in managing PLO affairs, as critics frequently charged, it was not apparent in his Spartan lifestyle or apparel. At all my meetings with him over a period of twenty-three years, I believe he wore the same threadbare uniform jacket and trousers.

In late November, ten months later, I received word that Arafat wanted further discussion. I boarded a commercial flight for Damascus. At my hotel I was met by Abu Hassan, Arafat's close associate who attended the January discussion. He escorted me to the same apartment where I first met the PLO chief. A few months later Hassan died in a car bombing in Beirut.

During this meeting—it lasted only two hours—Arafat authorized me to report to the White House the PLO terms under which a new Palestine would live at peace with Israel. I was amazed that he gave me this responsibility. I should not have been. All executive branch officials were forbidden even to talk to him on the phone.

As Arafat dictated, I wrote down his words, then read them back slowly several times to make sure they accurately reported his position. I kept asking, "Are you sure this is what you wish to say?" This is the text he approved:

> The PLO will accept a Palestinian state consisting of the West Bank and Gaza, with connecting corridor, and in that circumstance will renounce any and all violent means to enlarge the territory of that state. I would reserve the right, of course, to use nonviolent, that is diplomatic and democratic means, to bring about the eventual unification of all of Palestine. We will give *de facto* recognition to the State of Israel. We will live at peace with all our neighbors. November 30, 1978.

To me, his statement was historic. It was a major advance from positions the PLO had taken on previous public occasions. It impressed me as a solid basis for good-faith negotiations. If accepted by Israel, it could lead to peace without further violence. I believed that any objective observer would view it as a big step in the right direction.

After returning to Washington, I reported Arafat's peace terms during an appointment at the White House with Zbigniew Brzezinski, Carter's national security adviser. I knew him from several joint peace initiatives during the Vietnam War. He listened politely to my report but gave no sign that he considered Arafat's pledge a significant development. As I expected, my initiative brought harsh criticism from several congressional colleagues and from Jewish constituents in Springfield, Illinois. It elicited no response from the White House.

Arafat's pledge was dismissed as worthless by Israeli officials. When I encountered Israel's Labor Party leader Shimon Peres at a White House event a few days later, he declared that Arafat, during an interview on NBC's *Meet the Press*, disputed details of the pledge I had reported. I had watched carefully the same televised interview, and, giving Peres the benefit of all doubts, I knew he was at the least mistaken. I believe he lied.

A few days later the *New York Times* reported a dispatch from Paris that confirmed the accuracy of my recollection of Arafat's appearance on *Meet the Press*. Ibrahim Souss, the PLO representative in France, referring to Arafat's pledge to me, was quoted as saying, "If a Palestinian state existed, the PLO would stop violent attacks against the State of Israel and give it *de facto* recognition." Souss called the statement a "major concession" by the PLO leader.[9] Aside from the brief report in the *Times*, major media paid no attention.

Peres's unwarranted dismissal of my report was, to me, the first evidence that genuine concern for Palestinian human rights never existed among Israeli officials. They did not want good-faith negotiations. Instead, they wanted discussions to proceed inconclusively, affording Israel time to expand its already burgeoning illegal Jewish settlements inside Palestine.

I became convinced Palestinians had legitimate grievances against our government, but these complaints received no official U.S. understanding, much less redress. I also became convinced that a great nation like the United States should establish and maintain, as a matter of self-interest, direct communication with all states and major political entities like the PLO. At the time, I did not comprehend the immensity of Israeli influence on U.S. public policy, but I began to seek commonsense conditions on future U.S. aid to Israel. It was an uphill battle with no victories.

I visited Israel and several Arab states, interviewing leaders and people on the street. In a visit to Gaza, I witnessed firsthand the plight of more than a million Palestinians crowded into what amounted to an open-air prison. I also visited the West Bank where Palestinians were cordoned off behind fences, barbed wire, and checkpoints. I took part in international gatherings where the Middle East conflict was the central theme. All these experiences were depressing.

For years, Israeli officials maintained a policy of no-talk with entities hostile to their objectives. Such groups, like the Palestinians, were called terrorists because they opposed, sometimes violently, Israel's takeover of territory Arabs and their ancestors had claimed as their own for two thousand years. Under international law and United Nations doctrine, such takeovers are unlawful, a crime the U.S. government facilitates by permitting U.S. donations deductible from taxable income to be used to finance settlements.

As the result of pressure by Israel's U.S. supporters, the U.S. government adopted the same no-talk policy, which meant refusing to have any communication with PLO leaders like Arafat. The rule was treated as sacrosanct as one from a deity. The refusal made U.S. officials look juvenile or spineless or both. One evening in 1981, I took part in a nationally televised discussion in Hillsdale, Michigan, on the Israel-Arab conflict. It was hosted by journalist William Buckley with the Reverend Jesse Jackson as his main sparring partner. When my turn to speak arrived, I focused on the no-talk issue. "If Israel is serious about negotiating peace," I said, "it must deal directly with the Palestinian leadership. No one else is waiting in the wings to take the place of Arafat and the PLO." I was given no time to elaborate and headed back to Washington feeling that I had failed to make my argument clear. The next day in the House of

Representatives, Representative Neal Smith of Iowa told me he had watched the debate on television and congratulated me: "Your point was solid. By refusing to talk to Arafat, the undisputed leader of the Palestinians, Israel shows that it doesn't really wish to negotiate a peaceful settlement." Coming from a Democrat with whom I had no previous discussions, Smith's comment surprised and pleased me.

I found myself in a difficult and highly controversial project. I was trying to establish a mutually useful flow of information between Arafat and the U.S. government. I was never an agent, official or otherwise, for either party, but twice I found myself, at the private request of Harold Saunders of the State Department, transmitting official messages to the PLO chief. On both occasions, the U.S. government wanted Arafat to cancel PLO plans to have controversial issues called for debate and vote by the UN Security Council. In these telephoned conversations, I exchanged only a few words directly with Arafat. Most of our words were relayed through Mahmoud Labadi, Arafat's personal assistant, who was fluent in English. Arafat cooperated fully on both requests, issuing instructions to his diplomats at UN headquarters in New York. His cooperation was never acknowledged by the U.S. government. I never misled Arafat, and he never misled me. Labadi, like Abu Hassan, was killed months later in a car bombing in Lebanon.

In March 1978, I joined my Republican colleague, Charles W. Whalen of Ohio, in publicly challenging the legality of Israel's use of U.S.-donated military equipment. In a letter to Secretary of State Cyrus Vance, we stated that Israel, during its invasion of Lebanon, violated the terms of the Arms Export Control Act that prohibits use of U.S.-supplied weapons beyond legitimate self-defense. A month later Vance responded by writing that Israel "may have violated U.S. law." He did not elaborate, and I knew it was pointless to press the issue further.

In a moment of bravery, prompted perhaps by the Findley-Whalen letter, President Carter ordered his ambassador in Israel to warn then–Prime Minister Menachem Begin that if assaults by his forces in Lebanon did not stop, Israel's U.S. aid would be impaired. Begin immediately picked up the phone and ordered a halt in military operations in Lebanon.

Seniority on the Foreign Affairs Committee gave me the top Republican seat on the subcommittee that dealt with the Middle East. This position led to invitations to attend small huddles on public policy, sometimes in the White House with Carter. I met privately several times with President Anwar Sadat of Egypt and with his successor, Hosni Mubarak, and developed a cordial relationship with King Hussein of Jordan during meetings on Capitol Hill and in Amman, Jordan. One day in Washington, Sadat told me in a private conversation that Egypt would "gladly" forego his country's annual gift from Washington, worth over a billion dollars, if the U.S. government would put "serious conditions" on grants to Israel. No such conditions were ever imposed.

During the administrations of Presidents Lyndon B. Johnson and Jimmy Carter, I was occasionally in the White House with other colleagues for discussions of foreign policy. Most of my questions to presidents and their senior advisers warned of the cost to our national interest posed by our government's pro-Israel bias in Middle East policy. Responses were never candid or edifying. In a congressional group discussion with Johnson about Middle East policy, I asked, "What about the Palestinians?" The president did not respond, but James Abourezk, then a Democratic House member, later mentioned the episode and recalled saying to himself, "There is a gutsy guy."

One day a State Department official got huffy during a subcommittee meeting when I suggested scheduling further hearings on the White House request for an annual $2 billion thank-you gift to Israel for signing the Camp David Accords. Why pay Israel big money for doing something it wanted to do in its own interest, I wondered. No colleagues supported my suggestion.

Menachem Begin always impressed me as an arrogant, skillful conniver. During an informal Foreign Affairs Committee discussion,

I addressed him personally. Noting that Israel had returned the Sinai
to Egypt, I asked what further territorial concessions the Israeli
prime minister would accept to establish a durable peace with the
Palestinians. Begin responded by shouting, "We will never, never
surrender one tiny bit of Samaria or Judea [the biblical names of the
Occupied West Bank]."

On concluding the Camp David negotiations that produced
Egypt's peace treaty with Israel, Carter believed the accords included
a firm pledge by Begin for "autonomy" for the Palestinians, a status
Carter considered a major step toward statehood. It proved to be
an empty dream. The Israeli government subsequently blocked all
moves toward Palestinian autonomy or statehood.

My relationship with Carter's special emissary to the Middle
East, Robert Strauss, was cordial and, for a time, close. A charm-
ing man with a super-active pace, he told me he strongly opposed
the U.S. policy of having no direct talk with Palestinians. He said
he would have immediately opened direct discussions with Arafat
if Carter had approved. He added, "I know I could work out in
direct talks most of the difficulties we have with the PLO." Strauss
expressed the hope that I would be a useful bridge of unofficial
communications between him and Arafat.

Among my Arafat souvenirs is a handsome sandalwood statue of
a Palestinian woman bearing a jug. The PLO leader autographed the
base and asked me to deliver the statue to Strauss. When I called to
arrange delivery, Strauss sent word that, much as he wished authority to have direct talks with Arafat and would like the souvenir, he
felt he could not accept it because of the Carter no-talk policy. It
remains in my office.

One day, I encountered strong evidence of lobby influence. The
Foreign Affairs Committee was considering major aid legislation
for Israel, and, as usual, the legislation gave the president no leeway
in its administration. The aid was firmly pledged to Israel alone. I,
a Republican, offered an amendment that would let the president,
Democrat Carter, distribute some of the funds to other Middle East

states if circumstances warranted during the uncertain year that lay ahead. Committee Chairman Clement Zablocki ordered a show of hands on my proposal. I alone voted aye. All others voted no. I viewed the vote as evidence of troubling subservience to Israel's well-being, rather than America's.

The lobby-inspired policy forbidding U.S. administration officials from direct discussions with Palestinian leaders was strictly enforced by President Carter. He fired UN Ambassador Andrew Young, my former colleague in the House, in August 1979 because Young had a brief chat with PLO Ambassador Zedhi Terzi, a Palestinian I knew well. At the time, Terzi was the PLO representative to the UN, and his brief exchange with Young occurred when happenstance put the two of them together on a short ride in a New York City elevator.

The day after the incident, Secretary of State Cyrus Vance invited me to his office at the State Department for an update on my dealings with Palestinians. During our chat, Vance mentioned Young's violation of the no-talk rule. I said the incident seemed to me trivial, unrelated to any official matters, and should be overlooked. Vance said, "No, it is important. Andy has to go." He did not elaborate, but I knew the importance he cited derived from the foolish no-talk pledge that Carter had made to the government of Israel.

During one of my periodic public discussions with district citizens, a constituent questioned my willingness to associate with Arafat, in his words a "person widely considered worse than Genghis Khan." The group seemed satisfied when I explained that I sought only to be a bridge of communication, attempting to help Arafat gain a better understanding of the United States government and, hopefully, also improve American understanding of the Palestinians.

Over the years, I found it almost impossible to have a civilized discussion about Arafat or the PLO anywhere in America. Even today, twenty-six years after my departure from Congress, I find the public perception of Arafat as a terrorist as strong as ever. Recently, a medical technician winced as if in pain when Lucille pulled from her purse a photo showing us having dinner with the PLO chief. Shortly before Arafat's death, when a CNN commentator spoke of his failing health, she added that Arafat continued to sponsor terrorism while rejecting Israeli peace initiatives. She made no mention of Arafat's generous terms for peace, rejected by Israel.

19

◇◇◇◇◇◇◇◇◇◇◇◇◇◇◇◇◇◇◇◇

Confronting AIPAC

My Middle East activities became a central issue early in my 1980 campaign for reelection. Quincy Mayor David Nuessen contested my candidacy for the Republican nomination and was supported, not just by AIPAC, but by national lobbying groups who long had me on their "enemies" list. Fundamentalist Christians were attracted to Nuessen because he was strongly anti-abortion and supportive of Israel. Anti-abortion organizations opposed my nomination, even after the primary when State Representative David Robinson, the Democratic nominee, emerged as sympathetic to abortions.

Picketers displayed signs in the federal courtroom in Springfield where I was conducting a "town meeting." One sign accused me of murdering babies.[10] Two days later in Alton, anti-abortion protests interrupted me several times in mid-sentence. I never endorsed abortions, but I was convinced there are wrenching human dilemmas in which the procedure should be permitted. For that reason, I opposed sweeping prohibitions by law or constitutional amendment and thus incurred the opposition of well-funded groups.

Abortion and Arafat were the most popular targets of groups opposing me. Rev. Jerry Falwell, a popular TV evangelist, headed an organization called the Moral Majority that rated the voting record of members of Congress based on Falwell's definition of morality. My voting record put me, like my Republican colleague

John Buchanan of Alabama, a respected, ordained Baptist minister, in Falwell's not-so-moral minority.

My demand in 1979 for an investigation of the operations and profligate spending of Cotton, Inc., headed by J. Duke Wooters, prompted him to urge cotton growers to contribute to Nuessen's primary campaign. A U.S. Department of Agriculture official listened to a tape of Wooters's speech to assembled growers and concluded that this appeal for campaign financial aid to Nuessen might violate legislation under which Cotton, Inc., was established. This led to an investigation of the organization by the department's inspector general. A Commodity News Service report stated that the investigation would determine whether Wooters was linked to "extensive campaign contributions to Nuessen by California cotton growers."[11] Once Election Day arrived, the investigation stopped. I did not bother to ask why. Other more important issues were pressing.

Earlier that year, the postal service delivered a dress shirt from Cotton, Inc., that Lucille praised as "gorgeous." I mailed it back, not wishing to be obligated in any way to the organization. I was the target of fierce passions that political disputes sometimes yield. While on Capitol Hill, I received several explicit written death threats.

Wishing to be helpful in my campaign, President Anwar Sadat of Egypt taped a statement praising my work in Congress. Late in the campaign, I received a letter from Arafat in which he wrote: "Your adversary, David Nuessen, tries to defame you because of your relations with us. But God will always be with you, because you are dedicated to a cause of justice." Both messages were acknowledged with appreciation but not mentioned publicly.

My early support for Republican presidential candidates George H. W. Bush, who was then Reagan's chief challenger for the nomination, and later John B. Anderson, my Illinois colleague, displeased fervent supporters of the California governor. When Anderson left the Republican Party and became an independent candidate, I withdrew my support of his candidacy, but it got little attention.

My name appeared twice on the 1980 primary ballot. While being nominated as the 20th District Republican candidate for Congress, I was also elected delegate to the Republican Presidential Nominating Convention.

When the primary votes were counted, I was renominated by an uncomfortably snug 55 percent. After I won both positions in the primary, I announced I would support Reagan at the nominating convention. Voters on primary day overwhelmingly supported him and, besides, I believed he could defeat Democrat Jimmy Carter in November.

The fact that little-known Nuessen, in only three months of campaigning, received 45 percent of the votes both districtwide and in the Jacksonville area was a strong signal of trouble ahead. Those voting for Nuessen, in my view, did so mainly as a warning to me. The mayor carried his home county of Adams and nearly topped me in the district's largest county, Sangamon, where Republican leadership decided to withhold its customary support. According to the *St. Louis Globe-Democrat*, "Conservatives voted for Nuessen to send Findley a message that he was getting too liberal." It was an unprecedented sign of dissent that could be attributed to several issues beyond my dealings with Arafat. Early in my career, Congress approved a series of proposals for unprecedented federal authority—realms previously left to states. I opposed most of these groundbreaking decisions. But once a proposed new federal authority became the law of the land, I used my vote, where possible, to influence its scope and content. Some conservatives believed I should maintain my opposition to each such measure, despite the fact that, in effect, the legislative train had left the station.

Not all publicity was negative. My notoriety prompted Mike Robinson, an Associated Press reporter in Washington, to emphasize the modesty of our home-away-from-home in a Washington suburb. It resulted in a widely published report that accurately portrayed our unpretentious lifestyle: "[Findley] lives in suburban Falls Church, Va., in a brick bungalow with an aluminum awning over the door, potted petunias on the porch, and crabgrass in the lawn. Findley drives a 1968 Buick."[12]

In early May, the Lincoln Academy of Illinois, a prestigious group headed by Illinois Governor Thompson, elected me a Lincoln Laureate.[13] Months earlier, the Federal Republic of Germany presented me with its highest civilian award, the Commanders Cross, Order of Merit, commemorating my efforts to strengthen the role of Germany in the Atlantic Assembly, an affiliate of the NATO organization. Extended amid campaign turmoil, these honors were gratifying.

Dr. Edward Ragsdale of Alton, Republican chairman of Madison County and a leader in anti-abortion activities, openly backed Nuessen in the primary. He told the *Globe-Democrat* that if my announced support for the candidacy of Ronald Reagan proved to be a "gimmick," his forces would make sure that Nuessen would defeat me in the primary two years later.

After my narrow win, Nuessen called with his congratulations and offered to help me win the general election in November. He told reporters he was for me "one hundred percent."[14] Years later, chuckling, he told me that his mother was upset when she learned of his decision to contest me in the primary.

In July, we were unpacking our suitcases in the Detroit hotel for Illinois delegates for the Republican National Nominating Convention when we heard loud chanting from the lobby below. "Paul, Paul, he must go, he supports the PLO." With the primary election over, State Representative David Robinson, selected by Democrats as my opponent in November voting, arranged for college students to promote his cause even at the Republican convention. Their activities started with the demonstration inside the hotel lobby and a few harassing telephone calls to our room.

At the time, we were unaware of two other anti-Findley protests outside the hotel earlier the same day. The *Journal-Courier* in Jacksonville reported, "About a dozen Jewish women picketed the entrance to the hotel for a couple of hours two different times to protest Findley's pro-PLO stand. 'We will work to defeat this friend of the PLO,' the picketers told delegates as they entered and left the hotel.' The protesters identified themselves as members of the Zionist Organization of the United States."[15]

Fundraising advertisements on behalf of Robinson appeared in Jewish newspapers nationwide. They described me as a "practicing anti-Semite who is one of the worst enemies Jews and Israel have ever faced in the history of the U.S. Congress." This reckless charge reflected Israel's new definition that decried any criticism of the Jewish state as an expression of anti-Semitism.

The advertising worked well for Robinson's campaign bank account. Official reports showed that he received contributions from every state in the union. The advertising may have been a factor in the decisions of entertainer Bob Hope and former President Ford to withdraw from commitments to speak at campaign events on my behalf. In explaining their decisions, both cited the notoriety over my meetings with Arafat.

Hope's withdrawal occurred after the sellout of tickets to a Springfield luncheon where he was scheduled to speak. I offered ticket refunds, but none was requested. On short notice, my Republican colleague, Guy Vander Jagt of Michigan, filled in for Hope. A powerful speaker, he wowed the crowd with his oratory and prodigious memory.

Faced with an aggressive campaign heavily financed by what I believed were mainly Zionist supporters of Israel, I tried to turn this reality to my advantage. As proof that Robinson was being financed by people residing outside my district, I had my campaign organization print and distribute five thousand copies of Robinson's lengthy official document that gave details of receipts by his campaign committee, including each donor's name, address, and the amount contributed. Only a few donors resided within the congressional district that I represented. The document was well read.

Senator Charles Percy, then chairman of the Foreign Relations Committee, intervened successfully on my behalf to keep *Playboy* magazine from publishing my picture shaking hands with a woman who was also displayed on the same page in nude postures. California colleague Jerry Lewis informed me of the plan after overhearing a discussion at a restaurant the night before. Grateful for the tip but upset at the plan, I recalled being photographed a month earlier with a woman I had never met.

A congressional staff photographer I knew, trusted, and may have been tricked, asked me to pose with the woman, explaining only that a famous Japanese photographer wanted it for a magazine feature on women in lobbying. I agreed, never suspecting that the photograph would be published amid nudes. It would be embarrassing, so I quickly tried to stop publication. Aware that Percy was a friend of *Playboy* owner Hugh Hefner, I went immediately to the senator's Capitol Hill office. Luckily finding Percy at his desk, I explained my plight and asked if he would intervene with Hefner.

As I listened, Percy telephoned *Playboy* headquarters. Told that Hefner could not be reached immediately, the senator asked for Hefner's chief assistant. He explained my problem and asked him to prevent publication of my picture. When informed the issue of *Playboy* was already being printed, Percy said, "I know Mr. Hefner would not want to embarrass Congressman Findley, who supports progressive legislation and is in a challenging campaign. I want you to stop the presses, destroy any copies already printed, and remake the page without Congressman Findley's photograph. Let me know the cost of these changes. I will pay them in full." Hefner's assistant agreed to remake the page. I was surprised at his agreement and amazed at Percy's offer, as it could entail thousands of dollars. Even for a wealthy man like Percy, it was a remarkable commitment. When published, the page had only photographs of the lady minus clothing. I verified the change personally, although the magazine is not on my reading—or viewing—list. I read other periodicals to keep abreast of the news, so to speak. A year later, I asked Percy if he received a bill. He answered in one word: no.

The campaign made me realize as never before the political strength of the American Israel Public Affairs Committee (AIPAC).

It is a smooth functioning, efficient organization staffed by committed professionals who know the right buttons to tap—and when. It has a network of volunteers in almost every congressional district in the nation who respond quickly and skillfully to each call for help, whether it be pending legislation or a political campaign crisis. One of them, Dr. Ralph Nurnberger, became a close friend. He never tried to mislead me. AIPAC leadership was not always forthcoming. It claimed it did not take part in campaigns, but one of its staff members told me it devoted 75 percent of its resources in defeating Senator Percy's bid for reelection in 1984. Two years earlier, AIPAC director Thomas Dine openly claimed credit for my defeat. The organization's resource investment that year may have been 100 percent. Although AIPAC clearly exists for the sole purpose of supporting legislatively the State of Israel, a federal court, after lengthy delays, finally determined in 2010 that the organization's reason for being is not a foreign nation. Therefore, AIPAC need not publicly disclose information about its donors.

Beginning with Johnson's administration, all presidents have avoided a serious showdown with Israel's lobby, and Congress has done its bidding. For years I was virtually alone as a sustained critic on Capitol Hill of Israeli misbehavior. Periodically I received a word or two of whispered praise and encouragement from colleagues but rarely open support, except for Republican Paul "Pete" McCloskey of California, who spoke out forcefully. It was a lonely role—a sharp contrast with earlier years when Findley amendments won strong support across party lines. The people of the United States and their government were subservient to the will of the Israeli government. They still are, but this domination is rarely mentioned in public.

In late September 1980, Democratic candidate David Robinson and I squared off in a debate—the only one of the campaign—before a capacity crowd in the chapel on the Illinois College campus in Jacksonville. By then, Robinson's status as a conscientious objector to military service had surfaced, and the Vietnam War was still vivid in public memory. To qualify as a conscientious objector, he had to declare his opposition to military service in any war, not just the one in Vietnam. Instead of responding to the military draft for noncombat duty, Robinson requested and received permission to perform "alternative public service" in Illinois.

As I pondered what to say in the debate, I remembered that not all conscientious objectors are the same. I knew a young man named Mike Bischoff was a conscientious objector but he served in Vietnam as an unarmed medic. He frequently worked under hostile fire in rice paddies, perhaps risking his life more often than armed troops. Sharing the platform with Robinson, I said, "I know admirable people who are pacifists, and I defend the fundamental right of citizens to be conscientious objectors. But I ask Mr. Robinson and all of you here tonight to consider what would likely have happened in World War II if all Americans were conscientious objectors. When France and the Low Countries fell to Hitler's forces, could England have survived alone? With the United States unable to field an army, would Hitler have massacred all Jews in Europe, not just part of them, along with a lot of other innocent people? Remember, we know not what crises may arise in the future. How do you wish to be represented in Congress on war issues?" Robinson did not respond. I did not mention the subject again.

The chore of raising campaign funds—a task I never enjoyed—and seeking election-day votes took much of my time. I was glad when Election Day arrived. I defeated Robinson by a margin of 3 percent of votes cast, my tightest in years. My son Craig became a member of the Illinois General Assembly by a comfortable plurality, but political clouds on the horizon soon darkened for us both.

As I entered the reception area of my office on Capitol Hill one morning in late 1981, my assistant, Bob Wichser, gave me unsettling news. The long-delayed realignment of Illinois congressional districts was settled to my disadvantage. When he finished providing the details my only comment was, "That means trouble." I retreated to my private office and closed the door.

Continuing a trend of several decades, the new census found Illinois population lagging behind the national growth. Illinois would lose one more member in the House of Representatives. Under federal law, the state legislature, where my son Craig served, faced the chore of remaking congressional district boundaries, as well as changes in state legislative districts. After much wrangling, the legislature adjourned without reaching a decision on congressional district lines, leaving the final choice to a panel of three federal judges. Among three maps left pending when the legislature adjourned, the panel chose the one least advantageous to me. I lost all of Republican Morgan and Scott counties, and one-half of Sangamon County. Morgan was the most serious loss. It was where I'd been born and always received a strong bipartisan vote in each general election. The new district borders encompassed half of Democratic Macon County and all of largely Democratic Christian, Moultrie, and Shelby counties. Still worse, the realignment occurred at a time of economic recession, usually disadvantageous to the party controlling the White House, in this case Republican Ronald Reagan. Heavy industries in Sangamon and Macon Counties were hit hard. Large Fiat-Allis and Caterpillar plants were hurt by a U.S. embargo on trade with the Soviet Union and a general turndown in orders. Unemployment was rising in most communities, and farm commodity prices were down. The one bright spot was the absence of competition in the 1982 primary.

Democrats chose experienced politician Richard Durbin as my Democratic opponent. He was long active in politics and a close associate of ever-popular U.S. Representative Paul Simon, a Democrat widely and deservedly applauded as "Mr. Clean." Durbin had nearly defeated popular Republican State Senator John Davidson in a recent election, and narrowly lost a bid for election as lieutenant governor. Unlike Robinson, he was not controversial. He was a natural choice for Democrats to select as my campaign opponent. The Republican National Committee, controlled of course by President Reagan, supported my candidacy. He sent a letter describing me as "distinguished" and citing my "important leadership."[16]

Our contest attracted major media. The Associated Press, in a national news report on pro-Israel political action committee (PAC) donations to the Durbin campaign, announced that the total amount he received from these PACs by the end of August 1982 reached the historic high of $112,000. The leader of one PAC, who asked the AP to withhold his name, said flatly, "I hate Paul Findley." The reporter noted a penchant for sponsor concealment among the many political action committees that existed solely to advance the interests of the Jewish state: "The titles of most of the pro-Israel PACs do not mention Israel or anything related to it." He quoted my response to critics who derided me as hostile to Israel's existence: "Findley says he favors a U.S. guarantee of Israel's borders and insists his program would bring peace to the Mideast."[17]

Both of us received endorsements from party "heavy hitters." Republican Vice President George H. W. Bush and his wife Barbara, brushing aside pro-Israel protests from Texas, attended a successful fund-raising luncheon on my behalf in Springfield. Mrs. Bush stood next to me in the reception line and whispered that she and the vice president were glad to have me join the "grip and grin" circuit. Democrat and former Vice President Walter Mondale and Senators John Glenn and Ted Kennedy, all Democrats, showed up for Durbin. I had maintained cordial terms with Kennedy through the years and left a welcoming note for him at the Holiday Inn East in Springfield where we were both staying. Before leaving town, he responded with a warm handwritten note "wishing me well."

When I visited Jacksonville—no longer in my district—in early 1982 to attend a community celebration in my honor, an unsigned letter from Quincy contained a threat on my life. It led Jacksonville police to insist I wear a bulletproof vest during the event. The letter included these words, "I was in a tavern and heard some men making plans. They were hoods for certain and not drunk but drinking enough to throw caution to the winds. . . . These men sometime in the future are going to shoot you. . . . What they have planned for your families is unprintable." During the celebration I wore the vest, and events proceeded without disturbance.

AP reporter Mike Robinson, writing from Washington, provided this campaign appraisal: "[Findley's] reputation for honesty is untarnished after 20 years in the House," adding that my race with Durbin "shapes into one of the most heated in the nation."[18] The *Chicago Tribune* reported, "The race is one of four targeted by national Democrats which could swing from a Republican to a Democrat." It characterized my new district as 55 percent Democratic.[19]

The scrapbook my staff compiled is filled with clippings about my various 1982 activities and comments on both agricultural and foreign policy. Almost every published comment attributed to me was followed by a headlined dissent from my opponent. When election day arrived, victor and vanquished spent about $600,000 each, again setting an all-time record for Illinois congressional campaigns. My opponent hit hard late in the campaign. This prompted Bill Carl, my friend and permanent chairman of the Findley-for-Congress committee, to observe, "I can remember when you were nothing but a hero."

When the unofficial vote count was completed in the early morning after the polls closed, the totals showed me on the short end by 1,407 votes—less than 1 percent of the nearly 200,000 cast. I was dead tired and, realizing the contest was lost, headed straight for bed.

With a bit more energy, I would have gone to my campaign headquarters in Springfield to thank any supporters still gathered there and to telephone congratulations to the congressman-elect. I would like to have repeated, with a broad smile, the message of U.S. Representative Morris Udall of Arizona when he told news media he was dropping out of the Democratic presidential nomination race in 1976: "The people have spoken, the stupid bastards." Early the next morning, Diane and I stopped by Durbin's headquarters where I tucked a written note of congratulations under the locked door.

Two days later former colleague Graham Purcell, a Democrat from Texas, was waiting with members of my Capitol Hill staff at National Airport (now Reagan National) when Lucille and I arrived. Purcell and I had become good friends during our days together on the House Agriculture Committee. He brought smiles when he identified himself as the self-appointed undertaker to members of Congress defeated for reelection.

My defeat was a milestone in regional partisan history. Durbin's win marked the first time a Democrat occupied the Illinois 20th congressional district seat in forty years. It became Republican in 1942 when Sid Simpson, an automobile dealer in Carrollton, Illinois, defeated the bid of Democrat U.S. Representative James M. Barnes of Jacksonville for reelection. Barnes won the seat left open by the death of Democratic House Speaker Henry T. Rainey, also of Carrollton, a representative for most of thirty years.

Although upset with myself for failing to win a twelfth term, I soon found exciting challenges. A new door opened that gave me opportunities I would never have had if I remained in Congress. Back on Capitol Hill for a post-election day legislative session, a page summoned me to a phone in the Republican cloakroom. Waiting on the line was a veteran activist I had known and admired throughout my years on Capitol Hill. He urged me to write a book about Israel's U.S. lobby and suggested the title, *They Dare to Speak Out*. His only request was that I keep his name out of the text. He recommended that I meet soon with Professor Hisham Sharabi of Georgetown University, whom I had long admired as a leading spokesman for Arab American human rights. Soon after meeting the professor, I received a grant from the Middle East Peace Research Institute in Boston that helped me meet some of my expenses in researching and writing the book manuscript.

20

A New Door Opens

Suddenly, I learned that my personal bank account would receive a welcome additional boost. A flurry of donations, most of them one thousand dollars each, arrived at my campaign postal box, too late, sadly, to be useful in the campaign strategy. They totaled over thirty thousand dollars. All were from people in Texas and Mississippi who were, I assumed, employed by a construction firm doing business in the Middle East. None acted on my offer to return the checks, so I deposited them in a public service account bearing my name, drawing from it periodically to cover research expenses during my book project.

Information about my new account was easily accessible to the general public. This meant that it could come to the attention of some two thousand political action committees. At that time, the transfer from my fund to other similar accounts was authorized by law, and such transfers frequently occurred. It was noteworthy that none of these committees asked me for funds. I assume that none wanted to be known as benefiting from a former member of Congress well known as a critic of Israel.

I stayed in Washington, because most sources for my book lived there. As soon as I finished the text, Lucille and I sold our small bungalow in Falls Church, Virginia, and headed for a new residence in Jacksonville, Illinois, the heart of Findley Country as my posters identified it. One morning in the summer of 1983, while busy working on my book in a small office I rented in downtown Washington, I received a phone call from Harold Saunders, a former State Department diplomat. During the period I was viewed as Arafat's best friend in Congress, Saunders occasionally gave me, very privately, troubleshooting assignments with the PLO chief. This time Saunders, by then retired from government service, was at a desk at the American Enterprise Institute located near my office in downtown Washington. He was drafting a study of Middle East issues. For months he had been a principal source of inside information that would make my book-in-progress a bestseller. Like dozens of other sources, he agreed to be interviewed provided I not cite him as the source of specific data.

Saunders knew of my deep disappointment in failing to reform the costly pro-Israel bias in U.S. Middle East policy. Usually strictly business, this time he started our chat with an out-of-character, sentimental comment: "I can look out the window by my desk and see the small building on New York Avenue where I know you are working at the lonely task of writing a book about Israel's lobby."

It was indeed a task. Putting it together required all of 1983 and the first seven months of 1984, an unbroken stream of weeks that consisted of six workdays each. But it was not as lonely as Saunders might believe, because each of the more than one hundred people I called for information cooperated fully and thanked me for undertaking the project. Most people like to see their name in any book, but about half of my sources insisted on anonymity. Even the two excellent graduate students who helped me that summer insisted that I not divulge their identity. One of them has since climbed high on the ladder of diplomatic service. I understood their concern, as I had already experienced the ability of pro-Israel zealots to take aggressive action against critics of the Jewish state.

In fact, I had some concern about my own personal safety, as well as for the security of my research materials. As if to give credence to my concern, a bomb killed Alex Odeh as he entered the Los Angeles office of the American Arab Anti-Discrimination Committee the day after he publicly expressed sympathy for the plight of Palestinians. No violence related to my book project occurred, but security remained a concern. When a wallet was stolen from my office in broad daylight, I decided to keep copies of manuscript segments stored in the attic of our residence in Falls Church, Virginia.

During the summer of 1983, I interviewed I. F. "Izzy" Stone, the celebrated Jewish author and commentator. He provided a fascinating review of his own journalistic encounters with pro-Israel zealots over the years. I offered to meet him at his home for the interview, but he insisted my office—twenty blocks distant—was his usual distance on a morning walk. When he arrived, he spoke favorably about several of my legislative projects but expressed concern that a book on Israel's lobby by a former member of Congress might provoke anti-Semitism. He urged instead that I write a memoir on my own life and suggested I call it "Internationalist from the Corn Belt." I assured him I would write only about what the lobby actually did and use adjectives and adverbs sparingly. A slight man with thick eyeglasses and passion in his words, Stone sipped on a paper cup of tea as we talked.

My final major chore in 1984 was cutting the manuscript by more than one hundred typed pages. That done, I sent a copy to foreign correspondent Donald Neff, long a Middle East reporter for *Time* magazine and author of three books on Israel's wars with Arabs. On a long flight to Lebanon, Neff edited my entire manuscript. I sent another copy to Thomas Dine, director of the American Israel Public Affairs Committee, asking him to notify me of any errors he found in my text. He did not respond but unwittingly helped me greatly by having staff members comb the text for flaws. Luckily, I secured a copy of their detailed critique in time to make the manuscript error-free.

Meanwhile, I was sending book outlines and sample chapters to prospective publishers. More than twenty major firms rejected my submissions. Three of them explained candidly that my text was so controversial that publishing it would cause costly discord within their staffs and among traditional customers.

In a personal interview, one of the three, son of Arab immigrants, spoke with great passion about my book's importance. At one point, he dropped to his knees and beat the rug with his fists as he said, "It must be published somehow, but I simply cannot afford to be the one to do it." His passion may have been prompted partially by remorse. Planning a career as a book publisher, he changed his Arabic name to an Anglo-Saxon one, a step that he said helped business. Predicting accurately than no major publisher would handle my book, veteran literary agent Alexander Wylie of New York wrote, "It's a sad state of affairs."

One morning, good news arrived. Lawrence Hill, the owner of a small firm in Westport, Connecticut, offered to publish my book. When I accepted his offer, I asked him why he decided to "walk where others feared to tread." He said that he and his wife, a Jew, were both critical of Zionism and concluded that my book presented "an important issue in free speech." To my surprise, my book *They Dare to Speak Out: People and Institutions Confront Israel's Lobby* was reviewed prominently in the *Washington Post*, the *Christian Science Monitor*, and forty-eight other newspapers. It was reviewed as being "first class," "straightforward and valid," "undeniably impressive," "resolutely fair-minded," "responsible," and "thoughtful."[20]

Once Lawrence Hill began marketing it, the American Arab Anti-Discrimination Committee (ADC), chaired by former Senator James Abourezk and directed by Omar Kader, contracted with a New York City firm, Peggy Raub Publications, to organize a nationwide publicity tour for me. It began in April 1985 and continued for more than a year. ADC members and other individuals helped promote sales by calling bookstores nationally to inquire when copies of my book would be available. Arab organizations and individuals, some domestic and others abroad, made bulk purchases for complimentary distribution to U.S. opinion-makers and public libraries. My former colleague Pete McCloskey and his wife, Helen, were so pleased with my book they personally left copies on consignment at a number of bookstores in California.

Tahseen Khayat, owner of a leading publishing business in Beirut, arranged publication and distribution of *They Dare to Speak Out* in Arabic, as well as the serialization of its entire text in five leading Arabic dailies in the Middle East. I learned that Crown Prince Fahd of Saudi Arabia, later elevated to the monarchy, looked forward to each Arabic installment published in a Riyadh newspaper. President Hosni Mubarak of Egypt told me, with a smile, that he read *They Dare to Speak Out* from beginning to end in one long night. Years later, Jordan's King Abdullah II informed me that his father, King Hussein, summoned him from his U.S. university studies one day, handed him a copy of my book, and instructed him to read it carefully.

Khayat arranged the translation and serialization of two other books I wrote, *Deliberate Deceptions: Facing the Facts About the U.S.-Israel Relationship*, published in 1993, and *Silent No More: Confronting America's False Images of Islam*, marketed in 2001. His sister Bushra, owner of a bookstore in Abu Dhabi, was a helpful companion of the Findleys during several visits to the United Arab Emirates. *They Dare to Speak Out* was also published in German, Indonesian, Urdu, Farsi, and Malaysian editions. Saeed Butt, a retired Pakistani government official who read the English edition of *They Dare to Speak Out,* sponsored at personal expense the translation and publication of two thousand copies of an Urdu edition, then one thousand copies each of my two more recent books, also in Urdu. Only a few copies remained unsold in 2008. In July 2008, Butt reported that twenty-five thousand copies of an English edition of *They Dare to Speak Out*—he called it "pirated'—had been printed in New Delhi, India. It was followed, he wrote, by a second printing of "more than a few thousand." Foreign editions and additional printings of the original English edition brought total sales of the book to more than 325,000, a remarkable total for a nonfiction book. It was listed for seven weeks on the *Washington Post* best-seller list and was Lawrence Hill's most successful publication.

The high point of the publicity tour was my appearance on the NBC *Today Show*. Just before the show began, I asked Bryant Gumbel if I could mention a toll-free number where my book could be purchased. He responded, with a smile, "I can't stop you." So I slowly stated the number. In the days that followed, the phone rang constantly and several thousand books were sold.

During several television interviews, including my *Today Show* appearance, pro-Israel activists successfully demanded that broadcast time devoted to my book be shared by a pro-Israel critic. I addressed a number of audiences arranged by the ADC, the National Association of Arab Americans, and the Arab American Institute. I also spoke at numerous colleges. Each event was unique in setting and personalities. Anti-Findley picketing occurred at several stops. During the question period at one university, I was loudly identified as "the new Hitler."

While at home midway through my speaking schedule, a caller asked a question about my views on Middle East policy. When I paused in responding, he said, "That's enough. All I wanted was to hear what a slimy scum-ball sounds like." I became accustomed to such attacks and had no trouble putting them out of mind.

Most meetings were constructive and energizing. On our first visit to Dubai, United Arab Emirates, in 1986, I began lasting friendships with Wasfi and Linda Ataya, who hosted a supper in their residence. It was served in a tent on their spacious lawn. A giant, lonely tree topped with a playhouse for their young children and ablaze in multicolored lights was a major attraction. During the supper, I met two businessmen who became cherished, lifetime friends, Khalaf al Habtoor and Easa Al Gurg. Both were already prominent in Dubai's amazing business and cultural growth. Al Gurg, although not of royal blood, would soon become the long-serving dean of Arab diplomacy in London as ambassador of the United Arab Emirates. Al Habtoor already had underway a group of luxury hotels and other companies and had founded several schools and major international sports events. Among investments in higher education, he endowed a leadership center at Illinois College, where my papers and mementoes will be among those permanently lodged.

Within weeks of the publication of *They Dare to Speak Out,* my desk was piled high with letters from every state, twelve hundred letters in all. All were personal messages from readers disturbed by revelations in my book. All asked what they could do to help remove the costly pro-Israel bias in U.S. Middle East policy. Some were lengthy, anguished pleas, others were brief but sincere requests for guidance.

This correspondence prompted me to ponder what I could do beyond writing books and lecturing, and what I could recommend to those asking for advice. At the time, the largest and most active membership organizations dealing with Middle East issues were designed mainly to serve Arab Americans or U.S. Muslims. I knew that many critics of U.S. policy in the Middle East were non-Arab Christians like myself, and a number of Jews who considered U.S. policy reform in that region highly urgent. It occurred to me that such people would welcome membership in an organization with no ethnic or religious focus.

After consulting with friends with long experience in Middle East policy matters, notably Ambassador Andrew Killgore, retired foreign service officer Richard Curtiss, scholar John Duke Anthony, author Grace Halsell, and former colleague Pete McCloskey, I decided to start an advocacy group based in Washington, D.C. It would be committed to justice in the Middle East and bias-free policies in that region. It would be called the Council for the National Interest (CNI).

On Lawrence Hill's death in 1988, the Lawrence Hill imprint was purchased by Chicago Review Press/Independent Publishers Group in negotiation with Hill's associate publisher Shirley Cloyes.

In March 1990, during a visit to Saudi Arabia with our son Craig, I accepted a proposal from Sheikh Ahmad Salah Jamjoom, director general of *Al Madina* daily newspaper in Jeddah. He invited me to write a weekly column for publication in his Arabic language newspaper, as well as in an English language newspaper, the *Saudi Gazette*, published in Riyadh. Over a nine-year period, I wrote more than four hundred articles, each captioned, "Speaking Out." Through them, I attempted to convey understanding of America's political process and the influence of Israel's lobby in the making of U.S. Middle East policy.

In 1992, while continuing to write the weekly columns, I decided a sequel to *They Dare to Speak Out* might rally additional support to a worthy cause. That summer I wrote *Deliberate Deceptions: Facing the Facts About the U.S.-Israeli Relationship*, published by Shirley Cloyes, then publisher of Lawrence Hill Books. It is a reference book that separates fact from fiction. It presents each of the primary examples of mythology circulated as the truth by Israel's U.S. lobby and demolishes each by direct quotations from Israel officials or prominent U.S. Jews. In composing the text, I had major help from Donald Neff, the historian-journalist who had edited the manuscript of *They Dare to Speak Out*. Neff's comprehensive compilation of Middle East data dismissed each bit of mythology. The copyright to *Deliberate Deceptions* is now owned by the *Washington Report on Middle East Affairs*.

In 1993, immediately after the signing ceremony on the White House lawn with its famous handshake between Middle East leaders Yasser Arafat and Yitzhak Rabin, the PLO leader entered the White House for the first time. He was one of President Carter's guests of honor at a formal reception, the first such experience for the PLO chief. By this invitation, Carter effectively released U.S. officials from the no-talk rule.

I attended the outdoor ceremony but feared it was mainly a photo-op event organized by Rahm Emanuel, then an adviser to Bill Clinton and later Barack Obama's chief of staff. It led only to endless, inconclusive negotiations but at least produced a widely publicized handshake and gave Arafat a long-deserved measure of dignified recognition.

Hours later, the PLO chief invited several people, including former UN Ambassador Young and me, to his hotel suite where we had a jovial, upbeat discussion. He expressed hope the signed document would be a step toward peace. My book on U.S. Muslims, *Silent No More*, had just arrived in bookstores, and Arafat granted my request for a picture of him holding a copy. Without glancing down at the book, the PLO chief posed, holding it upside down. The photographer waited until Arafat turned it right side up. He laughed heartily at the misstep, then warmly greeted former UN Ambassador Young, by then a consultant in foreign trade, saying he hoped that this meeting would not, like Young's earlier encounter with a PLO official, threaten the former ambassador's employment.

After leaving Congress, I met with Arafat four more times. The first two were in Baghdad, during a period when the U.S. government was assisting Saddam Hussein, the Iraqi dictator, in his war with Iran. Both times we were warmly welcomed to quarters provided to the PLO chief by the Iraqi government. I had not been with him for several years, and on the first occasion he provided an upbeat report on prospects for peace. He said, as commander in chief of PLO military units, he had developed a system for smooth round-the-clock communication.

During our chat, we were all startled by a loud pop. It proved to be a defective lightbulb that shattered. I was in Damascus to address a gathering of the diplomats and foreign service officers arranged by Nizar Hamdoom, whom I met when he was Iraqi ambassador to the United States. During our second chat, even briefer than the first, Arafat presented Lucille with a handsome jacket fashioned by Palestinian artists. We were in Baghdad for the opening of the reconstructed Babylonian theater.

Another meeting with Arafat occurred in 2000 in a New York City hotel. After a dinner program observing the fiftieth anniversary of the United Nations, Arafat came to the distant table where I was seated. He embraced me, then took my hand and escorted me to his hotel suite for a discussion of peace prospects and plans at Bethlehem for the two thousandth anniversary of Christ's birth. When we entered, he lamented Israeli housing that nearly surrounded Bethlehem. He said he wanted me to attend the celebration early the next year and offered to make arrangements, an invitation I later had to decline. At one point, clearly exhausted, he sat silently with his eyes closed for several minutes. He was not the bubbling Arafat I had known at earlier meetings.

Our last meeting was in Jericho, Palestine, in the summer of 2003, when we accompanied a group of young leaders on a tour of the Occupied Territories. Jericho was our final stop. Our group had participated in a UN-sponsored conference in Amman. In the assembly hall of his modest headquarters, Arafat responded to questions while seated. Several times, he signaled to a colleague to respond. Sitting next to him, I noticed that his legs and lips trembled constantly. When the program ended, he walked quickly to an adjoining room. Unlike our other meetings, there was no private discussion. He was a tired, sick man.

In 1974, when I addressed a United Nations conference in Geneva, the audience included Dr. Ahmed Shuga'a, chairman of the Department of Arts and Sciences at Yemen's bustling Sana'a University. When I finished, Dr. Shuga'a came to the rostrum and asked me to lecture in Sana'a. I agreed and the next April I spoke to an audience in Sana'a University. By then the two Yemens, North and South, were united with Sana'a as the capital. In my remarks, I tried to explain why the United States, a superpower, was, in effect, financing Israel's abuse of Arabs. I wondered how many people in the Yemen audience believed a superpower of 280 million citizens could be manipulated by zealots for Israel, a small state of only six million. I was a curiosity, and so were the U.S. Middle East policies I criticized.

In October 1997, Shuga'a sent word that the University of Sana'a had approved an honorary doctorate degree for me, the university's first such recognition of a foreigner. My family and I visited Sana'a a month later for the presentation ceremony. After an overnight stay at the venerable Queen of Sheba Hotel, Shuga'a escorted us to the auditorium building where his colleagues had erected welcoming signs in English on large sheets of canvas. Government and university officials, together with several foreign diplomats, attended. Special guests, including the Findleys, were garbed in the distinctive green academic robes of the university. Mine, a treasured item, now decorates my office door. After the ceremony, we were taken by automobile to Taiz and Aden, where I was scheduled to address other groups. Highway flooding delayed our arrival in Taiz by an hour, but on arrival we found the large lecture hall still filled. At Aden, a local citizen told me he recalled my first visit to South Yemen. In March 1999, I ceased writing weekly articles for publication in Arab states so I could give full attention to completing a book on U.S. Muslims.

In 2007 my warnings about the harmful impact of Israel's U.S. lobby on American society gained heightened credibility with the publication of the bestselling book *The Israel Lobby and U.S. Foreign Policy,* coauthored by two eminent political scientists, Dr. John Mearsheimer of the University of Chicago and Dr. Stephen Walt of Harvard University. It has been translated and reviewed widely. When I telephoned Mearsheimer to congratulate him, he said they were encountering criticism similar to what I had experienced. Thanks to university tenure policies, he said, "At least I didn't lose my job." In remarks to a Washington, D.C., gathering in October 2008, Walt acknowledged my pioneering work when he said, "Paul was there first." He said that I deserved "enormous credit" for this "most comprehensive analysis" that showed that some lobby tactics were "not healthy for the United States." Although coolly, sometimes rudely, received by most critics, the Mearsheimer/Walt book and the authors' subsequent articles and media appearances constitute a major step toward the civilized conversation about Israel's U.S. lobby that American society so badly needs.

They augmented substantially the small circle of people willing to speak out candidly on Middle East challenges. Shortly before her death in 2000, author Grace Halsell, a powerful voice for Middle East justice, told me, "We have to hang together, because there are so few of us." Those willing to criticize Israel openly are still few in number. Those who speak out must brace themselves for rude treatment.

Mearsheimer lectured in 2007 at the Portland Hilton, Portland, Oregon, a city of 350,000. His news conference, announced in advance to all twelve local television, radio, and newspaper outlets, drew only one reporter, who represented a neighborhood journal for seniors. Mearsheimer told the reporter, "This media response is nothing new. Reporters elsewhere have been warned about writing about me." Mearsheimer first experienced lobby influence on media when the Chicago Council on Global Affairs, responding to complaints, cancelled a public lecture it had already publicly announced for him.[21]

After leaving the White House, Jimmy Carter, with a pro-Israel record second to none, became a tireless and fearless champion of the human rights of Palestinians. He is a steady source of inspiration, bravely advocating a truly independent state in the West Bank and Gaza for Palestinians and opening helpful direct talks with Hamas and Hezbollah, the chief local challengers of Israel's excesses. For this political bravery, he, a lifelong Democrat, is shunned by his own political party. At the 2008 Democratic presidential convention that nominated Barack Obama, convention managers limited Carter's appearance to a brief walk-on.

Early in the Obama administration, the president and nearly all members of Congress jumped dutifully through the hoop held by Israel's lobby. A House of Representatives resolution drafted by the lobby denounced a widely applauded UN war crimes report. The report fixed most of the blame on Israel for its deadly bombardment against the Gaza Strip just weeks before Obama's inauguration. The Israeli assault left fourteen hundred Palestinians dead, contrasted with four Israelis killed by homemade Palestinian rockets launched from Gaza. The resolution denounced the report and its author, the respected South African Justice Richard Goldstone, a Jew.

The disapproval resolution was opposed by only thirty-three House members. In the Senate, it was approved in voice vote. President Obama expressed no objection to the resolution or the Israeli bombardment. Months later, he briefly entered the Middle East thicket by demanding a halt in the construction of illegal Jewish housing within Israel-occupied Palestine and by declaring his support for an independent Palestine. In a vivid demonstration of America's subservience to Israel, Israeli Prime Minister Benjamin Netanyahu defied Obama's demand by swiftly ordering the construction of still more illegal housing. The chastened president fell meekly silent.

In January 2010, General David Petraeus, chief of U.S. Central Command and America's most popular U.S. military figure, warned Congress that "Israel's intransigence on the Arab-Israeli conflict was jeopardizing U.S. standing in the region." He said it threatened the security of U.S. forces.[22] When I read his words, I believed for a moment they would be the critical tipping point on U.S. policy in the Middle East. With the nation's stellar military figure in effect sounding the alarm against Israel's mistreatment of Palestinians, I believed members of Congress and major media personalities would quickly magnify and amplify Petraeus's words. It would surely stiffen Obama's backbone, if not those on Capitol Hill. But no. Petraeus's warning fell on deaf ears. After a mild flurry of news stories, it disappeared a few days later—perhaps the most awesome example of our nation's silent subservience to Israel. Whether Obama will ever issue an ultimatum to Israel and stand resolutely behind it remains to be seen.

When Israel came into being in 1948, with U.S. blessing, I paid no attention. I was just getting established as the manager of a weekly newspaper in country Illinois. In a few short years, the Jewish state would dominate the U.S. government. Nineteen years later in the 1967 Six-Day War, during which Israel's military forces routed Arab armies and seized the remainder of Palestine, I was an innocent bystander. At the time, I was a new member of the House

Committee on Foreign Affairs. I had never been to the Middle East and knew little about Islam or Israel. On June 9 that year, I recall listening as Lester Wolff, a Jewish representative from New York, made a brief statement on the House floor. He said Israeli forces mistakenly struck a U.S. Navy ship in the Eastern Mediterranean the day before, and Israeli officials apologized. Only a handful of members paid attention and none spoke up. I turned to issues in Vietnam.

From that moment, happenings aboard the USS *Liberty* on June 8, 1967, were thoroughly concealed from the public.

21

∞∞∞∞∞∞∞∞∞∞∞∞∞∞∞∞

Fateful Cover-Up

Decisions were made swiftly in the White House Situation Room on a fateful day, June 8, 1967. They were ugly, bloody, incomprehensible. They powerfully influenced events to this day. It was a day President Lyndon Johnson faced broad challenges, especially the worsening war in Vietnam and fast-rising antiwar protest in America. In Vietnam, the U.S. death toll was steadily rising, and in America, most citizens saw the conflict as a hopeless quagmire. On the domestic front, Johnson was frantically trying to keep Jewish leaders from joining the antiwar protest. A long-standing supporter of Israel, he had already provided Israel with secret aid for its conquest of Arab land.

Johnson's orders that day ignored the murder of U.S. sailors and sanctioned malfeasance and deceit. If presented as fiction, the account would be dismissed as beyond possibility in the real world. To this day, the truth remains largely hidden by a cover-up ordered by Johnson and left firmly in place by his successors.

I did not become aware of the day's momentous events until 1979, twelve years later when I read *Assault on the Liberty,* a book by retired Lieutenant Commander James M. Ennes. It is a graphic, eyewitness account of Israel's premeditated attempt to destroy a U.S. Navy intelligence-gathering ship and its entire crew in the Eastern Mediterranean—an unprecedented, almost unbelievable criminal act Israel committed against its only major benefactor in the world.

Evidence published in Ennes's book and amplified greatly by facts that surfaced in subsequent years provide overwhelming proof of Israel's guilt. I read the text from start to finish during a long flight to Eastern Europe. I rubbed my eyes in shock and sorrow. Although thoroughly footnoted, I wondered how this could happen. Detailed disclosure of this awful chapter in history is more important today than ever before. Johnson's secret decisions that day played a major role in making the United States totally subservient to Israel. The facts remain little known.

The attack on the USS *Liberty*, a lightly armed vessel, occurred in international waters in the Eastern Mediterranean. The ship's identity was well marked. Its U.S. flag fluttered in a brisk breeze throughout bright daylight hours of Israel's early reconnaissance from air and its subsequent assault from air and sea. The attack began in early afternoon and lasted more than an hour. When Israeli aircraft shot *Liberty*'s U.S. flag to pieces, a larger one was immediately hoisted in its place. Flying low, the planes strafed the deck with rocket fire and napalm, disabled all antennae, punctured the hull with over eight hundred holes, then shot to pieces the rubber life rafts lowered into the sea when the ship seemed doomed.

An Israeli torpedo boat, firing at close range, blasted a thirty-nine-foot hole only inches above the water line.[23] Miraculously, just before the ship's electrical equipment went dead, Technician Terry Halbardier crawled across the open deck amid lethal strafing and strung a cable from a damaged antenna to the transmission cabin. This made possible the broadcast of a lone appeal for help. Wounded by shrapnel during his crawl, Halbardier's bravery saved the *Liberty* and crew from total destruction. One more torpedo hit would have sent the ship and crew to the bottom of the sea.

The distress message was heard aboard the USS *Saratoga*, a carrier patrolling near Crete. In response, several critical U.S. decisions were made and carried out in rapid sequence. The *Saratoga*'s captain, Joe Tully, ordered fighter aircraft launched to defend the

Liberty and reported the launch to carrier group commander Rear Admiral Lawrence Geis aboard the flagship carrier *America*. Geis relayed the information to Washington.[24]

From the White House, President Johnson, seated in the Situation Room, responded quickly with an astounding order. Although aware the *Liberty* was still under attack, he directed Geis to cancel the rescue attempt. After vainly protesting the order, the admiral ordered cancellation.

On the *Saratoga*'s bridge, distraught sailors watched as the planes turned back. On the ship's radio they heard final frantic pleas for help from the *Liberty*. Amid the pleas were background sounds of shells exploding.[25] Minutes later, Israeli authorities, by then aware of the *Liberty*'s radioed plea for help, halted the attack.

Aboard the *Liberty*, 34 U.S. sailors were dead and 171 seriously wounded.

Two veterans gave me details of the verbal exchange when Johnson ordered callback. Radioman Tony Hart, a nineteen-year navy veteran serving at a U.S. radio relay station in Morocco, listened directly and intently to the entire conversation between President Johnson and Secretary Robert McNamara in the White House and Admiral Geis at sea.

This is what Hart recalls McNamara said to Geis, "Get those planes back on deck." Geis replied, "But the *Liberty* is still under attack and needs help." McNamara repeated, "Get those goddamn planes back on deck." Geis, aghast at the order, said, "Mr. Secretary, I wish to appeal that order to higher authority." McNamara told him, "I already have the president's authority to call the planes back. He is right here." Hart recalls Johnson then said to Geis, "I don't care if the ship goes down, I'm not going to war with an ally over a couple of sailors." The admiral said, "Aye, aye, sir." When wounded *Liberty* survivors were brought aboard the *America*, Geis expressed his regret to them at being required to call off the rescue. Until his death, the admiral agonized over what, despite the presidential order, he might have done to help the *Liberty* crew.

Over the years, I have attended several reunions of *Liberty* survivors and remain in close communication with several of them. During a recent gathering, retired Commander David Lewis, the senior *Liberty* intelligence officer, provided new details. He was critically injured in the assault and, after being airlifted to the *Saratoga* sick bay, he was summoned to the private cabin of Admiral Geis for details on the callback. The deeply shaken admiral told Lewis in privacy that he feared he would be ordered to remain silent about his verbal exchange with Johnson and McNamara. He wanted Lewis, as a senior officer on the *Liberty*, to know exactly what was said.

The only difference in the recollections of Lewis and Hart relate to several of Johnson's words. Lewis said Geis recited the president's words as follows: "I don't care if the ship goes down. I am not going to embarrass an ally over a couple of sailors." Hart recalled Johnson saying, "I don't care if the ship goes down, I am not going to war over a couple of sailors." Either version is shocking. The Lewis version was secondhand. The Hart version, firsthand.

The commander told me, "Johnson's order was probably the first time in history U.S. military forces were refused permission to help defend a U.S. Navy ship under attack."[26] Israeli officials, caught in a premeditated crime against a U.S. Navy ship, admitted the attackers were Israeli, then apologized after falsely claiming the assault was a case of mistaken identity.

Johnson accepted Israel's lie without protest, although convincing evidence the assault was deliberate was already available at highest levels of his administration.[27]

The president quickly dispatched Admiral Isaac C. Kidd and staff to the Eastern Mediterranean to carry out what from the start was a bogus Court of Inquiry. Its finding was ordered in advance by Johnson. Kidd was instructed in advance to issue a finding that cleared Israel of any blame.

In compliance, Kidd and staff traveled to the Mediterranean, where the admiral personally threatened surviving crewmen, some of them still in hospital beds. Seaman John Hrankowski, one of the badly injured survivors, described the scene. "Admiral Kidd first took off his admiral stars to appear more relaxed in chatting with the sailors. Then he put on the stars and his uniform cap and said sternly, 'If you tell anyone what actually happened, you will pay a fine, or go to prison, or worse.'" Hrankowski recalled, "We trembled. I was scared. He didn't have to explain what the word 'worse' meant."[28] After a week's tour that included only limited, superficial interviews, Kidd's group issued a finding that absolved Israel of any wrongdoing.

In 2007, retired navy Captain Ward Boston, the chief legal officer who had traveled to the Mediterranean with Admiral Kidd, publicly confessed that both he and Kidd privately believed at the time of the inquiry the assault was deliberate. By then, Kidd was deceased. In a public, sworn statement distributed widely, Boston stated that before the inquiry began, Johnson ordered Kidd to issue a finding that cleared Israel of blame.[29] Kidd's inquiry report was a fraud, but even today U.S. officials cling to the fiction of mistaken identity, acting as if Boston's confession never occurred. Official navy records have been scrubbed clean of any reference to the launching of rescue aircraft, their callback on presidential order, or conversations or documents related to the attempted rescue of the *Liberty*.

Kidd, already a distinguished senior four-star admiral, should have refused the presidential order. He should have upheld time-honored tradition by refusing to engage in deceit. No military officer is compelled to violate law. He should have brought a glorious end to his career by resigning his commission on principle and explaining to the public why he did. By doing so he would have enlightened the American people—and the Congress—on the crime committed by the government of Israel and likely prompted our government to proceed carefully in any future dealings with Israel.

Instead, Kidd and Boston were complicit themselves in gross, damaging deceit. Boston deserves credit for righting the record, although forty years after the assault on the navy ship.

In late 1983, I had a glimpse of Kidd's personality. While preparing my book on Israel's lobby, I interviewed him and was shocked at his jovial attitude toward the *Liberty* assault and his condescending reference to survivors as "kids."

The known facts about the *Liberty* leave vital questions unanswered. Why would Israel accept the high risk of public disclosure when it attempted to destroy the *Liberty* and its crew? One theory: Israel planned to begin its invasion of Syria the next day and did not want to risk the *Liberty*'s intelligence team getting an advance tip on its plans and relaying the information to the White House which, at the time, was attempting to bring about a cease-fire. That theory seems implausible, however, because premature disclosure of its plan would not likely have kept already victorious Israel from quickly gaining control of Syria's Golan Heights, nor would that territorial attainment have been worth the high risk of public disclosure of Israel's decision to sink the *Liberty*.

Commander Lewis told me he believes Israel wanted to sink the ship with no survivors and subsequently blame the crime on Egypt. This, he said, would have created fury in the United States so intense that Congress would declare war on Egypt and its Arab allies. Noting that Israelis had eliminated the Arab war machines by the time they attacked the *Liberty*, he added, "They wanted us to be in the war only to consolidate their gains. They feared that without active [U.S.] support [of Israel] world opinion would have forced Israel to withdraw from captured lands." Lewis believes Israel's scheme, if successful, would have locked America tightly and permanently with Israel and against Arabs.[30] Another theory is that Israeli authorities feared the *Liberty* crew might learn about Israel's secret execution of hundreds of captured Egyptian soldiers and other prisoners then underway in a nearby desert.

Forty years later, the cover-up was lifted but only slightly. Halbardier received the Silver Star medal and a citation for bravery, the twelfth issued to a *Liberty* survivor but the first to identify Israel as the attacking nation. The others referred only to "foreign" air and naval forces.[31]

In a supreme example of irony, Israel's attempt to destroy the U.S. ship and crew did not damage the U.S.-Israeli relationship. The cover-up was so swift and successful that U.S. support of Israel's agenda actually emerged greatly magnified. Prior to the assault, U.S. aid to Israel was, by current standards, miniscule, less than eighty million dollars a year. After the *Liberty* assault, aid to Israel increased from that trickle to a rising flood—unconditional financial, military, and diplomatic support worth billions. I keep close watch on official statements.

Why Johnson ordered callback of rescue aircraft and cover-up remains unclear, but important facts are beyond dispute: Israeli forces committed premeditated murder. No U.S. administration has questioned Israel's false claim of mistaken identity. Despite repeated pleas by surviving crewmen and others, no federal official or body has undertaken thorough hearings on what actually happened.

In May 2010, survivor Joe Meadors, a *Liberty* signalman, had another experience under Israeli military assault. He was one of several hundred unarmed volunteers aboard the seven-ship *Free Gaza* flotilla that sought to breach an illegal Israeli blockade of the Gaza shore and deliver needed food, medicine, and construction supplies to beleaguered Palestinians suffering near-starvation conditions. Israeli commandoes boarded the ships in international waters in a blatant act of piracy, killing nine volunteers and wounding more than twenty others. Meadors escaped injury. Also aboard and uninjured was retired Ambassador Ed Peck, a distinguished retired diplomat who served several years as a board member of the Council for the National Interest.

Over the years, as I became acquainted with survivors of the *Liberty*, I asked key congressional leaders to undertake public hearings, arguing it was the least Congress should do for surviving crewmen who bravely kept the ship afloat. With one exception, the members of Congress I approached did nothing but listen.

Representative Charles Bennett of Florida, a senior and respected chairman of the sea power subcommittee whom I had known and admired for years, was candid. When I visited his office and urged him to schedule hearings, I witnessed the angry side of the usually affable and cordial representative. He stood from his desk chair, hit the floor with his cane, and thundered, "Hearings would do nothing but embarrass some of my constituents." When I heard the words Geis attributed to President Johnson—"I am not going to embarrass an ally over a couple of sailors"—they seemed a grim echo of Bennett's. I could hardly believe these callous words came from Bennett's lips. I could only imagine how thoroughly intimidated he was by a group of constituents.

The crime Israel inflicted on the *Liberty* crew and the towering malfeasance of their commander in chief are almost beyond belief. In his own words, the president of the United States placed a higher value on shielding Israel from deserved blame for a war crime than on protecting the lives of navy personnel under his command. His cover-up caused hundreds of high-ranking military officers and other government officials to give official credence year after year to lies they knew were harmful to the U.S. national interest.

Johnson's purpose may have been to protect the Jewish state from embarrassment, but his cover-up may have had additional motivation. Its success shielded him from the high risk of condemnation and even impeachment. In a Senate trial for high crimes, his misconduct would certainly have been found worse than the misdeeds that brought President Bill Clinton to impeachment and trial, or those that led Richard Nixon to resign from the presidency.

Presidential reaction to the assault on the *Liberty* might have been different if John F. Kennedy had occupied the Oval Office. Just before his assassination, Kennedy was in strained standoff with Israel. He strongly opposed Israeli possession of nuclear weapons. Almost to the day of his death, he was sending stern messages to Tel Aviv, demanding unsuccessfully that Dimona, the Israeli area devoted to research and production of nuclear facilities, be open to inspection by international agencies.

After the assault on the *Liberty*, U.S. pressure against Tel Aviv ceased. Before the assault, Johnson, long a passionate supporter of Israel, maintained an intimate relationship with New Yorker Arthur Krim, a wealthy Jewish businessman and national Zionist leader, and his wife, Matilda. Both had close connections with Israeli officials and were frequent guests in the White House. They even established a residence near the Johnson ranch in Texas and communicated with Johnson during the days leading up to the Six-Day War. Matilda was an overnight guest in the White House when the assault on the *Liberty* occurred.

As Johnson made decisions on June 8, 1967, he obviously concluded that accepting the Israeli lie of mistaken identity in the *Liberty* disaster was the best way out of a complex and personally threatening situation.

It is instructive to speculate on what might have happened if Johnson had not ordered the rescue aircraft to turn back. By the time they could reach the *Liberty*, Israeli aircraft and torpedo boats would have had ample time to flee. The *Saratoga* pilots would have radioed for immediate help for *Liberty* survivors, many of them critically injured. With its guilt exposed, the government of Israel would have to drop its phony claim of mistaken identity. Perhaps it would launch a new lie, claiming that "rogue" officers carried out the assault without authority. They might even announce that the guilty personnel were already imprisoned and receiving psychiatric examination. Despite the new lie, however, the American people would surely be furious at the Israeli government for permitting the lengthy and costly "rogue" assault and insist Congress put limitations and conditions on any future dealings with Israel.

Instead, the day's events marked a decisive, fateful, fundamental wrong turn in U.S. foreign policy. U.S. sailors were killed in cold blood, and the murderers were rewarded with higher levels of unconditional U.S. support. Israeli officials had reason to believe they could get by in the future with any misdeed—even murder of U.S. citizens—without even a U.S. rebuke.

I had no awareness of these ominous developments until years later. The cover-up quickly led to fateful, costly U.S. subservience to Israel—religious bias in foreign policy so blatantly Israel-centric and unfair to Arabs and Muslims that it continues to fuel anti-American hostility worldwide.

Early steps in this peculiar relationship with Israel occurred when the U.S. government became a partner in crime by looking the other way in 1974. That year, Yitzhak Rabin, during his first term as Israeli prime minister, quietly authorized illegal Jewish settlements on Arab land seized during the 1967 war. It was an example of deceit. I never trusted him or his words on the occasions I met him in Washington and Tel Aviv.

Comprehensive pro-Israel bias became the inflexible rule in Washington. Our government provided the massive, unconditional aid at all levels that enabled Israel to destroy and humiliate Palestinian society. In 1992, when Rabin campaigned successfully for a new term as prime minister, he bragged openly of starting illegal settlements years earlier. Anti-American passions began to skyrocket when U.S. forces, under pressure from Israel, invaded Iraq and Afghanistan. Anti-Muslim fears began to sweep across America.

By 9/11, Yasser Arafat was in the twilight of his career. Israel had virtually imprisoned him in a house arrest in Palestine's West Bank. A combination of Israel-imposed restraints and declining health kept him from moving freely from one capital to the next, as was his custom.

Historians should accord high marks to Arafat as a champion of human rights. Once he organized the PLO in 1964, he seemed to give no thought to anything else, risking his own life time and again. He doubtless made mistakes, but he persevered against heavy odds with singleness of purpose in his quest for the dignity and rights of Palestinians.

In fundamental ways, Arafat's tactics differed from those of Mohandas Gandhi, Nelson Mandela, and Reverend Martin Luther King Jr. Despite bloody, sometimes lethal opposition, the three preached and practiced nonviolent resistance as their undeviating path. Arafat did not. Given local circumstances, perhaps he thought he could not. From the inception of the PLO until his death, Arafat considered himself commander in chief of the movement's ragged, poorly armed, poorly organized, and dispersed military forces, even during his long exile from Palestinian territory.

Was Arafat a terrorist? If so, the colonists who rebelled against King George III in 1776 may deserve the same label. To the PLO leader, the violence he frequently authorized was never terrorism, but a lawful exercise of the right of people to struggle forcibly to regain control of their ancestral homes from an occupying power.

Was he a great leader? By any reasonable standard, the answer is yes. A wide variety of personalities gathered under the PLO tent. He, and he alone, kept them together. He was also a remarkable survivor. One day he told me of surviving a plane accident in North Africa. He said that when a crash landing seemed imminent, his aides aboard the limping aircraft tied him up in every blanket and pillow they could find. When the plane hit the ground, the fuselage broke in two pieces. He told me, "I walked away without serious injury." Often in the crosshairs of would-be assassins, he had at least the nine proverbial lives before he succumbed to what his associates believed was deliberate poisoning.

I was deeply touched when televised news one evening showed former President Carter placing a wreath on Arafat's grave in Ramallah, Palestine. Will Arafat be remembered favorably? Certainly by most Palestinians. Sadly, no one has emerged as the unchallenged new voice against oppression, a role Arafat filled until his death in 2004.

Today, the U.S. government is widely despised in the Muslim world—and among many people of other faiths—for its pro-Israel bias. The gulf between the United States and the Muslim world widened when Israel, with open support of the U.S. government, killed over eighteen thousand Arab civilians in and near Beirut in 1982, bombarded nearly half of Lebanon in 2003, and all of Gaza in the winter of 2008 to 2009. But no U.S. government in forty years has voiced serious objection, much less suspended aid to Israel in protest.

The influence of the Jewish state throughout American society is now so profound its misbehavior may bear the seeds of Holy War, a religion-based struggle of unpredictable violence between Muslims and mostly Christian Americans allied with Jewish Israel. If that statement seems far-fetched, reflect on the fate of the *Liberty* and consider the powerful new anti-American passions that might erupt worldwide if military forces of either Israel or the United States commit acts of war against Iran.

Stephen M. Walt, the Harvard professor who coauthored an examination of the influence of Israel's lobby, recently disclosed an exquisite example of subservience. He reported that applicants for positions in the Obama administration had to pass a pro-Israel litmus test: "Every appointee . . . must endure a thorough background check by the American Jewish community." He added, "Groups in the lobby target public servants like [Ambassador Charles] Freeman and [former Senator Chuck] Hagel because they want to make sure that no one with even a mildly independent view on Middle East affairs gets appointed."[32]

22

∞∞∞∞∞∞∞∞∞∞∞∞

Seeds of Holy War

In 2005 a Cornell University survey disclosed a shocking level of anti-Muslim bias in American society. Forty-four percent of those surveyed were so frightened by false perceptions of Islam that they favor government restrictions on the civil liberties of all U.S. Muslims, a religious community of more than six million.[33]

The poll came to my attention during a visit to the United Arab Emirates, five years after my book *Silent No More: Confronting America's False Images of Muslims* was published. It was one of the most disturbing revelations in years. It meant that nearly one-half of our citizens believe all U.S. Muslims too dangerous to be accorded the rights proclaimed in the Declaration of Independence and guaranteed in the U.S. Constitution.

Five years later, the numbers remain just as troubling. A January 2010 Gallup survey of 1,006 households disclosed that nearly one-half—43 percent—admitted to being prejudiced about Muslims and troubled about Islam. Fifty-three percent of respondents said their view of Islam was "not too favorable or not favorable at all." Pollsters noted, "The 43 percent is probably an underestimation."[34] The results give U.S. Muslims new reason for anxiety.

All citizens should accept the findings as a wake-up call. Religious bigotry grows quickly like a deadly cancer and misdirects public policy as well as individual behavior. Our pro-Israel bias is considered worldwide to be anti-Arab and anti-Muslim and deplored,

271

except in Israel and America. It is little noted in the United States because major media uniformly ignore news that puts Israel in a bad light but routinely headline reports that link the words "Islam" and "Muslim," however falsely, with mayhem. As a result, U.S. Muslims fear for their safety while our nation's moral standing plummets.

Dispute over Palestinian land is at the root of today's worldwide turmoil. During the four decades since the Six-Day War, the government of Israel has kept an iron grip on all of Palestine, specifically the territory called Greater Israel that Jews controlled only briefly more than two thousand years ago. Today's Jewish occupiers claim this real estate as their own, basing it on their widely disputed interpretation of biblical passages. Millions of U.S. Christians are similarly duped.

The illegal occupiers are a minority and not representative of majority views in Israel, but they are politically powerful. They consist mostly of ultraconservative Jews who claim Palestinian land was God's gift in perpetuity to Jews. They claim their messiah will not come until Greater Israel is fully reestablished. Accordingly, they fiercely resist the establishment of another independent state on any part of Palestine.

One day in 1981, after the president led a White House cabinet-room discussion of agricultural issues with farm-state congressmen, I learned firsthand what President Reagan thought of the Jewish occupiers. When formal discussion ended, I found myself temporarily cramped in the doorway with the president. For a moment, he was my captive. I looked directly at him and said, "Mr. President, I believe the Palestinians deserve a homeland of their own." He paused, then asked, "But where would they go?" He was serious. I was stupefied.

Did the president believe the Palestinians had no right to stay where they were, land their ancestors considered home for two thousand years? That was his unmistakable message. I realized he accepted the Zionist claim that the land long owned by Palestinians was the God-given property of Jews only. Reagan was a

Presbyterian, like myself, a denomination that has almost unanimously rejected this Zionist claim. Perhaps he held fundamentalist views at heart, despite his church affiliation. His comment made me appreciate the immensity of the task facing those who work for the day when Palestinians can once again be free and unmolested in their own historic homeland.

Jews are not alone in expecting the return of a messiah. Millions of fundamentalist U.S. Christians believe their messiah, Jesus Christ, wants them to support Israel until his return to earth. On his return, they believe Jesus will defeat the forces of evil on the Plain of Armageddon, and, at that moment, all Jews will be converted to Christianity or destroyed. Estimates of the number of Christians holding these extreme views range from twenty million to sixty million. During my service in Congress, I found them to be numerous, deeply committed, and politically active. Although the U.S. government occasionally states its opposition to Jewish settlements in occupied Palestine, the Internal Revenue Service ignores an absurdity by allowing U.S. citizens to deduct from taxable income contributions they made to Jewish organizations that indirectly fund expansion of settlements.

The Cornell survey exposes the massive obstacle to removal of pro-Israel bias in U.S. Middle East policies. With nearly half of our citizens fearful of Islam, a U.S. administration determined to establish evenhanded policies in the Middle East, where Muslims predominate, faces the daunting hurdle of overcoming deeply rooted stereotypes that cast all Muslims as dangerous.

Since the survey, President Barack Obama, a Christian whose paternal family was Muslim, has offered words of conciliation to the Muslim world, but these and similar expressions from a few other sources have been submerged by a steady flow of televised clips, newspaper headlines, and talk-radio declarations that falsely link Islam with suicide bombings and the killing of innocent people. Several 2010 surveys showed one in four U.S. citizens mistakenly believe Obama is a Muslim. Admiral Mike Mullen, chairman of U.S. Joint Chiefs of Staff, wrote that the Muslim community "is a subtle world that we don't fully—and we don't always attempt to—understand."[35]

Anti-American sentiment in the Muslim world arises mainly from three interrelated factors: first, the presence and behavior of U.S. troops in countries where Muslims predominate; second, the anger that spreads when U.S. combat operations kill Muslims, both civilian and military; and third, U.S. complicity in Israel's abuse of Muslims in Palestine and elsewhere. Our military combat operations in Iraq, Afghanistan, and Pakistan are, with few exceptions, directed entirely against Arabs, most of them Muslims. These acts of war blight many thousands of families and breed anti-American protest. This unchallenged reality fuels prejudice and hate both here and abroad.

In America, citizens seem conditioned to demonize whoever is officially designated as our enemy. Today, such designees are almost all Muslims. U.S. killing of Muslims is shocking. More than one hundred thousand Iraqi civilians have been killed since U.S. forces invaded Iraq in 2003. In addition, the U.S. aerial blockade of Iraq during the decade preceding the invasion caused critical shortages of medical supplies, medical personnel, and food. The shortages were a factor in the high toll of infant deaths estimated at a half million.

Since the U.S. assault on Afghanistan began in 2001, our bombers, artillery, drones, and troops have killed more than 7,500 civilians in Afghanistan. In Pakistan, attacks by U.S. drones and bombers killed at least 450 civilians in the first half of 2009. Moreover, the U.S. government must accept major responsibility for 1,005 civilian deaths during Israel's assault against Lebanon in 2006 and 1,400 civilian deaths caused by the Jewish state's onslaught against Palestinians in Gaza the winter of 2008 to 2009.

Almost all these deaths were Muslim, and both assaults were openly supported by Washington. In addition, the United States is held responsible for the violent deaths of thousands of Palestinians and Lebanese caused by the series of U.S.-financed Israeli assaults on Lebanon in 1982 and since. Almost all those killed were Muslim.[36]

Through lectures and published articles, I have strongly protested these atrocities.

Professor Stephen Walt of Harvard University estimates that in the last thirty years 10,325 Americans—mostly victims of 9/11 and U.S.-initiated combat operations in Iraq and Afghanistan—have been killed by Muslims, while at least 288,000 Muslims have been killed by American combat forces. This is a ratio of thirty Muslims killed for each American lost. The totals include military as well as civilian dead. Walt chose low estimates of Muslims killed.[37]

The dead are not just statistics. The agonized shriek of a bereaved Muslim mother or wife is just as penetrating and soul-wrenching as that of a bereaved Christian or Jewish mother or wife. Each death, like every other death in wartime, blights the lives of close friends beyond immediate family members. This means several million Muslim families already harbor lasting resentment and anger against the United States.

Osama bin Laden, the reputed leader of Al-Qaeda, calls 9/11 payback for U.S. complicity in Israel's long-standing abuse of Palestinians and its massacre of about eighteen thousand civilians during its 1982 assault on Beirut, Lebanon. He said he got the idea of destroying the World Trade Center in Manhattan while watching tall buildings in Beirut fall during the Israeli bombardment. U.S. Representative Paul McCloskey witnessed evidence of U.S. complicity when he visited Beirut soon after the assault. He told me he was angrily accosted by Lebanese who showed him fragments of munitions used in Israel's bombardment. They were marked "made in the USA." In a September 2009 radio broadcast, bin Laden said; "As I have said so many times for over two decades the cause of the quarrel with you is [U.S.] support for your Israeli allies who have occupied our land, Palestine. . . .[it] prompted us to carry out the 11 September events."[38]

Brewing revenge came two decades later when a small group of professed Muslims caused the awful carnage of 9/11. U.S. military combat focus against Muslims prompts fears in many people in the Islamic world that the United States, largely Christian, is leading a new crusade against Islam. Muslims are well informed of the blood-shed Christian Crusaders inflicted on Muslims centuries ago.

Perceptions are powerful. Foreign troops are seen as proof that local officials are actually puppets of a foreign power. In both Afghanistan and Iraq, U.S. generals are viewed as the real government. In Palestine, U.S.-backed Israeli occupiers are viewed as the real government. Only when foreign troops are gone will local citizens believe their government is free of foreign control.

Foreign troops stir emotions that range from anxiety to outrage. A recent study of all suicide bombings worldwide since 1975 yields important findings: First, suicide bombings occur almost entirely in countries like Iraq and Afghanistan where foreign troops hold the upper hand; and second, they cease when the troops leave.[39] In my watch over media, these findings are not published.

The full story of 9/11's origin remains incomplete, but tentative conclusions provide an instructive case study of how U.S. religion-based bias can lead to awesome bloodshed. Charged with the horrible destruction of 9/11 is a small group of professed Muslims. Its leader, Khalid Sheikh Mohammed, told U.S. captors his main motivation was "hatred of America's long-standing pro-Israel bias" in U.S. Middle East policies.[40]

September 11 produced instant, lasting anti-Muslim fury throughout the United States that reverberates nine years later. Each U.S. death is inevitably mourned by scores of outraged relatives and other friends, anger that intensifies anti-Islamic stereotypes that surfaced in the Cornell University poll.

Pakistani journalist Ansar Abbasi recently told a senior State Department official calmly but bluntly, "You should know that we hate all Americans." He added, "Thousands of innocent people have been killed because Americans are trying to find Osama bin Laden."[41] And innocent Muslims who are U.S. citizens have been subjected to unwarranted violations of civil liberties, racial profiling, and lengthy detention without due process. The Council on American Islamic Relations, the largest Muslim advocacy group whose chapters frequently hear me speak, reported in 2009 a "growing level of anti-Muslim prejudice and stereotyping."[42]

In Afghanistan, U.S. military forces face difficulty enlisting local support for war measures against the Taliban and bin Laden. Instead of viewing him as an enemy, many Afghans remember him as a patriot who—with CIA support—helped force Soviet forces to retreat from Afghanistan a few years ago. Despite hating the Taliban's un-Islamic harsh treatment of women, some Afghans have positive memories of the organization's success. After Soviets were forced to leave, the Taliban dethroned warlords and ended both petty and major crime when it controlled 80 percent of Afghanistan just before the U.S. invasion in 2001.

Al Jazeera international television network recently surveyed Pakistanis on what they considered to be the greatest threat to their country. Fifty-nine percent named the United States. Only 11 percent picked Taliban militants.[43] Many Pakistanis support the Taliban and resent U.S. support of repressive Pakistan regimes. Dr. Wolf Fuhrig, a retired professor in my hometown who has frequently visited Arab countries, found on recent visits a sharp increase in anger toward America. In earlier years, local citizens expressed hatred of U.S. government policy, not the American people. Now the fury is directed against all Americans. On visits home, two Illinois College exchange students whose families reside in Palestine found the same shift in sentiment.[44]

Until a decade after leaving Congress, I had no awareness of "Islamaphobia," a popular name for anti-Muslim bias in the United States. The challenge posed by false images of Islam first came to my attention in 1989, when I lectured in Cape Town, South Africa. I shared the platform in a giant arena with my host, Sheikh Ahmed Deedat, known worldwide as a charismatic spokesman for Islam. More than thirteen thousand attended. His lecture, like mine, reviewed Israel's abuse of mostly Muslim Palestinians. The evening was a major bookselling event. Over two thousand copies of the Quran and nearly nine hundred copies of my book, *They Dare to*

Speak Out, were sold. After the program, participants were hosted in the home of a Muslim businessman, where evening prayers were said and a midnight dinner served.

Three days in South Africa were a learning experience. In talks with Deedat and his staff, I became aware of the close linkage of the principles of Islam with Christianity and Judaism, as well as with the Declaration of Independence and U.S. Constitution. The next day, Deedat's staff arranged a guided tour of the city and surrounding countryside that gave us a glimpse of the ugly class structure of apartheid that still ruled South Africa. Because of their ancestry in India, the Deedat family lived in an area reserved for the second level of four segregated classes. White people were at the top. Blacks occupied the bottom two. On one side of a highway, we found blacks struggling to survive in makeshift shacks with no plumbing. On the other side were handsome, modern mansions for whites only.

In 1995, I attended a weeklong seminar in Malaysia. It was a life-changing experience. I was one of forty-two people, four from the United States, who discussed "Western Images of Islam." I had been writing articles about my experience with Deedat and in them recognized the importance of interfaith understanding. Upon arrival in Penang after a tiring ride halfway around the world, Lucille and I found a warm, relaxing welcome in the home of John Mohideen, a civil rights lawyer, and his wife, Muslimah. Arriving at their home for a reception, we made new friends and experienced a new treat—fried bananas.

The seminar was convened by Dr. Chandra Muzzafar, a Muslim convert from his youthful days as a Hindu in India. Now a citizen of Malaysia, he heads the Foundation for a Just World, speaks powerfully from a wheelchair, and writes just as powerfully in the foundation's newsletter. At week's end, he asked delegates to state what each would do at home to help correct false images of Islam. When my turn came, I promised to draft a concise statement useful to U.S. Muslims as they dealt with false images. As we left Malaysia, convinced that false images of Islam were a major barrier to reform of

U.S. Middle East policies, I knew I was hooked. I bore a profound new challenge and felt compelled to give it full attention.

At home, my first project was drafting "A friendly note from your Muslim neighbor." Its concise language lists important beliefs and principles that link Christianity, Judaism, and Islam, then it corrects in nonconfrontational words the most common stereotypes of Islam. In drafting the note, I became aware that Muslims, like Christians and Jews, are pledged to God, peace with justice, cooperation, charity, family responsibility, and tolerance toward people of other faith traditions. Islamic teachings abhor terrorism and subjugation.[45] In recent years, as I became personally acquainted with scores of Muslims, I found broad commitment to these rules but little knowledge of this commitment beyond the Islamic community As I address Muslim audiences, I distribute copies of this "friendly note," and urge each recipient to make copies to pass out as daily opportunities arise. I also state other ways Muslims can help erase hostility toward Islam: attending Christian services and afterward offering to meet with church groups to answer questions about Islam; demanding corrections when media convey false images of Islam; and wearing pins or rings that show Muslim affiliation, thus visibly linking the person's good behavior with Islam.

At the time, the principal Muslim organizations in America— the Islamic Society of North America (ISNA) and the Islamic Circle of North America (ICNA)—focused mainly on personal service to members. I have addressed national conventions of both groups. Serious efforts at outreach did not begin until 2006. In 2009, ISNA achieved one of the Muslim community's groundbreaking steps in outreach when Rev. Rick Warren, a leading Christian mega-church pastor, spoke at its annual convention.

Beginning in 1998, I devoted most of three years to writing a book about U.S. Muslims, *Silent No More: Confronting America's False Images of Islam*. In it, I dealt with stereotypes, explained the plight of U.S. Muslims, provided details of their religious commitment, and listed their contributions to American society, as well as the indignities and burdens they bear. In preparing the text, I consulted leaders of principal Muslim organizations and Ahmad Osman, a U.S.-educated native of Sudan and editorial director of the book's publisher, Amana Publications in Beltsville, Maryland.

Helpful suggestions came from Easa Al Gurg, a leading diplomat and businessman in the United Arab Emirates; Zainab Elberry of Nashville, a native of Egypt who is revered as an unofficial ambassador of Islam; and her Morocco-born husband, Nour Naciri. One day, to underscore the cordial connection of Islam and Christianity, Al Gurg, by then the United Arab Emirates ambassador to Great Britain, sent me a copy of the Quran keyed to twenty-seven places in the text in which Jesus is celebrated. Nihad Awad, national director of the Council on American Islamic Relations (CAIR), Professor Agha Saeed, founder of the American Muslim Alliance (AMA), and ISNA's Syeed helped me with research and marketing. *Silent No More* was published in August 2001 by Amana. Sales now exceed fifty thousand.

In one home, my book was eagerly read. After speaking in 2004 to a gathering in Westminster, London, a man told me he had been spending evenings in Durban, South Africa, reading *Silent No More* aloud to Ahmad Deedat, by then paralyzed and bedridden. He said the Muslim leader had been unable to speak or move his limbs for several years but had worked out a laborious system of communicating by blinking his eyes. In 2007, Deedat's son Yousef wrote that his father, using the eye-blink system shortly before his death, composed this message for me: "My dear brother Findley: I may never see you again. I feel I have already left the outside world behind. Your book brought that world back into my room. Thank you, my brother." Yousef wrote that "the intense meaning" of his father's message moved him deeply.

A month after *Silent No More* first appeared, American society was engulfed in the horror of 9/11. The perpetrators were identified as Muslims, which to many Americans instantly—but wrongly—linked Islam with the awful, senseless carnage. At a news conference at the National Press Building in Washington, leaders of major U.S. Muslim organizations immediately deplored the assault as a gross violation of the principles of Islam and condemned those responsible. Their declaration received no coverage in major media.

The assault spread and strengthened false images of Islam. It led to harsh practices of official bias against law-abiding Muslims. In its immediate aftermath, I stirred hometown passions by declaring in an op-ed in *Jacksonville Journal-Courier* "this indefensible and cowardly assault on America was payback for bad U.S. policy, specifically our pro-Israel bias and complicity in Israel's lethal abuse of Arabs." I said it was a terrible warning that our government must reform its policies in the Middle East. That Sunday I delivered the same message in a sermon in the local Congregational Church. To my surprise, my statements provoked unprecedented anger among some of my neighbors. It was so fierce a clergyman I had met only once offered Lucille and me his rural residence as a temporary refuge. We declined his offer, because police volunteered special surveillance of our home.

A friend told me, "We needed time to mourn those killed before you tried to educate us on why it happened." He may have been right, but I sense that even today Americans have difficulty believing that our government could be so immorally wrong as to help Israel commit awful crimes against its Arab neighbors.

Printed here are selections from my statement. I present them because they distill my accumulation of that thing called truth. This is what I believe:

Nine-eleven would not have occurred if the U.S. government had refused to be complicit in Israel's humiliation and destruction of Palestinian society. The catastrophe could have been prevented if any U.S. president during the past forty-two years had suspended all U.S. aid until Israel withdrew from Arab land it illegally held since the 1967 Six-Day War. Israel's U.S. lobby is powerful and intimidating, but any determined president could prevail and win overwhelming public support for suspension of aid by telling the American people the truth. . . . The U.S. government is now reviled in many countries, because it provides unconditional support despite Israel's violations of the United Nations Charter, international law, and the precepts of all major religious faiths, including Judaism.

Nine-eleven had its origin years ago when Israel's U.S. lobby began its unbroken success in stifling debate about the U.S. role in the Arab-Israeli conflict. For fifty years, open discussion of the Arab-Israeli conflict has been almost nonexistent. Members of Congress act like trained poodles, jumping through hoops held by Israel's lobby. As a result, all legislation dealing with the Middle East is heavily biased in favor of Israel and against Arab/Muslim entities. Lobby intimidation even silences most U.S. Jews who object to the lobby's tactics and Israel's brutality.

Terrorism almost always arises from deeply felt grievances. If they can be eradicated or eased, terrorist passions are certain to subside. The U.S. government has made no serious attempt to redress Arab/Muslim grievances, or even to identify them. Israel is headed by a scofflaw government that should be treated as such.

In 2003, Israeli lobby influence was so dominant it brought the official, president-appointed 9/11 Commission to its knees. In a telephone conversation with my former colleague, Lee H. Hamilton, then director of the Woodrow Wilson Institute, he ruefully reported that on two different days he and co-chairman Thomas S. Kean proposed scheduling hearings where testimony on possible motivations for 9/11 could be heard and examined. Both times they dropped the proposal when other commission members voiced strong objection.

The co-chairmen should have scheduled hearings despite colleague protests. A printed public record of candid discussion could have helped the American people understand grievances that prompted 9/11. An unidentified brave member of the commission staff inserted in its official report a vital statement of motivation expressed by Khalid Sheikh Mohammed (KSM), identified by the commission as the chief organizer of 9/11: "By his own account, KSM's animus toward the United States stemmed not from his experiences [in the United States] but rather from his violent disagreement with U.S. foreign policy favoring Israel."[46]

This finding alone justified thorough hearings on motivation. Instead, the salient fact remained obscure and unreported. It appears in the center of a long paragraph on a page devoted to other items. I must conclude that commission members who objected to hearings did not want public disclosure of why the assaults occurred and that a staff member slipped this important statement in a place unlikely to be noted by commission members. Like much of American society, the commissioners were afraid to risk the ire of Israel's lobby.

During a White House news conference in January 2010, Helen Thomas became one of the few journalists of national prominence to focus attention on terrorist motivation. During a news conference called by President Obama she repeatedly pressed John Brennan, Obama's specialist in counter-terrorism, to explain why the Christmas Day would-be "crotch bomber" tried to kill himself and everyone aboard an airliner near Detroit. Taken aback, Brennan mumbled unresponsive words each time Thomas raised the question "why?" Like the 9/11 commissioners, Brennan seemed afraid to mention pro-Israel bias as the principal motivation for assaults on the United States. Nothing can justify 9/11. It was a ghastly criminal act that demanded aggressive prosecution and punishment of those guilty. It did not warrant heavy bombing of isolated, impoverished, largely illiterate Afghans. They lacked the resources to fill any significant role in foreign activity, much less high-tech skills that produced the 9/11 crime. But because people charged with 9/11 were identified as Muslims, the assault intensified anti-Islam stereotypes throughout America. It also elevated thorough dissemination of inaccurate information about Islam to a high level.

The task of correction deserves highest priority by our nation's leaders. For example, it would be proper and timely for the House of

Representatives to celebrate a current, historic reality, the presence of Keith Ellison of Minnesota and André Carson of Indiana as the first Muslims elected to Congress. I have personally observed ample precedent for a celebration. During my experience on Capitol Hill, the House of Representatives recognized several members whose careers provided testament to the religious diversity of this nation.

A vast educational project must be undertaken, with Muslims taking a leading role. They remain misunderstood strangers in our midst. Most Americans have never knowingly met a Muslim, visited a mosque, or heard or read a verse from the Quran. They are unaware of constructive contributions that Muslims make to our society. Our non-Muslim leaders, elected and appointed, must alert the public in clear language to the deadly threat posed by anti-Muslim stereotypes and emphasize Islam's broad links with the other two major monotheistic religions, Christianity and Judaism.

The stakes are high. Present demographic trends put in doubt whether Israel can survive many more years as a Jewish state. Expansion of Jewish settlements in the territory Israel controls may soon rule out any possibility of a viable independent Palestine. Birth trends forecast within twenty years a Palestinian majority within the territory Zionists cite as Greater Israel. If that occurs, the Jewish state will then be under great international pressure to end the second-class status of Palestinians. It may ultimately force Israel to extend full citizenship to them, thus ending it as a Jewish state. If its officials refuse, Israel will descend still deeper into racist colonialism, a spectacle the American people will finally refuse to support.

In a cruel project designed to avert that demographic tide, Prime Minister Benjamin Netanyahu embarked in 2010 upon what may become massive expulsion of non-Jews from occupied Palestine, including East Jerusalem. This draconian step is a blatant violation of international law, Geneva Conventions, and the principles clearly expressed in the United Nations Charter.

Only a modest measure of protest has developed in the United States, shocking inaction in a nation pledged to equal justice under law. As the world's only major benefactor of Israel, the U.S. government has readily at hand tools to frustrate this ugly example of ethnic cleansing. At this writing, the silence in Washington is deafening.

If ethnic cleansing can be halted, the two-state objective—Israel and a new Palestine, living securely side-by-side—takes on new appeal and urgency. It was presented formally in a plan conceived and first announced in 2002 by Crown Prince Abdullah of Saudi Arabia. Under his proposal, all Muslim states would extend full recognition and diplomatic relations to Israel, in exchange for Israel's withdrawal from territory it seized in the 1967 Six-Day War. The new Palestine would establish its capital in East Jerusalem. It was endorsed by twenty-two countries where Muslims predominate, as well as by the Palestinian Authority and Hamas, the organization elected to govern Gaza. After becoming king, Abdullah renewed the proposal in 2007. He wisely insists the parties agree on the general goal before negotiation of details. His proposal is an urgent message of common sense.

Former *New York Times* foreign correspondent Chris Hedges reports that strident voices irrationally warn of Islamic terrorism. He cites emotional messages issued by "self-described former Muslim terrorists now born-again Christians." They are Walid Shoebat, Kamal Saleem, and Zachariah Anani, who stir passions of fundamentalist audiences. Hedges warns, "These men are frauds, but that is not the point. They are part of a dark and frightening war by the Christian right against tolerance, that, at the moment of another catastrophic terrorist attack on American soil, would make it acceptable to target and persecute all Muslims, including the some six million who live in the United States. These men stoke these irrational fears."

Author Diana West wrongly argues that "Islam's and the West's [belief systems] are so diametrically opposed that our interests cannot intersect [with Islam's]." She calls for "a multi-level campaign to reverse jihad's ultimate goal," which she wrongly declares is "to extend Islamic law by both violent and other means." She cites a Pew poll showing that 87 percent of mostly Muslim Pakistanis "support the death penalty for those leaving Islam."[47] This misleading conclusion about the penalty for apostasy—leaving one's faith—arises from tribal fantasy, not from Islam. Salam al-Marayati, director of the Muslim Public Affairs Council, states, "Nothing in the Quran calls for death for apostasy. It is shunned by all faiths, but judgment is left to God, not people."[48]

Overcoming such misdirected warnings is a momentous task. If the political and military status quo continues unchecked, the world risks war arising from the excesses of radicals on both sides. The sad truth is our government has done nothing since 9/11 to recognize legitimate Muslim grievances, specifically the bias in U.S. Middle East policy that is blatantly pro-Israel and anti-Muslim. Mohammed Bashardost, M.D., an immigrant from Afghanistan who supplied research for my book, *Silent No More*, cites "Holy War" as "the most challenging task of our times." He declares, "President Obama has no choice. He must adequately, properly, and courageously address the seeds, roots, and causes of Holy War." Bashardost received his medical degree at the American University in Beirut where he witnessed "the good, bad, and evil," on one occasion "an indiscriminate Israeli bloodbath of defenseless Palestinian women, children, and seniors." He believes U.S. troops in Afghanistan have little understanding of local culture and tradition, especially deep-seated opposition to foreign troops that have controlled most of Afghanistan for twenty of the last twenty-five years.

Bashardost provides insight into modern Afghanistan: "Patriotism and sacrifice are parts of social life, rooted in religion and culture. If a person is killed while defending his homeland or kills someone invading his country, he is considered fully entitled to the great mercy of almighty God." Like many other people, Bashardost may not fully comprehend the grip Israel's lobby has over American society. Only a few members of Congress are willing to reject its demands. Lobby influence over the president is almost as great. In its constant fear of offending Israel's lobby, Congress, the presidency, and major media prompt nationwide alarm when radical, professed Muslims engage in suicide bombing or are suspected of attempting to do so. Our government frantically overreacts by scrapping long-cherished civil liberties and attempting to place our nation in a protective cocoon constructed by the Department of Homeland Security.

As a lifelong Republican, I am pained to recognize that my party is playing the terrorism card, trying to defeat Democrats by mislabeling them "soft on terrorists." Other official statements deepen fear.

After denouncing rendition, Obama has kept it as a presidential option. He states some insurgents will be held in detention indefinitely without due process. In 2010, the Obama administration announced approval of the policy of targeted killing of people suspected to be "threats to security." In a shocking departure from constitutional guarantees, Director of National Intelligence Dennis Blair told a congressional committee in February 2010 that the U.S. government, "with executive department approval," may "deliberately target and kill U.S. citizens who are suspected" of involvement in terrorism. "We don't target people for free speech. We target them for taking action that threatens Americans." He added, ominously, "If we think direct action will involve killing an American, we get specific permission to do that."

He left the impression that permission for killings will be sought only from higher authority within the executive branch, not from Congress or federal courts. Asked to comment, attorney Brent Wickum, who has defended several detainees at Guantanamo Bay, said, "They kill somebody and don't need to offer any justification." Constitutional scholar and longtime friend Francis A. Boyle of the University of Illinois writes that "this extra judicial execution of human beings" violates the U.S. Constitution and international law. He adds, "The U.S. government has now established a death list for U.S. citizens abroad akin to lists established by Latin American dictatorships during their so-called dirty wars."[49] This policy is frightening evidence of a presidency gone amuck. It violates principles of justice and morality imbedded in the Constitution, law, precedents, and international treaties.

Every suicide bomber violates basic principles of Islam, first by taking his own life, and second by killing innocent people. Christian-Muslim-Judaic doctrines are violated every day by professed followers, with total killings of innocent people by Christians far outstripping such killings by the other two. Religious issues are often clouded by ethnic bias. The result is a toxic mixture that will keep rising in explosive potential. Radicals on both sides of the religious divide will try to rule discourse and action. Anti-Islam violence could quickly erupt in the United States and Israel, matched throughout the Muslim world by fury against an emerging U.S.-Israel axis. The seeds of Holy War might yield the bitter fruit of humankind's most deadly folly ever.

23

∞∞∞∞∞∞∞∞∞∞∞∞∞∞∞∞∞

Banishing Jungle Law

In early pages I cite the nationwide influence during my college days of Clarence K. Streit. His book *Union Now,* published in 1939, thrilled me and many others of my generation, because it presented a commonsense plan to prevent future wars and promote the rule of law in world affairs. It would attain this authority through the permanent federation of major democracies. Inspired by the success of the U.S. federation, he proposed a new level of government with precise but limited powers.

It was especially appealing to young men, like me, who were headed for military service in World War II. It won immediate popularity, prompting Streit to leave a successful career as foreign correspondent for the *New York Times* to devote his full time to promoting "union of the free."

He died at the age of ninety on July 6, 1986. Hours earlier, a grand display of fireworks signaled the end of the three-day celebration that opened the restored Statue of Liberty in New York Harbor. The coincidence was a perfect salute to Streit's life. This apostle of liberty did not live to see his federation dream fulfilled, but he kept the "*flambeau* of liberty," as he often called his plan, burning brightly until his last breath.

A deep-seated ambition to advance Streit's plan was the most important factor that prompted my early dream of election to Congress. During my first seventeen years on Capitol Hill, it was the major focus of my legislative endeavors. Beginning in 1978, my attention was diverted to the high cost of America's Israel-centric foreign policy, but Streit's vision remained vivid in my mind. His plan is a roadmap that will someday lead the world to embrace the rule of law and abandon military conflict, properly tagged the law of the jungle.

During a memorial service in the U.S. Capitol a few days after Streit's death, I was asked to speak. I started with these words, "My book of memories is sprinkled with green ink." In the audience, Arthur Burns, former chairman of the Federal Reserve System and a lifelong supporter of Streit's proposal, chuckled audibly. He knew what I meant. His book of memories, like mine, included many handwritten notes from Streit, always written in the apostle's hallmark, green ink. In his often lonely quest for federation, Streit never deviated from ink color or from the basic elements of federation described in his book. He recognized the inherent limitations of national sovereignty and proposed a commonsense solution.

He was confident that once begun, the federation ultimately would become worldwide, as other nations accepted reforms that made them eligible for membership. Streit's book proposed a three-person executive, a two-chamber legislature, a vast free-trade area, and unified foreign, defense, currency, trade, and postal services. It was a grand design, political union of the world's principal military power centers that were experienced in the rule of law. The sponsors believed that, once established, the new union's strength would prevent major wars and preserve individual liberties within an ever-expanding realm.

It stirred so much enthusiasm worldwide that Streit formed and headed two organizations of supporters. I signed up as a member of one of them—Federal Union, Inc.—and remain on the board of directors of its successor, The Streit Council for the Union of the Democracies, still well led by Don Dennis, whom I joined on Streit's magazine staff in 1946. The other organization Streit founded, The International Movement for Atlantic Union, had even broader international membership. His early supporters included a large number of business, diplomatic, academic, and political leaders in the United States, France, Britain, British Commonwealth states, Low Countries, and the Scandinavian ones. Among them were Britain's Anthony Eden and France's Foreign Minister Maurice Schumann, the voice of Free France during World War II.

Justice Owen J. Roberts resigned from the U.S. Supreme Court during World War II to devote his full time and energy to promotion of the federation goal. Arnold Toynbee, the British historian, once told Streit, "The federation you envision is inevitable." Streit made the cover of *Time* magazine and engaged in nationwide radio discussions of his proposal. President Franklin D. Roosevelt invited Streit to the White House for a chat.

As a college student, I endorsed his proposal in a column published in the campus newspaper, then entered the text in a national college contest sponsored by Streit's Federal Union membership organization. It won second prize, a train ticket to Washington, D.C., and the promise of a day with Streit. On Christmas Day 1941, I reached the capital. The next day, after lunch with Streit at the National Press Club, I squeezed through a door in the House of Representatives gallery to hear British Prime Minister Winston Churchill's stirring speech to a joint meeting of Congress. It was one of the great thrills of my life, adding fuel to my already blazing interest in politics.

In a somber conversation, Streit told me he felt I had taken the place of his only son, killed just days earlier in an auto accident. During the forty-six years that followed, Streit was an important, inspiring part of my life. My endorsement of Streit's plan prompted support from my scientist brother William. Among my souvenirs is a long article, reprinted from the *Illinois Technograph*, a publication of the University of Illinois College of Engineering. In it William, then an instructor, summoned scientists to demand an end to national sovereignty so a new federation could have sufficient authority to function effectively.

In my second term in Congress, I began identifying Streit supporters on Capitol Hill. To my surprise, I discovered several dozen. We knew federation would spark controversy, as had a resolution introduced in each of the previous seven Congresses by former presidential candidate Senator Estes Kefauver of Tennessee. We proposed a "blue ribbon delegation" of U.S. citizens authorized to meet with similar groups from other NATO nations to consider steps toward federation. Proposals formulated in convention were subject to ratification by member nations. Although only exploratory, it contemplated a giant step in statecraft. No hearings were held.

My active work for federation began in 1963 when my Republican colleagues authorized me to form a twelve-member Republican Committee on NATO and the Atlantic Community. Two years later they approved a Republican-financed trip to Paris with me as chairman to study the disarray in NATO. The same year, I joined a small, unofficial, bipartisan group called Members of Congress for Peace through Law (MCPL). Representative Patsy Mink of Hawaii, a Democrat, was one of its leaders. We were colleagues on the House Agriculture Committee, where she won bipartisan applause by occasionally distributing a sampling of pineapples to members. This acquaintance quickly led me to Mink's project in world law. The group, mostly Democrats, gathered for discussion once a month. The objective was to promote enforceable world law as the proper and sure avenue to durable peace. When I joined the group it had fewer than twenty members. When I left Congress in 1983, it had grown to include more than one hundred. Its purpose fit my campaign for Atlantic Union and my objection to using acts of war to advance foreign policy objectives. While a member, I was first alerted to America's long-standing pro-Israel bias.

In 1966, the House Foreign Affairs Committee held hearings on my resolution advocating Atlantic federation. It differed from Kefauver's mainly by recommending the U.S. delegation be co-chaired by former presidents Truman and Eisenhower. In a letter to me dated April 6, 1966, Eisenhower gave explicit endorsement to the concept:

"I strongly favor your undertaking. Let there be no doubt about this. Second, I warmly appreciate the invitation to share the chairmanship of the delegation with former President Truman and would like very much to be able to do so. . . . [but cannot because] considerations of health have imposed upon me very explicit medical disciplines for some considerable time to come. . . . I wish your undertaking well and wish I could personally help to advance it as you have suggested."

Buoyed by this endorsement, Streit organized an Atlantic Union Conference in Springfield in June 1966. He demonstrated his own wide influence by securing as principal speakers Canada's most popular politician ever, Prime Minister Lester B. Pearson, and U.S. television's most popular personality, NBC *Today* host Dave Garroway. Pearson was a principal author of the North Atlantic Treaty. Garroway shared supreme popularity with his faithful companion, a Chimp named J. Fred Muggs.

During his address, Pearson forecast that "in the longer sweep of history, both Europe and North America will come to realize that their respective affairs can best be harmonized in a wider union." He urged, "We can begin with the 'like-minded' Atlantic nations who have already acquired a sense of community and a habit of cooperation, but it must ultimately include all mankind. The world is too small for less, yet we continue to boggle at even the first careful steps. We must develop common, unifying political institutions that would provide for collective foreign and economic policies, as well as genuinely collective defense. Nothing less will be adequate to meet today's challenge of jets and rockets and hydrogen bombs."

His remarks received coverage in major print media but not the detailed attention they deserved. After he spoke, Streit presented leadership plaques to Pearson, former U.S. Senator Frank Carlson of Kansas, and posthumously to Ambassador Adlai Stevenson II. State Treasurer Adlai Stevenson III, who later became U.S. Senator, received the plaque as a memorial to his father.

In a private conversation, Pearson gave me insight into Canadian politics that matched my experiences in Illinois. He recalled a speech he delivered in a rural constituency in which he expounded at length about his role in creating the North Atlantic Treaty. When he finished, a local citizen came to him and said, "This talk about NATO may be well and good, but if you don't do something about postal service around here, you may have to find another job."

Garroway stated that reading Streit's latest book, *Freedom's Frontier*, made him "a new man." He added, "Nothing since has been as exciting."

In 1967, Representatives Clem Zablocki of Wisconsin, Morris Udall of Arizona, Don Fraser and Albert Quie of Minnesota, and I reintroduced the Atlantic Union resolution. The House Foreign Affairs Committee held hearings but took no further action. A year later, support of the resolution edged up to 114. Forty-one Democrats and the same number of Republicans were cosponsors. In addition, twenty additional Democrats and twenty Republicans pledged support.

The same year, Senator Barry Goldwater, Republican candidate for president in 1964, and four future Republican presidential candidates—former governors William Scranton of Pennsylvania, Nelson Rockefeller of New York, and Mark Hatfield of Oregon and former Vice President Richard Nixon—declared their support. On the Democratic side, endorsements came from three presidential prospects, Senators Robert F. Kennedy and Eugene McCarthy, and Vice President Hubert H. Humphrey. Nixon, Rockefeller, and McCarthy had long been Streit supporters. Notably missing was a response from Republican Governor Ronald Reagan of California.

In offering his support, Goldwater predicted that while the quest is "a must," it will be lengthy: "I strongly support the federation idea, but I am not optimistic about it coming about in the next few years." He added in his inimitable way, "When it happens, most of our population may be light tan."

Federation received sharp criticism in some quarters. In an editorial titled "Illusions Die Hard," the *Chicago Tribune* rejected it as a "pipe dream." The *Tribune* opined, "The author of the resolution is Representative Paul Findley, an Illinois Republican, who usually makes pretty good sense. Joining him as sponsors are four other Illinois Republicans: John B. Anderson, Edward J. Derwinski, Robert H. Michel and Donald Rumsfeld. But hold on to your hats. Listed as other sponsors are Barry Goldwater, former Vice President Richard Nixon, and, less surprisingly, Governor George Romney of Michigan and Governor William W. Scranton of Pennsylvania." Puzzled and seeming to verge on apoplexy, the editor signed off with one word "Crazy."

In 1972, Don Fraser of Minnesota and I introduced identical resolutions, using the same wording as the 1967 version. This time the House Committee on International Relations recommended passage, but the House Rules Committee, in a five-to-four vote, declined to forward it for consideration by the full House. In 1973, the resolution was again reported favorably by the renamed International Relations Committee.

I knew Nixon supported the Kefauver bill while a House member. I decided to request a private appointment to encourage his public endorsement, mailing my request on December 27, 1972. I knew it would not be easily attained, so the same day I sent an information copy to Bill Timmons, the president's chief of congressional liaison. Two days later, letters from Timmons and his associate, Dick Cook, acknowledged my request.

Copies of these went to Henry Kissinger, Nixon's national security adviser. On January 3, 1973, presidential assistant Raymond Price entered the correspondence. He received a memo from David Parker, the official in charge of presidential correspondence, asking that he give it "appropriate" handling. On January 11, David Gergen, now a CNN commentator, wrote to Timmons offering to arrange an appointment for me with a White House staff member. The same day Parker wrote me a letter, with copies to Timmons, Cook, adviser Helmut Sonnenfeldt, and Price. It stated, "We cannot be encouraging about setting up the meeting you request." He added, "The president has asked that arrangements be made for

one of his top advisers in the National Security Council to meet
with you, if you wish." In the next document, a "correspondence
file" from General Brent Scowcroft, Kissinger's assistant, to Parker,
Scowcroft requested that a memo be sent to me no later than January 30. The rapid flow of communications here and there continued
every few days until February 26.

The interview finally occurred at 10:00 A.M. on March 2. It was
worth the wait. During a lively and, in my view, helpful discussion
that stretched beyond ten minutes, Nixon reiterated his support for
Atlantic Union and pledged to send me a letter to that effect. As
we talked, he took extensive notes on a yellow pad. At one point, I
mentioned a view Eisenhower expressed to me during a recent chat
at Gettysburg. The former president told me four U.S. divisions then
stationed in West Germany could safely be reduced to one.

In my file is a packet containing copies of twenty-seven documents recording the progress of my request through the phalanx
of aides who seemed to feel the duty to block intrusions on presidential time. Gaining the appointment was grueling but instructive.
Clearly, the preparation of the documents cost taxpayers a sizable
bundle. Years before, the process was simpler. Representative William Springer, a veteran Republican from a neighboring district, told
me his experience securing a White House appointment during his
first term in 1951. Wishing to talk personally to President Harry S.
Truman about veterans' legislation, he telephoned his request to the
White House. Before the day was over, he received this telephoned
response: "The president will see you tomorrow morning at ten."

Perhaps Nixon's elaborate system for clearing appointment
requests insulated the chief executive too thoroughly from outside
influences and even from reality, leaving him prey to notions of
being above law and custom.

The Senate approved a version of the Atlantic Union Resolution
on a voice vote without debate, a painless advance because it was
sponsored by Senate Majority Leader Mike Mansfield of Montana
and Republican Minority Leader Hugh Scott of Pennsylvania, both

longtime Streit supporters. In the House, even legislation supported by bipartisan leadership can provoke a storm.

After committee approval occurred, Fraser and I privately discussed the resolution with each member of the Rules Committee prior to its public hearing. Perhaps these interviews helped, because the committee—for the first time—approved the resolution for House floor consideration. I sent a brief, personal note to every House member, mentioning my long years of commitment to the federation goal. Democrat Jack Brooks of Florida responded in writing, stating he was impressed with my personal appeal and would cooperate. Another good friend, Graham Purcell of Texas, did the same. With a smile, he later told me that, in doing so, he felt like he was joining a secret cult. To many members, Streit's proposal was too radical for serious consideration.

The main sponsors decided in advance to avoid full discussion of the text of the Atlantic Union resolution during debate on the rule, expecting that it would be approved without argument. Procedures on the rule rarely drew more than a handful of congressmen to the House floor. This one proved to be the exception.

On April 10, 1973, a month after my appointment with Nixon, the rule was called up for consideration on the House floor. During a contentious debate, the chief critic was Republican colleague Peter Frelinghuysen of New Jersey, a member of the International Relations Committee who had opposed the resolution at each stage of its progress. To illustrate the great potential reach of our proposal, he quoted from Streit's statement supporting an earlier version of the resolution: "I would strongly favor including in such a Union's powers not only the common defense but a common foreign policy, a common currency, a common market." Frelinghuysen then said, accurately, that the resolution contemplated "a transformation of present relationships into a union and the transfer of certain aspects of national sovereignty to this new supranational entity." He then characterized it as "an unwise and unrealistic goal." To my dismay, another Republican, Craig Hosmer of California, offered this gem of ridicule: "This resolution is a quixotic, emotional anachronism, and it ought to be laid to rest by a decisive negative vote."

Veteran Democrat Claude Pepper of Florida, Republican Tom Railsback of Illinois, and I offered supportive remarks. Pepper said, "This resolution is a step toward a goal the freedom-loving and peace-loving nations of the world have been moving toward for a long, long time, however slowly. It is a step which must be taken if we are to provide for the welfare of our people and have peace in the world." He warned, "There will be those who wish to go back to our days of isolation." Railsback said, "Some type of international institution must be set up to deal with the problems that are supranational in scope." I summarized the bipartisan support among candidates for the presidency and quoted the positions of President Nixon and former President Eisenhower.

The pending rule to clear the way for a full debate in the House of Representatives failed by thirteen votes. The tally was 197 affirmative, 210 negative. Although disappointed, I rejoiced in the strong affirmative total. Voting for a step toward this possible conveyance of national authority were Republican leader Gerald Ford; Republican whip Les Arends; three future speakers of the house, Thomas "Tip" O'Neill, James Wright, and Thomas Foley, all Democrats; and a future presidential candidate in the House delegation from Illinois, Republican John B. Anderson. Quite an accomplishment.

Scanning the recorded vote, I noticed the names of several members who, like Brooks, were in the affirmative column for rule approval but unlikely to vote for the resolution itself. Twenty-six members did not vote. If all members had voted, I concluded the margin of defeat would have been at least a dozen votes larger.

In early 1976, in the wake of a sharp protest over the touchy issue of national sovereignty by the national office of the Veterans of Foreign Wars, the International Relations Committee rejected by a narrow vote my motion to report the resolution once more. Several members who voted for the resolution told me they had received troubling protests from constituents, as well as from the VFW. The committee vote was a clear signal that much broader support would be needed to return the resolution to the floor.

In June that year, Streit organized a luncheon chaired by Vice President Nelson Rockefeller in the U.S. Capitol, during which he presented the $7,500 Union of the Free Award to me for advancing the federation idea. Rockefeller and Streit were the main speakers. The guests included several diplomats, military officials, and members of Congress, plus Elizabeth Taylor, a new supporter of Atlantic Union.

With the full agreement of major cosponsors, I put the Atlantic Union Resolution on the shelf, hoping in time to win the support of the VFW and other dissenting groups. None of us could visualize an early improvement in congressional support.

After Streit's death, his widow, Jeanne, invited me to choose any book from his library as a keepsake. My choice: John Fiske's *The Critical Period in American History*. Copyrighted and printed in 1898, it bore Streit's handwritten inscription—in green ink, of course: "C. Streit, NY 1934." It was complete but in pieces, with pages heavily marked and the oft-repaired binding connected to only the last chapters of the book. It was obviously Streit's most important source of information about the period in which the U.S. federal union took shape, 1783 to 1789, and likely his most important inspiration for *Union Now*.

Like the book, Streit was well-worn and somewhat tattered in his last days, but his mind was as sharp as ever. In *Union Now*, he set forth the standards and principles of the federation of his dreams, most of them drawn from America's successful federation of formerly independent states. Through the years, other organizations surfaced, endorsing federation but proposing changes in specifics. Some recommended immediate union of all major nations worldwide, no matter what their experience in self-government might be. Others suggested gradually transforming an alliance like NATO, step by step, into a federal government. Streit offered arguments against each proposed variation.

Throughout his long life, he remained optimistic. Each day offered a development that in his mind became a new touchstone for action. If he became discouraged, it was never apparent. He seemed always at my door with new suggestions for action. He had disappointments, of course. He was nominated frequently for the Nobel Peace Prize and the Presidential Medal of Freedom. Neither came his way, although he richly deserved both.

He was in the glorious tradition of Old Testament prophets, proudly carrying his *flambeau* aloft. One day, I heard Streit make a profound observation. "When the U.S. federal union came into being in 1789, the Clipper Ship was in its glory days. Today, two centuries later, physical science has progressed to rockets, television, and nuclear energy, but political science is still stuck in the age of the Clipper Ships." He noted that many contemporary problems were clearly beyond the reach of sovereign national governments, acting individually or through weak associations, like the United Nations and NATO.

At the top of the list was the challenge posed by the steady increase in nations possessing nuclear weapons. Some warheads are small enough to be carried in a small suitcase but powerful enough to destroy a giant city. The specter of a bomb being detonated by a rogue group, deranged individual, or as the result of accident will haunt humankind until all warheads are disabled. A new level of government with sufficient worldwide strength to enforce a law against such weapons is, in my view, the only realistic hope. In 1946, Winston Churchill alluded to the nuclear challenge. He expressed his hope the United Nations would attain the power to enforce the rule of law and become the world's sole repository of nuclear warheads.

Safe management of spent nuclear fuel and other toxic by-products of nuclear energy is nonexistent in the world. International laws must be established and enforced. Our ever-shrinking world requires an authority able to police sea-lanes and enforce law if a new tyrant should threaten its neighbors. No individual nation, not even a superpower, should attempt to meet this responsibility.

Military drones—unmanned bombers—should be outlawed. They are a frightening new tool of mass destruction. The United States now uses them to fire missiles into Afghanistan, Pakistan, and Yemen and in earlier years used them in Bosnia. Britain and Israel also use drones, and other nations will soon follow.

The United Nations is not the answer. It is not a government and seems destined to remain an organization of independent states. It is a debating center that can occasionally express multinational consensus and is important as such.

International federation is not a new idea. After his presidential years, former President U. S. Grant lectured on behalf of a federation of English-speaking nations. In recent years, Walter Cronkite, America's respected news commentator, became a strong voice for federation. Shortly before his death, while speaking to the Democratic World Federalists organization in San Francisco, Cronkite said, "Today, the notion of unlimited national sovereignty means international anarchy. We must replace the anarchic law of force with a civilized force of law."[50]

As I reflect on my career, my main regret is my failure to maintain leadership in the advancement of federation during my last five years on Capitol Hill, while, hopefully, also giving attention to the daunting task of reforming U.S. Middle East policy. I find it deeply distressing that our vast community of politicians, scholars, organizations, and think tanks seems almost bereft of people calling for the civilized force of law that Cronkite and Streit championed. Federation would solve the Middle East conflict. Israelis and Palestinians, like other people, would run their own local affairs, but enjoy security provided by the federal government through its power to prevent acts of war from any quarter. War, I believe, would become a thing of the past.

Perhaps only a handful of readers have previously heard of Clarence K. Streit. He is one of the most remarkable people of my acquaintance. Streit ranks high among people of this age that future historians will remember fully and favorably. Federation is inevitable, I believe, because nothing less can peaceably manage problems that no single nation can master. When federation comes, it will include more than the NATO nations contemplated in the Atlantic Union Resolution advanced in Congress forty years ago. It will be transworld in scope, not just transatlantic. Streit's books and other writings will be revived. Perhaps legislative endeavors undertaken a half-century ago for the advancement of Atlantic Union will be remembered, not as a failure, but as a constructive step forward.

As world leaders ponder what to do about challenges that reach beyond the competence of individual nations or fragile alliances, they will find rich inspiration in Streit's legacy. A U.S. president with wisdom and courage will someday, I believe, help frame a strong new international political institution able to enforce the rule of law. The only question is whether this act of wise statecraft will occur before humankind struggles with still more military and economic upheavals. Such a nightmare may already be at our doorsteps.

If schemers of the neo-con mentality that dominated foreign policies during the George W. Bush administration return to power, the U.S. government could quickly seek the trappings of empire, enmeshing our people in new wars, delaying indefinitely progress toward the "civilized force of law" that Cronkite envisioned. In this new war, if it comes, our likely main partner will be Israel, along with remnants of NATO entrapped as reluctant copartners.

Is America in the early stages of an ugly, bloody struggle for empire?

Epilogue

∞∞∞∞∞∞∞∞∞∞∞∞∞∞∞

Nation in Peril

Since my boyhood, America has made great strides in physical science, standard of living, social progress, and banishing racism. Of all the thousands of votes I cast in Congress, those for civil rights bills were the most satisfying. They expressed my conviction that varied pigmentations of skin are blessings from the Creator, not shadings of superiority or inferiority.

Still, I had mixed feelings when I left Capitol Hill. While pleased over advances, I was distressed over loose ends left dangling dangerously. Among them were foreign policy blunders like preemptive war, religious bias in foreign policy, continued development of nuclear weapons, and neglect of looming famine.

Today, a quarter-century later, the loose ends remain largely untouched, and some dangle more perilously than before. Despite the certainty of imminent worldwide food shortages, serious programs to prevent famine are nowhere on the U.S. agenda. Our calamitous bias in U.S. Middle East policy seems more entrenched than ever.

Military might, not moral and legal right, continues to settle major challenges in world affairs. No one with influence lifts a finger to establish an international system strong enough to enforce the rule of law worldwide.

In Washington, both chambers of Congress ignore constitutional responsibilities. Instead of taking the lead in tying up loose ends, members often respond to lobby pressure by careening in the opposite direction, fueling instead of redressing anti-American passions. There is little sign these days Congress will disenthrall itself from misbehavior and neglect by undertaking the positive, constructive roles in both domestic and foreign policy that the framers of the Constitution envisioned.

The peril of Holy War is little noted in America because the lobby for Israel effectively limits free speech. It is a pernicious curiosity that a small band of scofflaws in Jerusalem and Tel Aviv have manipulated America, an advanced society of three hundred million people, so thoroughly that most citizens are unaware of their own subservience.

When Israel is involved in any issue, free speech is almost non-existent in the halls of Congress, academia, pulpits, and even at coffee counters in the smallest villages. Hardly a voice of concern and protest about Israeli criminal behavior can be heard anywhere in the United States.

Fear is a major element. Except for those aligned with Israel by religious scruples, almost all Americans are afraid to speak out in candor, fearful that uttering the slightest rebuke of Israel will bring the reckless charge of anti-Semitism. Rare indeed is a U.S. citizen, especially any in public life, willing to declare the government of Israel what it truly is: a scofflaw state.

It is a grim state of affairs for all humankind. When will our government take the moral high road in Middle East policy? Partly because of litmus testing, the U.S. national scene is bereft of people able and willing to take charge. This loathsome censorship is a main impediment to America's liberation from domination by Israel.

Local protests against Arab authorities that began with the revolution in Tunisia in early 2011 and spread quickly to Egypt, Yemen, and Jordan arose partly from outrage over the plight of Palestinians. American Jewish leader and scholar Henry Siegman wrote on February 17, 2011, in the *London Review of Books*, "While the Israeli-Palestinian challenge is not the prime cause of the current upheavals [against authoritarian governments], the failure of the Arab regimes to halt Palestinian dispossession is not far from the top of the list of popular grievances." If democracy takes root in Arab states, strong domestic demand for a viable, independent Palestine is certain to follow.

The best immediate hope for a just peace may come in a massive, resolute awakening among Israeli patriots, like activist Uri Avnery, who see clearly the certain demise of Israel as a Jewish state when demographic tides raise Arabs to a majority in the territory now controlled by Israel. That moment may spark a dreadful civil war in the Holy Land.

Inspired by the great transformation of South Africa in recent years that brought white Afrikaners and black Zulus together in equal political standing, Israeli Semites and Palestinian Semites surely have the ability and the wisdom to establish a peaceful and enduring accord. Wise and courageous men and women must take control of public policy in the Holy Land and organize a mutual program of confession, forgiveness, and reconciliation. If South Africans can dismantle ugly colonialism, Israelis can do the same, working hand-in-hand with Palestinian counterparts.

Loose ends in public policy include two I neglected while in office. One is the ominous growth and influence of America's military-industrial complex. The other is the growing threat to representative government posed by Washington-based lobbies that dominate financing of congressional campaigns.

In President Eisenhower's farewell address to the nation in January 1961, he warned, "We must guard against the acquisition of unwarranted influence, whether sought or not, by the military-industrial complex." He referred to the massive growth of military-related spending that began in World War II. It was not a one-line, sidebar-type observation. He added, "The potential for the disastrous rise of power exists and will persist. We must never let the weight of this combination endanger our liberties or our democratic processes. We should take nothing for granted."[51]

It is noteworthy that he made a last-minute change in text. An early draft warned of the "military-industrial-congressional complex." Before delivery, he deleted the word "congressional."[52] Whatever his reason for deletion, congressional funding of the Department of Defense (DOD) and related government programs is a major element in this persistent threat. The complex gets what it wants with hardly a murmur of protest or evidence of serious oversight. No member of either chamber makes serious, sustained attempts to restrain the DOD's size or influence. Neither Congress nor the president exerts the vigilance Eisenhower urgently recommended.

Early in my career I experienced the DOD's subtle but effective touch in outreach to Congress. A representative of the department called at my Capitol Hill office, offering me an instant commission as a lieutenant commander in the navy reserve. All I had to do was sign up for brief duty once a year. As one who left the navy in 1946 as a lowly—but proud—lieutenant junior grade, immediate endowment with two-and-one-half gold stripes on uniform sleeves was alluring. I quickly declined, however, fearing acceptance would cloud my judgment when DOD budgets came up for consideration by Congress.

During Eisenhower's presidency, the DOD had an annual budget slightly under $41 billion.[53] The Soviet threat was real. Most of its intercontinental ballistic missiles were aimed at the United States, and some U.S. politicians warned that Soviet Sputniks would soon outmatch U.S. missiles. Warsaw Pact nations of Eastern Europe were fully under Soviet control.

Today, the Soviet Union does not exist, with its main surviving component, Russia, struggling in economic difficulty. The Warsaw Pact is also nonexistent, and none of its former members are hostile to the United States. No threat to U.S. territory exists. No nation except North Korea can be cited—or sighted—as a threatening enemy on any point of the compass.

Still, the annual outlay for the DOD mounts ever higher. Just under $800 billion—over $2 billion a day—its 2010 budget is greater than the aggregate military budgets of all the world's other

military powers. It is far greater, even after adjustment for reduced
dollar value, than it was during Eisenhower's Cold War presidency.
When defense-related budgets of other departments and agencies
are added, the annual U.S. outlay for the military-industrial complex is nearly one trillion dollars. In addition to feeding the needs
of the DOD, our arms industry gives America the dubious honor of
being the world's leading merchant of war-making instruments.[54]

The DOD is a giant government within a giant government, but
is treated as sacrosanct by Congress and most citizens. It controls
mighty armed forces and massive inventories of nuclear weapons, as
well as a variety of intelligence agencies, some of which have their
own secret foreign operations. It operates 3,800 installations in the
United States, including several institutions of higher learning, like
the War College, and sometimes duplicates activities of other parts
of the federal government. Its bounteous contracts lure hundreds of
colleges, universities, research institutions, and manufacturing plants
into becoming cheerleaders for the DOD's growth. Its economic ten-
tacles are a powerful political influence in every state in the Union.[55]

As in the greatest days of the British Empire, the sun never sets on
the Department of Defense. It is the *de facto* policeman of the world,
implementing a far-reaching security doctrine inaugurated unwisely
and without congressional sanction in 2002 by President George W.
Bush. In compliance, the DOD now maintains 737 military bases
scattered worldwide.[56] Each foreign base risks empire-like trouble
simply by being there, because, as every foreign leader knows, the
U.S. president always has at his fingertips the means to commit acts
of war instantly from any of the 737 bases, foreign or domestic.

Early in my career on Capitol Hill, I learned that not even a superpower like the United States should attempt to police the world. A
world policeman is needed, but policing should be undertaken only
by a strong international institution, not individual nations. One
need only note the inconclusive misery our nation has experienced
trying to police Vietnam, Iraq, and Afghanistan. No such institution exists and no prominent citizen calls for its creation. Nor does

any leader echo Eisenhower's warning about the peril implicit in the immensity of today's military-industrial complex. Cutting the DOD budget by one-half would be a constructive first step in taming this giant bureaucracy. Even if that reduction were accomplished, the DOD's military budget would still be the world's largest by far.

The new Department of Homeland Security in its quest for dangers within our border, has established an enormous bureaucracy whose sole job is to search for terrorists, snooping that keeps unwarranted fear at a high level. Hunters for domestic terrorists—cynics call them snoopers—occupy floor space three times the size of the giant Pentagon building.

Still worse, there are disturbing signs that President Obama, surrounded by generals, has been misled into accepting the delusion that terrorists can be defeated by the bombs and missiles employed by an occupying military force. Instead of halting U.S. combat operations and redressing grievances, Obama brandishes swords anew. He expands U.S. combat forces in Afghanistan, extends war measures into Pakistan, and threatens Iran.

All current U.S. combat operations are directed against Muslim countries. Many people—not just Muslims—perceive a growing threat of violent struggle between Christendom and Islam. Unwarranted fear and bigotry haunts our nation. Pundits and politicians warn recklessly of an "Islamist" threat. Anti-American passions flourish as we continue foreign military combat that kills Muslims by the thousands and our government remains complicit in Israel's abuse of Arabs. We should reduce our foreign military bases to those operated in genuine collaboration with the host country and never initiate acts of war anywhere except to meet precise treaty obligations or to protect U.S. territory or citizens from imminent attack.

Another challenge I neglected is the threat to representative government posed by large gifts to congressional campaigns from Washington-based lobbyists. Today, most candidates get much of their support, if not dominant funding, in big checks from special interest lobbies headquartered far from their constituencies. Donors expect these investments to pay dividends as votes are cast on Capitol Hill. Arriving on the House floor one day, I asked Representative Tennyson Guyer, a witty colleague from Ohio, how he had voted on a pending amendment. He responded, with a grin, "I haven't yet been financially advised." He was kidding and quickly told me how he had voted. But many votes in Congress are "financially advised," a reality that prompts this troubling question: whose interests do representatives really represent? Before answering, keep in mind that members of Congress whose reelection campaigns are fully financed by their constituents have become a rarity.

Early in my congressional career, I voted for legislation intended to limit congressional campaign expenditures to forty thousand dollars in each election. It became law, but the Supreme Court ruled it unconstitutional, holding that the right to support politicians financially is an expression of constitutionally protected free speech. As a result, all legislative attempts at limiting campaign spending, including the recent McCain-Feingold Act, have been ineffective. Only an amendment to the Constitution altering the First Amendment can permit Congress to establish effective limits.

America's gravest peril lies in the severe damage caused by religious bias in U.S. Middle East policies. This bias led to abject subservience to a small foreign nation, presidential decisions that trash long-cherished civil liberties, and staggering sacrifice in blood and treasure. The submission is so deep-seated our government makes no attempt to find out why we are hated. Or why some insurgents go to terrible extremes in venting their passion. Even in our War on Terror, U.S. officials never mention—much less try to redress—the grievances of those we attempt to destroy. Few Americans are aware the chief architect of 9/11 told a U.S. official interviewer he was motivated to organize that massive massacre by his intense hatred of biased U.S. policies that favor Israel.[57]

Almost every major official, elected or appointed, in our government is burdened with the baggage of subservience. Over the years, each has cast votes or taken public positions that demonstrate submission. So far, they are shielded from blame by a combination of public ignorance and fear. Most Americans are unaware of the depth and extent of Israel's influence over our government. Most of those who know the facts are afraid to speak out.

Any serious study of insurgent motivations would inevitably bring to public attention facts unfavorable to Israel—a focus all government officials will avoid like a plague. Fear of retribution makes even presidents back away from a corrective showdown. The vast majority of members of Congress and others employed on Capitol Hill, as well as senior officials in other government offices, tiptoe with trepidation where Israel is concerned. They fear even a word of criticism of Israeli behavior may lead to reckless charges of anti-Semitism that threaten careers.

The gross cost of this bias since 1975 is towering. In March 2010, it exceeded $3 trillion. This includes $1.6 trillion as the direct cost of aid to Israel since 1975. It also includes, using low estimates, the $1.5 trillion cost of combat and related military operations in Iraq, Afghanistan, and Pakistan—costs that would not have been incurred in the absence of pressure from Israel and U.S. neocons. The estimates of course include the cost of managing federal debt, as all aid to Israel and Israel-inspired war expenditures have increased public debt. The words are trillion, not billion.[58]

This cost hits your family hard. Our nation consists of about seventy-six million households. Dividing that number into $3 trillion yields $40,000 as the per-family cost of subservience to Israel. Ponder that statistic—$40,000 for your family and every other U.S. family—with no end in sight.

Still worse than dollar costs, this subservience has led Washington to scuttle individual rights long protected in our Constitution. Rendition, targeted assassinations without due process, and racial profiling come to mind. Each stains the name "America." Each is a reason to weep.

This is not the America I modestly but proudly helped defend in World War II. For the first time in my life, I am deeply troubled about our nation's future. In my youth, I never doubted that our country would survive the Great Depression and be victorious over Nazi Germany and Japanese imperialism. Today, I hope—and believe—most Americans inherit the patriotism and common sense of their forebears, but they have not yet grasped the magnitude of today's danger. Most of them have no awareness of the financial cost and cancerous afflictions caused by subservience to a small scofflaw foreign nation. Given the truth, I am sure they will rise up and correct these wrongs. They must be awakened.

The time has come for plain talk and clearheaded action. We must free our nation from unwarranted fear. We must retrace our steps to the moral high road where America belongs. We need leaders of undaunted courage and citizens who will participate resolutely in our political system. Reviewing my sixty years in public policy, in and out of elective office, I cannot imagine a higher calling or a more satisfying life than striving for justice in the partisan mainstream. I am a Christian, but I do not believe my faith—or anyone else's—is the only avenue to the Creator's blessing. Differences in religious faith are distinctions to be understood, not twisted and condemned. Years ago, Dr. Malcolm Stewart, my teacher of religion during college days, sent me a profound call for inter-faith understanding: "I do not believe there will be peace in the world until there is peace among the leaders of the major religions . . . until they come to understand each other."

Today, America is awash in bigotry and religious hatred. Desperately needed is open discussion of how this ugliness is related to U.S. Middle East policy and Israel's role in its making. But Israel's lobby effectively prohibits any criticism of the Jewish state in the chambers of power. Instead of constructive discussion, dangerous silence prevails. We must heed the warning stated by Joachim Prinz just before Rev. Martin Luther King Jr. delivered his speech in 1963 at the Lincoln Memorial in Washington, D.C. Prinz said, "When I was the rabbi in the Jewish community in Berlin under the Hitler regime . . . the most important thing that I learned was that bigotry and hatred are not the most urgent problem. The most urgent, the most disgraceful, the most shameful, the most tragic problem is silence."

The slings and arrows of partisan combat are trivial when contrasted with the opportunity to work on behalf of worthy causes in the political mainstream. There is satisfaction when one's proposal is adopted, but exhilaration comes when one stands on ramparts, virtually alone, seeking an objective that is urgently needed. Never despair. If the goal is not attained today, there is always tomorrow.

Those who enter that challenging mainstream as candidates or volunteers find the experience priceless no matter who wins. They gain friendships and understanding of the political world and contribute to the well-being of this nation. In all tomorrows, America will need candidates for public office and supporters who possess vision, courage, and common sense. These men and women need only one campaign slogan. It is found in Scripture: "Seek justice, only justice."

Notes

1. Paul Findley, *A. Lincoln: The Crucible of Congress* (New York: Crown, 1979), 162–163.
2. Oral history of House pages at 2009 page convention in Washington.
3. Reston, James R., *The Lone Star: The Life of John Connolly* (New York: Harper and Row), 551–553.
4. States News Service, February 10, 1979.
5. UPI, February 9, 1979.
6. Remarks at Luxembourg conference, December 10, 2009.
7. Victor Gilinsky, veteran member of the Nuclear Regulatory Commission, e-mail December 15, 2009.
8. Paul Findley, *They Dare to Speak Out: People and Institutions Confront Israel's Lobby* (Westport, CT: Lawrence Hill, 1985), 1–12.
9. *New York Times,* December 20, 1978.
10. *State Journal-Register,* July 12, 1978.
11. Commodity News Service, June 4, 1980.
12. Associated Press, September 2, 1978.
13. *Quincy Herald-Whig,* May 4, 1980.
14. *Quincy Herald-Whig,* March 19, 1980.
15. *Jacksonville Journal-Courier,* July 17, 1980.
16. Letter, May 5, 1981.
17. Associated Press, April 10, 1982, *News-Democrat*, Belleville.
18. AP dateline Washington, August 30, 1982.
19. *Chicago Tribune,* September 5, 1982.
20. *The Monitor*, the *Washington Post, The Jerusalem Post, The Boston Globe, Library Journal*, the *Detroit Free Press.*
21. *Chicago Tribune,* September 5, 1982.
22. Mark Perry, *Democracy Now!*, March 17, 2010.
23. WRMEA, September 10, 2009, p. 25.
24. Ibid, p. 26.
25. Ibid.
26. Conversations with Lewis and Hart on August 23, 2005.
27. James Ennes, 1991 interview with Ambassador Dwight Porter; e-mail text to author from Ennes, December 13, 2009; May 17, 2004, statement by J. R. Gotcher; text to author from Ennes e-mail, December 13, 2009.

28. Telephone interview with Hrankowski in Rochester, New York, May 18, 2010.
29. The San Diego *Union Tribune*, June 6, 2007.
30. E-mail to author from David Lewis, September 17, 2005, confirmed by phone that day.
31. WRMEA, September 10, 2009, p. 26.
32. Foreign Policy.com, *Ha'aretz*, December 4, 2009.
33. Associated Press, Ithaca, NY; *Belleville News-Democrat*, December 18, 2004, p. 7A.
34. Gallup Group survey, The Religion News Service, January 25, 2010.
35. *Joint Force Quarterly*, U.S. Department of Defense, August 28, 2009.
36. Not included in this summary of fatal injuries are the deaths of military personnel on either side of combat. For example, as this is written, U.S. troop deaths in Iraq total 4,295. Deaths among British and other coalition forces total 318.
37. Stephen Walt, "Why do they hate us?" The New Foreign Policy.com, November 20, 2009.
38. Posted September 14, 2009, by Prof. Juan Cole on his *Informed Comment* blog.
39. Richard Pape, *Dying to Win: The Strategic Logic of Suicide Bombings* (New York: Random House, 2006).
40. 9/11 Commission Report, p. 147.
41. William Pfaff syndicated article from Paris, August 23, 2009.
42. CAIR DC bulletin, April 9, 2009.
43. William Pfaff syndicated column, Paris, April 9, 2009.
44. Personal interviews with Wolf Fuhrig, Samer Anabtawi, and Jafar Qutob.
45. Text in *Silent No More,* Appendix A.
46. 9/11 Commission Report, p. 147.
47. West syndicated column, *Jacksonville Journal-Courier*, September 21, 2009.
48. Phone conversation and e-mail, September 22, 2009.
49. Inter Press Service, February 5, 2010.
50. Democratic World Federalists bulletin, Summer 2009, vol. 8, no 3.
51. Public Papers of the Presidents, Dwight D. Eisenhower, pp. 1035–1040.
52. Source Watch, www.imdb.com/titlett0436971, July 9, 2009.
53. DOD National Defense Budget Estimated (Green Book) Military Comptroller 2040 Budget, pp. 92 and 104.
54. Arnaud de Borchgrave, editor at large, UPI, Washington, August 6, 2009.
55. Ibid.
56. Ibid.
57. Khalid Sheikh Mohammed, quoted in the 9/11 Commission Report, p. 147.
58. *The Christian Science Monitor*, December 3, 2009; About.com, "US Liberal Politics," March, 29, 2010.

Acknowledgments and Family Notes

<><><><><><><><><><><><><><><><><>

This book is a by-product of a long life of varied endeavors, during which many people helped guide my steps. I entered every keystroke of this text, but those who helped me find and arrange the words remain gratefully in my thoughts. Chief among them is Lucille, my loyal and loving wife and best counselor, who proofread all drafts, wondering at times if a final one would emerge.

My special thanks to Cynthia Sherry, a longtime friend and now publisher of Chicago Review Press, owner of the Lawrence Hill Books imprint. She and text editor Michelle Schoob ably prepared the manuscript for publication. Prior to that step, my draft benefited from recommendations by Janet McMahon, news editor of *Washington Report*; Oregon journalist George Beres; and Shirley Cloyes, editor of the first edition of my bestseller *They Dare to Speak Out*. Friend of many years Tahseen Khayat, owner of All Prints Publishing House in Beirut, published in Arabic this book and three of my previous volumes. Whenever my Dell crashed, professional fireman Bryan McGee, between fires, brought it back to life.

Providing inspiration through the years: President Jimmy Carter; Senator James Abourezk; Capitol Hill staff leader and lifelong wise counsel Stephen Jones; *Washington Report* founders Andrew Killgore and Richard T. Curtiss; CNI president Gene Bird; dean of White House correspondents Helen Thomas; consumer activist Ralph Nader; founder of *If Americans Knew* Alison Weir; U.S. Reps. Dennis Kucinich, Ron Paul, and Paul "Pete" McCloskey; national director of the Council on American Islamic Relations Nihad Awad; director of the Muslim Public Affairs Council Salam al-Marayati; American Muslim Alliance founder Agha Saeed; and survivors of the USS *Liberty*. The list could be thrice as long and still not be complete. These people form a mighty chorus for interfaith and interracial goodwill. Perhaps in time it will rise in number and volume until it triumphs in halls of power. Studying their work is a priceless learning experience.

Acquaintance with people of different races and religious faiths helped me shed, totally I hope, any trace of self-righteousness. Mizin Kawasaki, M.D., introduced me via the Internet to Buddhism, scientist and tennis partner Vithal Ayyagari to Hinduism, Uri Avneri to the true spirit of Judaism, and scores of Muslims at home and abroad to the beauty of Islam.

Thanks to the generosity of Dubai businessman Khalaf Al Habtoor, my files and artifacts will be maintained in the campus Leadership Center where Illinois College's seventeen alumni who also served in Congress will be commemorated. When I first met Habtoor twenty years ago, I also began a long friendship with three other Emirates leaders. One is Easa al Gurg, Dubai busnessman who served for years as Emirates ambassador in London. The others are Ruler of Sharjah Sheikh Sultan bin Mohamed al Qasimi, who created the beautiful new American University of Sharjah, and Ahmed Khalifa al Suweidi, now retired, who led negotiations that created the United Arab Emirates and then continued for years as its acting foreign minister.

Our children have always been a great source of pride. Craig followed my footsteps first in country journalism, then in politics. He is now a trustee of a large community college and a member of the Illinois Prisoner Review Board. He and wife Karyl have two children: Liz, who is a college student; and Andy, who, with his wife Grace, are parents of Dominic, whose arrival makes Lucille and me great-grandparents.

After high school, Diane went to a university in Ft. Collins, Colorado, to study art. It was a permanent move, broken only by an art semester in the Florence, Italy, region. Today she is one of Ft. Collins's leading artists and active in community programs. She and husband Thomas McLaughlin have two children, high school teacher Cameron and university student Henry.

My mother would be glad to know that all four of our grandchildren are in teaching or heading that way. Of her five children, four became teachers. I was the black sheep, choosing journalism and politics.

—Paul Findley

Index